Arnulfo L. Oliveira Memorial Library

Broken
Boundaries

The Key to the Rehearsal.

Broken Boundaries

Women & Feminism in Restoration Drama

Katherine M. Quinsey

Editor

The University Press of Kentucky

Frontispiece: Nell Gwyn rising from the dead to speak the epilogue to Dryden's *Tyrannick Love,* published as the frontispiece to *A Key to the Rehearsal* (1714) in *The Dramatick Works of his Grace George Villiers, late Duke of Buckingham* (1715), vol. 2. By permission of the Department of Special Collections, Stanford University Libraries.

Editorial and Sales Offices: The University Press of Kentucky
663 South Limestone Street, Lexington, Kentucky 40508-4008

00 99 98 97 96 5 4 3 2 1

Library of Congress Cataloging-in-Publication Data

Broken boundaries : women and feminism in Restoration drama / edited
  by Katherine M. Quinsey.
        p.   cm.
    Includes bibliographical references and index.
    ISBN 0-8131-1945-6 (alk. paper). —ISBN 0-8131-0871-3 (pbk. :
alk. paper)
      1. English drama—Restoration, 1660-1700—History and criticism.
    2. Feminism and literature—England—History—17th century.
    3. Literature and society—England—History—17th century. 4. Women
    in the theater—England—History—17th century. 5. Women and
    literature—England—History—17th century. 6. Theater—England—
    History—17th century. 7. Gender identity in literature. 8. Sex
    role in literature. 9. Women in literature. I. Quinsey, Katherine
    M., 1955–
    PR698.F45B76 1996
    822'.409352042—dc20   96-5329

Manufactured in the United States of America

Contents

Illustrations

Acknowledgments

Special thanks go to my research assistant, Maria Magro, for her exhaustive, precise, and intelligent proofreading of this volume in manuscript, and to Mrs. Lucia Brown and her team at the University of Windsor for their admirable efficiency in preparing it for press. Above all, as editor I should like to express my deep appreciation for the grace, efficiency, and professionalism shown by each of the contributors to this collection, in every stage of our working together: they have embodied scholarship in all its best senses.

Introduction

Katherine M. Quinsey

*R*estoration drama is overwhelmingly concerned with questions
of gender identity, sexuality, and women's oppression, to a degree and
a depth not seen in a comparably popular form of entertainment before
or since. It stands out among the mainstream literary and artistic forms
of its time in its unusually direct, probing, and fluid way of engaging
certain radical questions: questions about the place of women in social
and familial structures, about male/female relations, about the nature
of women—and men—themselves. It is a remarkable index to the
centrality of the "woman question" in this period that this most popular
verbal form of entertainment, a peculiarly self-conscious form that
blurs, even erases, the boundaries between its fiction and the social
world of the audience, should be dominated by gender issues.
Restoration drama is deeply embedded in its social matrix, yet in both
its authorship and its production, as well as in its challenge to
fictionality and its unresolved dialogic interplay, it continually separates itself from that matrix, reflecting and generating social change.

The late seventeenth century is a pivotal period in women's social
history and feminist awareness, to some extent culminating a process of
ontological questioning of gender begun much earlier, and thus differing
significantly from later eighteenth-century vindications of women's rights.
It is now a commonplace that the seventeenth century spans the shift from
an earlier concept of gender as a variation in an essentially unified human
nature to a hardening of gender categories, which theorized female as
distinct in essence from male in all levels of existence—biological,
spiritual, intellectual, and social. It has also been generally observed that
the cataclysmic changes in the intellectual, political, socioeconomic, and
religious frameworks of seventeenth-century England were not extended
to matters of gender; as old frameworks of authority were fundamentally
altered, those supporting patriarchal social and economic structures were
merely reconfigured. Indeed, within seemingly more egalitarian socioeconomic and political models, the equation of women and property—

women's status as chattels and as passive channels of property exchange—was entrenched, and female power and autonomy were markedly lessened. The Restoration period, however, which saw traditional order outwardly restored but conceptual and discursive frameworks radically and permanently altered, is characterized by its discursive instability: a volatile mixture of question and (sometimes violent) reassertion, action and reaction, searching skepticism and conservative affirmation. This period bridges the differing essentialisms of the Renaissance and the eighteenth century with a fluid and dynamic questioning of the assumptions underlying both. Such questioning—which in its cutting through to the roots can only be called feminist—both springs from and itself promotes the unsettling of frameworks of perception in all areas of intellectual and social life. Consideration of the feminist questions in Restoration drama, then, should promote a reexamination of all the intellectual, political, and socioeconomic shifting taking place in the period.

Restoration drama is perhaps the most telling popular expression of these radical uncertainties. It probes, shifts, and juxtaposes frameworks of value, exposing the arbitrary nature of certain social structures even in the act of affirming them. Encouraged by the physical presence of women onstage as actresses, the increased and varied representation of women in the audience, and the entry of women into the public sphere as writers, and driven by the larger and deeper ideological shifts underlying these phenomena, this drama enacts a deeply ambivalent engagement with questions of female subjectivity, greatly expanding speaking roles for women and playing almost obsessively on the presence of women in the theater. The depth and extent of its interest in sexual roles, relationships, and identities can be seen in its adaptations of Renaissance models, such as John Dryden and William Davenant's *Tempest,* which multiplies the number of women characters and alters Shakespeare's plot substantially to play with notions of sexual identity, sexuality, and sexual roles. In all its modes, tragedies and comedies alike, Restoration drama focuses on the sexual basis of social structures—marriage, family, patrilineal succession—in a representation characterized by the unsettling and reexamination of assumptions. These cracks in the patriarchal structure coexist with attempts to reaffirm that structure, sometimes through violent reassertion of male prerogatives, sometimes through subtle reformulations of economies of power. A changing awareness of female subjectivity, and new anxieties about the nature of feminine identity, generated in part by the voice and presence of the actress, lead to attempts to restrain, contain, and construct that subjectivity in various ways. This process results in a volatile and unresolved dramatic interplay, in which the body of the actress, the women in the audience, and potentially feminist questions in the text about marriage, social structures, and gender roles and identity become the loci of anxiety, question, and assertion, in a fluid interaction of affirmation and critique, statement and subversion.

The recent flowering of interest in gender and sexuality in the eighteenth century has produced to date no collected study of feminist issues in this drama per se. This volume is indebted to some valuable revisionist historical work showing the extent and involvement of women in the theater as actresses, playwrights, spectators, and patrons (see Schofield and Macheski; Roberts; Maus), particularly to Jacqueline Pearson's study, which considers both women as playwrights and women as represented onstage in the period, thus highlighting the subject/object dichotomy that informs all female representation in this drama. The concerns of this book have also been sparked by recent theorizing of the body, sexuality, and gender, especially in performance and in this period (Straub; Braverman; Butler; Zimmerman; Weber; Stallybrass; Jardine), and by precise and challenging readings of the political implications within the dualities of contemporary discourse, both dramatic and otherwise (Staves; Markley; Brown). The main purpose of this collection, however, is to examine, from a comprehensive and fundamentally empirical perspective, the shifting forms of specifically feminist issues as they are enacted within both text and theatrical production in the Restoration period. The feminist critique focuses on the political, on assertions of and resistance to the ideology that devalues women in all its forms; this volume examines that critique both as it is enacted and as it is negated or appropriated, undermined or affirmed, in drama by playwrights of both sexes, and in the dynamics of production and the theatrical world. Thus the collection will foreground issues that, although apparently central to both the audience and the genre, have only been marginally considered. In so doing it should help revise current historical and theoretical understanding of both Restoration discourse and the society it represents.

The essays in this volume examine feminism in Restoration drama from a holistic and multiple perspective, using a variety of historical and theoretical approaches. They examine a wide variety of plays, considering not only comedy (most frequently associated with the woman question) but also tragedies, heroic plays, tragicomedies, and the interplay and adaptation of these different modes. The essays are grouped in the categories feminism in plays by women, feminism in plays by men, and feminism in theory and history of performance. This arrangement reflects both the interactive and extratextual nature of the genre and the multivocality of feminist discourse in this period, a multiplicity seen also in the various feminisms that inform the essays themselves. Subjects vary from female rewriting of Renaissance tradition and the inscription of feminist issues therein, to the ambivalences of feminist discourse in drama by mainstream male writers, to the interplay of voices between male and female playwrights, to the problematic relation between feminist critiques in the drama and changing social and political constructions, to feminist questions as enacted beyond the authored text in staging and audience dynamics, considering in particular the impact of the actress and the increased visibility of the female spectator.

The opening section on female-authored plays borrows its title from a male-authored satire on antifeminist reaction to women writers: the saying "A Pen in the Hand of a Woman . . . is an Instrument of Propagation," spoken by Henry Fielding's Justice Squeezum in *Rape upon Rape* (II.v; 101), equates women's writing with uncontrolled sexuality and reproduction, working through the familiar trope of the pen as the male instrument of both writing and sexual reproduction. Ironically, this misogynist gibe also suggests both the creative power of female writing and the effects of its distribution, as it continually challenges and undermines dominant masculinist frameworks of perception. The essays in Part 1 show how female dramatists of the Restoration appropriate and adapt male dramatic tradition—through rewriting of plays, through complex intertextual relationships, or through exploitation of existing dramatic conventions—and how in so doing they expose and challenge the ideology that generates and informs the tradition. In a fascinating instance of Restoration feminism's providing an early link with questions of race and cultural diversity in its challenge to the hegemonic framework, Jacqueline Pearson examines how Restoration women rewrite Renaissance plays to problematize stereotypes of race and gender, focusing particularly on Mary Pix's precise and comprehensive recuperations of *Othello*. Pix is generally considered relatively conservative, affirming patriarchal norms (Pearson 171–80), but Pearson shows how she works through a precisely articulated web of intertextual connections to question and dissolve the deeply rooted assumptions concerning femaleness and blackness that inform male dramatic tradition.

Women's writing of this period engages two dominant forms of masculinist discourse: first, libertinism, whose apparent commitment to individualism and the celebration of free sexuality masks a deep devotion to patriarchal domination and which overtly, sometimes violently, constrains, restrains, constructs, and even negates female sexuality and subjectivity; and, less obviously, scientific empiricism, which promotes gender-based oppression under the guise of objective inquiry. The rewriting and interrogation of these modes of thought are the focus of essays on the plays of Catherine Trotter, Delariviere Manley, and Aphra Behn. Rebecca Merrens examines the way in which Manley and Trotter resist a repressive tragic tradition that constructs women as the cause of the tragic disruption of patriarchal community and masculine integrity. Manley and Trotter show the roots of the tragedy to lie within the self-defeating and inconsistent nature of those patriarchal economies themselves, and they celebrate women who embody political and sexual power. Merrens also demonstrates the mutually constitutive nature of seventeenth-century scientific empiricism and dramatic tradition in their containment and objectification of women.

Three essays on Behn, the premier female dramatist, explore, from radically different perspectives, the nature and development of Behn's feminism, particularly her problematic relation to the libertine code. Dagny Boebel's detailed Bakhtinian-deconstructive reading of *The Rover* demonstrates how both the carnival context and women's speech, by destructuring accepted sign-signified connections, disclose patriarchal hierarchy as arbitrary fantasy, not metaphysical truth. The play also exposes the libertine concept of carnival as another form of patriarchal hierarchy brutally oppressive of female subjectivity and suggests an alternate, feminist concept of carnival that liberates women from the patriarchal system of signification. Peggy Thompson studies the development of Behn's feminism through her adaptation of traditional romantic endings, which increasingly resist comic closure and the marriage script and in their indeterminacy reflect Behn's own resistance to the restrictive script written for women in the social world offstage. Robert A. Erickson's study of Lady Fulbank as one of the few women "writers" in Restoration drama to create a successful script within the authorial script places Behn in relation to libertine drama as exemplified particularly in William Wycherley. Erickson also examines Behn's feminist rewriting of the libertine code to assert female subjectivity, integrity, and creative power.

Although the writing, performing, and publishing of plays by women in itself embodies a feminist critique, problematizing the relation of those plays to the patriarchal system they inhabit, it is remarkable that plays by men focus almost to an equal extent on what can be considered women's issues. Male-authored drama demonstrates a radical ambivalence in engaging feminist questions, an ambivalence suggested in the title of this section: "chased desire" encapsulates the duality of male expectations of the female as the object of sexual desire who must at all costs remain chaste, and as the object of masculinist definition and codification who is nonetheless perpetually elusive in her otherness. In male-authored drama, feminist questions may be resisted and repressed in reassertions of patriarchal conventions and prerogatives, which vary from violent oppression to subtle reconstruction and containment of the feminine; or they may exist as an unresolved force in the play, unsettling the dominant framework, undermining and questioning those same conventions; or male-authored plays may address feminist questions directly and sympathetically. Essays in this section cover a range of these responses. In an instance of how more aggressive forms of reassertion of patriarchal dominance occur in times of political and class insecurity, J. Douglas Canfield examines the cit-bashing plays of the Exclusion Crisis and demonstrates that class aggression, traditionally enacted through misogynistic appropriation of the female body, is rewritten with new intensity during this time. As both patriarchal and aristocratic privilege are emphatically asserted, male potency is seen as the proof of "natural" class dominance, and the female body and female sexual desire become constructed as entirely complicit ciphers in the transmission of this authority. Yet the metaphor and reality of rape and seduction in these plays also expose the power assumptions common to both sides and thus undermine any essentialist claims to legitimacy. The same aristocratic-patriarchal ideology receives a much more ambivalent treatment in Dryden's *Conquest of Granada*. In my essay I show that, within its redefinition and reaffirmation of patriarchy, the play focuses on a female figure who calls that order into question, contrasting the identity assigned through patriarchal construction of woman to the identity achieved through the expression of female subjectivity and will. The play is structured around this contrast, and the establishment of the hero's self and identity is intimately linked to it. Indeed, he and all the other men in the play become implicated in an oppressive system against which female subjectivity seeks to define itself.

After 1688, postrevolutionary ideology, Lockean ideas of equality, and with them the demystification of the monarchical structure helped create a climate of debate that generated an efflorescence of writing on feminist issues. This phenomenon can be seen not only in the rise to prominence of female playwrights such as Pix, Trotter, and Manley but also in a shift in focus in male-authored drama—most notably in the plays of Thomas Southerne, which turn libertine convention against itself and dramatize extensively something arguably like a feminist politics. Even the more apparently libertine and conservative plays of William Congreve and George Farquhar, however, reflect some of the feminist questions being raised in contemporary literature, as seen in James E. Evans's study of *The Way of the World* and *The Beaux' Stratagem*. Evans shows how both plays question the "private Tyranny" of existing marital convention in terms that suggest Mary Astell's distinction between the assumptions of equality in the Lockean social contract and the reality of oppression in the marital sexual contract.

This late seventeenth-century debate on women's nature and rights, however, paradoxically coexisted with a hardening of gender constructions, whereby the nature of male and female were redefined in a new configuration of traditional assumptions. Woman was essentialized as naturally modest, chaste, and pure, man's complement—and subordinate—in mind as well as body (see LeGates; Pollak; Shevelow). Thus female subjectivity itself was constructed so as to reinforce the "naturalness" of male domination. Accounts of female influence in "purifying" the drama, then, reveal a doublethink whereby the power and expression supposedly accorded women in this period—which did allow them some reaction against the misogyny of libertine conventions—are co-opted into attempts to contain and construct them in a manner consistent with dominant patriarchal ideology. (The same assumptions are evident in latter-day accounts of this moralizing feminine influence in 1690s drama [e.g., Smith]; these have been recently reexamined and thoroughly historicized by David Roberts [chap. 5].) This doubleness is particularly evident in male efforts to control and limit female interpretation, particularly of the subversive dualities of Restoration dramatic dialogue. The dilemmas and constraints placed on the female auditor by the conjunction of paternalistic expectations and libertine text are outlined in Patricia Gill's analysis of Congreve. She argues that the structuring of the response of the female auditor, whereby she is excluded from moral awareness if she does not understand the dialogue yet is incriminated as immoral if she does understand and interpret for herself, is paralleled in the depiction of the heroines of Restoration comedy, who must be "knowledgeable without being in the know"—a double construction that is part of an attempt to confine the act of female interpretation, uniting both fictional female character and real female auditor into an impossible fiction reflective of male desire.

The final three essays focus on the single most powerful element in Restoration drama's shift to a gender-centered focus: the appearance of the actress onstage, as a physical and speaking female presence, a presence that blurred or crossed or erased a number of boundaries. Her body became the site where questions regarding gender roles and identity could be enacted; the immense popularity of cross-dressing in female roles not only reflected an appeal to spectators' libidinous tastes—indeed, even these arose from complex sexual and social responses, as women spectators were also enthusiastic—but also became a means of questioning notions of female identity and the limitations attached to it, and of exploring and defining boundaries in sexual roles, sexual identity, and sexual attraction. The presence of the actress fundamentally altered the Renaissance dynamic of fictionality and the open-ended play on gender ambiguity it promoted (see Jardine; Zimmerman; Stallybrass; Garber). Her presence raised questions of the nature of female subjectivity and desire, as a female voice and body informed what was said and touched off in male spectators an intricate complex of response, interpretation, construction, and constraint. In the presence of the actress, the boundaries between fiction and extratheatrical "reality" were continually broken, blurred, or exploited. One of the most famous examples of this is the epilogue to Dryden's *Tyrannick Love,* in which Nell Gwyn reveals under the character of virtuous Valeria her own distinctly unvirtuous one—"I am the ghost of poor departed *Nelly*"—undermining the play's strenuous assertions of female virtue. The (usually well-publicized) offstage life of the actress, which continually inhabited her fictional parts, generated uncertainties regarding the consistency of female identity and the relation of public role to inner self. Furthermore, the presence of the actress also blurred the boundaries of fictionality in her relationship to the women in the audience, who were equally objects of viewing and of dramatic interest, as is evident throughout Samuel Pepys's diary and other memoirs of the period. John Macky wrote that "in the 1st *Row* of *Boxes* sit all the Ladies of Quality; in the second the Citizens' Wives & Daughters . . . so that between the Acts you may be diverted by viewing the Beauties of the Audience" (2:109–10, cited in Roberts 81). Thus the presence of women onstage became the locus for a whole complex of questions on the inherent theatricality of social roles, as dictated not only by gender but also by class.

The essays in Part 3 examine performance, production, and extratheatrical discourse as they reflect these questions. In particular they show how the Restoration actress—and the Restoration spectatrix—enact and embody the ambiguous status of women as both subject and object. In her study of representations of attempted rape in male-authored plays, Jean I. Marsden shows how the body of the actress becomes a site for the violent reassertion of male dominance, both in the attempt itself and in the convention of the victim's self-destruction that follows it. This process implicates the audience in a kind of doublethink, as it depends on a blend of sexuality and suffering that exalts the moral purity of the victim while sharing in the prurient desires of the villain. In these scenes theatrical spectatorship becomes a form of voyeurism reflecting its own gender-based economies; such scenes have a coercive effect on the female spectator, forcing her either to deny her sex or to indulge in a masochistic identification with the victim. The intersecting ambiguities of female status, of the theatrical dynamic that allows room for female subjectivity while at the same time reinforcing the status of women as sexual, economic, and spectatorial objects, are closely analyzed in Laura J. Rosenthal's essay on the actress and the spectatrix in Restoration adaptations of Shakespeare. She explores the problematics of female spectators' identification with female characters and with the actress and examines the "active and unsettled tensions" in which the female subjectivity represented onstage might provide a sense of empowerment for the female spectator, while at the same time the various forces that objectify women, both within the text of the play and in the performative focus on the body of the actress, compromise and contradict that subjectivity. Finally, Cynthia Lowenthal examines the audience's interpretation of the interplay of the actress's offstage life—itself frequently both fictional and "real"—and the actress's representation of characters onstage in her study of the extratheatrical discourse surrounding celebrities Anne Bracegirdle and Elizabeth Barry. Lowenthal shows how the specularized yet subjective presence of the actress—her reality within a fictional role—raised the question of the fictionality of all social status. Barry and Bracegirdle were used to counteract that uncertainty, as they were "read" through their representation of characters onstage and, simultaneously, through their own status as "known" objects offstage, in such a way as to reinforce class essentialism.

The representation of gender issues in the Restoration period is marked by an instability reflecting more general ideological shifts taking place at the time and evident in all aspects of experience. Out of that shifting dynamic of question and assertion, constructions of sexuality and gender appear that still govern social and intellectual structures today. In the range and multiplicity of these essays, this collection aims to chart some of the elements and relationships within that earlier, more volatile period and so to examine the roots and limitations of long-lived eighteenth-century assumptions.

Works Cited

Astell, Mary. *The First English Feminist: Reflections upon Marriage and Other Writings*. Ed. Bridget Hill. New York: St. Martin's, 1986.

Braverman, Richard. *Plots and Counterplots: Sexual Politics and the Body Politic in English Literature, 1660-1730*. Cambridge: Cambridge UP, 1993.

Brown, Laura. *Ends of Empire: Women and Ideology in Early Eighteenth-Century English Literature*. Ithaca, N.Y.: Cornell UP, 1993.

Butler, Judith. "Performative Acts and Gender Constitution: An Essay in Phenomenology and Feminist Theory." *Performing Feminisms: Feminist Critical Theory and Theatre*. Ed. Sue-Ellen Case. Baltimore: Johns Hopkins UP, 1990.

Dryden, John. *Tyrannick Love; or, The Royal Martyr*. 1670. *The Works of John Dryden*. Vol. 10. Ed. Maximillian E. Novak and George R. Guffey. Berkeley: U of California P, 1970. 105-93.

Fielding, Henry. *Rape upon Rape; or, The Justice Caught in His Own Trap*. London, 1730. Rpt. in *Complete Works of Henry Fielding, Esq*. Vol. 9. Rpt., New York: Barnes and Noble, 1967. 72-158.

Garber, Marjorie. "The Logic of the Transvestite: *The Roaring Girl* (1608)." *Staging the Renaissance: Reinterpretations of Elizabethan and Jacobean Drama*. Ed. David Scott Kastan and Peter Stallybrass. New York: Routledge, 1991. 221-34.

Jardine, Lisa. "Boy Actors, Female Roles, and Elizabethan Eroticism." *Staging the Renaissance: Reinterpretations of Elizabethan and Jacobean Drama*. Ed. David Scott Kastan and Peter Stallybrass. New York: Routledge, 1991. 57-67.

LeGates, Marlene. "The Cult of Womanhood in Eighteenth-Century Thought." *Eighteenth-Century Studies* 10.1 (Fall 1976): 21-39.

Macky, John. *A Journey through England in Familiar Letters*. 2 vols. London, 1714.

Markley, Robert. *Two-Edg'd Weapons: Style and Ideology in the Comedies of Etherege, Wycherley, and Congreve.* Oxford: Clarendon, 1988.

Maus, Katherine Eisaman. " 'Playhouse Flesh and Blood': Sexual Ideology and the Restoration Actress." *ELH* 46 (Winter 1979): 595-617.

Pearson, Jacqueline. *The Prostituted Muse: Images of Women and Women Dramatists, 1642-1737.* Manchester: Manchester UP, 1988.

Pollak, Ellen. *The Poetics of Sexual Myth: Gender and Ideology in the Verse of Swift and Pope.* Chicago: U of Chicago P, 1985.

Roberts, David. *The Ladies: Female Patronage of Restoration Drama, 1660-1700.* Oxford: Clarendon, 1989.

Schofield, Mary Anne, and Cecilia Macheski, eds. *Curtain Calls: British and American Women and the Theater, 1660-1820.* Athens: Ohio UP, 1991.

Shevelow, Kathryn. *Women and Print Culture: The Construction of Femininity in the Early Periodical.* New York: Routledge, 1989.

Smith, John Harrington. "Shadwell, the Ladies, and the Change in Comedy." *Modern Philology* 46 (1948): 22-33.

Stallybrass, Peter. "Transvestism and the 'Body Beneath': Speculating on the Boy Actor." *Erotic Politics: Desire on the Renaissance Stage.* Ed. Susan Zimmerman. New York: Routledge, 1992. 64-83.

Staves, Susan. *Players' Scepters: Fictions of Authority in the Restoration.* Lincoln: U of Nebraska P, 1979.

Straub, Kristina. *Sexual Suspects: Eighteenth-Century Players and Sexual Ideology.* Princeton, N.J.: Princeton UP, 1992.

Weber, Harold. *The Restoration Rake-Hero: Transformations in Sexual Understanding in Seventeenth-Century England.* Madison: U of Wisconsin P, 1986.

Zimmerman, Susan. "Disruptive Desire: Artifice and Indeterminacy in Jacobean Comedy." *Erotic Politics: Desire on the Renaissance Stage.* Ed. Susan Zimmerman. New York: Routledge, 1992. 39-63.

PART 1

Instruments of Propagation: Plays by Women

Blacker Than Hell Creates:
Pix Rewrites *Othello*

Jacqueline Pearson

*I*f *Hamlet* was the Shakespearean play most central to the reading and self-fashioning of readers of the Romantic period—if William Hazlitt and his contemporaries felt that "it is *we* who are Hamlet" (4:23–24)—then in the Restoration the play most integral to consciousness and culture was *Othello*. It was the only one of Shakespeare's major tragedies to be performed throughout the period in more or less the form that Shakespeare wrote it, with "no important variations from the original printings" (Odell 1:38), while *King Lear* appeared only in the fundamentally recast form of Nahum Tate's version (1681) and *Macbeth* and *Hamlet* in somewhat less radically altered texts by Davenant (1674, 1676). New printed editions of *Othello* appeared in 1681, 1687, 1695, and 1705, and in the early eighteenth century it was one of the most regularly acted plays, appearing in every season but two of the thirty-one between 1710 and 1742 (Odell 1:224). Clearly something about *Othello* had a deep appeal to performers, readers, and audiences in the Restoration.

Some of the reasons for this are obvious. Alone among Shakespeare's mature tragedies, *Othello* is a domestic play in which heterosexual love is shown in contention with, and is ultimately given priority over, a public world of war and politics. It therefore duplicates more completely than any other of the mature tragedies the typical range and interests of serious drama of the Restoration. Formally, the play's appeal to Restoration audiences is also readily explicable. Indeed, *Othello* is one of the key sources for Restoration tragedy, suggesting a number of elements that became central to the development of the genre after 1660: the single action, the exotic foreign background, the sharply paired and contrasted characters, the cunning but covert villain, the importance of issues of patriarchal authority. It was even decisively influential in visual terms, by originating, for example, the potentially titillating "couch scenes" so popular in Restoration tragedy, in which the female body is displayed and fetishized.[1] Finally, if Susan Staves is right in suggesting that the typical Restoration hero is "strangely passive" (42), a victim of forces beyond his control, then Othello provides an influential prototype.

Perhaps there were other reasons, too, for the special Restoration fascination for *Othello* and its images of exotic racial outsiders. Throughout the sixteenth and seventeenth centuries the highest classes of English society were vigorously exogamous. Charles II's mother was French, his grandmother Danish, his wife Portuguese. Class similarity was ultimately more important than national difference, and it is possible that the idea of an ethnically different partner acquired glamorous associations with royal and aristocratic practices. Moreover, the dependence of the Royalists on foreign allies during the Civil War, and the Interregnum exile of many Royalists, might well have initiated a reconsideration of the relationship between domestic and alien, those like us and those unlike us. During this period foreigners might well be friends and lovers, fellow Englishmen rivals or opponents. (This kind of scenario is dramatized, for instance, in Aphra Behn's *The Rover*.) Indeed, there was a tradition of associating the Stuarts with images of racial difference. Ben Jonson's *The Masque of Blackness* (1605) was written to be performed by Anne of Denmark and her ladies, who appeared in it as "twelue *Nymphs, Negro's*" (7:170–71). It is likely that in Behn's *Oroonoko* (1688) the fate of the royal black protagonist is used to figure that of Charles I (see Guffey). Additionally, because of his dark complexion, Charles II acquired a number of nicknames suggestive of racial difference, like the Black Boy (Falkus 13). As a result, in Restoration literature racial difference and racially different characters might well have acquired positive associations, with aristocracy and royalism generally and with the Stuart dynasty in particular, which challenged more traditional negative ones.

It is possible, too, that *Othello* offered a model that was particularly attractive to women writers. Mary Pix, for instance, goes so far as to use the play and its images of racial difference as a touchstone for female taste and even chastity and marital concord. In *The Innocent Mistress* (1697), for example, the vulgar and shrewish Lady Beauclair hates the theater, finding it "Nonsense," for "the first thing I saw was an ugly black Devil kill his Wife, for nothing" (24).[2] This not only reveals her lack of sensitivity; it also parallels her culpable failure to live harmoniously with her husband and even predicts the comedy's surprising conclusion, that she is actually a bigamist, for her first husband, who had been supposed dead, fortuitously reappears. We might have guessed as much, however, for no genteel woman could respond so insensitively to *Othello* and its images of racial and gender difference.

Interestingly, seventeenth- and eighteenth-century women writers seem to have identified less with (white, female) Desdemona than with

Othello himself. Male writers might impose on women an identification with Desdemona, but this is usually patronizing or even positively insulting. The Earl of Shaftesbury in 1710, for instance, uses the comparison to highlight women's alleged frivolity, perverse sexuality, and marginality to the world of literature, as he criticizes women's liking for travel books by imagining their female readers as "a thousand Desdemonas" pursuing black lovers (cited in Cowhig 13). The mixture in Desdemona of disruptively assertive sexuality and passive self-denial possibly disturbed women too much for her to be a useful model for them. In any case, Shakespearean tragedy is so androcentric a mode that assertive women writers had virtually no choice in reading but to identify with male characters and viewpoints, as does, for instance, Mary Wollstonecraft (see Wolfson 18).

The characterization of Othello, however, seems to have been uniquely useful to seventeenth-century women. Quotations from and allusions to *Othello* are very common in the works of Restoration and early eighteenth-century women writers, and they are attributed to women in the works of men. In Charlotte Charke's *The Art of Management* (1735), for instance, her fictional alter ego Mrs. Tragic identifies with and quotes Othello (19–20), and so does the jealous Belira in Delariviere Manley's *The Lost Lover* (1696) (26) and the female warrior Locris in Charles Hopkins's *Friendship Improv'd; or, The Female Warrior* (1700) (47). The appeal lies, I think, in the fact that *Othello* offers suggestive ways in which racial difference can be used to trope gender difference. Passive, manipulated, ultimately choosing the private world of love over the public world of war, a member of a disempowered group, subject to intense prejudice when he transgresses the limits of his proper sphere, Othello could be viewed as symbolically feminized, even as providing potentially resonant self-images for women writers who were also aware of prejudice and were anxious about transgressions of their assigned roles. Moreover, if women are traditionally associated with nature, men with culture (see Ortner), then the "super-subtle Venetian" Desdemona and Othello the "erring barbarian" (I.iii.356–57) might be seen to reverse this relationship, though Shakespeare's tendency is finally repressive, since the consequence of a reversal of "normal" gender relations is catastrophic.

Women dramatists of the Restoration in fact went further than *Othello* and ransacked the canon of pre-1660 plays for those that concentrate on images of ethnic otherness. It does not seem to have been previously recognized that the revision of such plays forms a significant element in the corpus of women's drama from the mid-1670s to about 1705; this does not seem so visibly the case for plays by male writers. Such plays include Aphra Behn's *Abdelazer* (1676), a revision of the anonymous *Lust's Dominion; or, The Lascivious Queen* (1599–1600?); *The Revenge; or, A Match in Newgate* (1680), probably by Behn, which rewrites John

Marston's *The Dutch Courtesan* (1605); and the two plays by Mary Pix that will take central place in this essay, *The Conquest of Spain* (1705), which rewrites William Rowley's *All's Lost by Lust* (1616–19; published 1633) but makes important alterations, and *The False Friend; or, The Fate of Disobedience* (1699), which seems to offer an original plot but which, I shall argue, is deeply and significantly imbued with echoes of *Othello.* The appeal of such plays to women dramatists probably lay in the sympathetic identification they allowed between women and other cultural outsiders. Racial and ethnic difference provided useful tropes for gender difference, and in the identification both are reformed. Women first significantly entered public, political discourse in Britain and America in the eighteenth century in the movements that opposed slavery (see Ferguson). Restoration texts in which women focus on images of ethnic difference can be read as an enabling mechanism for this emergence.

In this essay I wish to investigate the range of ways in which Restoration women use images of ethnic difference, especially to figure gender difference. I have written elsewhere about Aphra Behn's treatment of ethnic difference and her repeated use of themes and images of racial otherness; I have examined her replacement of a privileged white, male point of view with a range of different ethnic and gendered viewpoints ("Gender and Narrative," esp. 186); and I have been particularly interested in her dismantling of those binary oppositions through which a patriarchal culture maintains itself in power and excludes its Others. Such self-interested oppositions as black/white, male/female, are replaced with what a twentieth-century feminist has called "multiple, heterogeneous *difference*" (Moi 104–5), which celebrates difference rather than using it to naturalize oppressive hierarchies. Now I want to extend this examination to a less obviously radical dramatist, Mary Pix, and to show her subverting these binary oppositions with vigor but also with an extraordinary intertextual subtlety. First, however, it will be necessary to offer a brief introduction to images of ethnic otherness in male-authored seventeenth-century tragedies, in order to suggest the kind of views that playwrights like Pix and Behn could go on to subvert.

The ethnic Other in early seventeenth-century texts tends to be associated with stereotypes of "cruelty" and "lasciviousness" (Kabbani 19), and also with "credulity," "jealousy," and treachery (Jones 22, 79). These stereotypes are apparent even in those few plays that challenge them. Shakespeare is himself deeply interested in images of ethnic otherness and is sometimes prepared to challenge clichés. *Titus Andronicus,* for instance, begins by contrasting the civilized Romans with the "barbarous" Goths (I.i.28), but by the end of the first act the Gothic queen has already showed an understanding of the civilized values of mercy and compassion, while the civilized hero Titus has become "barbarous" (I.i.378). However, by the end of the play this problematization of issues of civilization and barbarism has been swamped by a fairly simple identification of the ethnic outsider with typical outlaw sexuality, rape, adultery, violence, and cruelty.[3] The black Aaron, whose name associates him with Judaism and thus with religious as well as racial otherness, in particular becomes an embodiment of evil (see his speech at V.i.124–44), a "devil" (V.i.145), and, in a phrase later remembered in the characterization of (white) Iago (*Othello* V.i.62), an "inhuman dog" (*Titus* V.iii.14).

Similarly, it seems to me that in *Othello* Shakespeare begins by problematizing the stereotype of blackness, but he finally chooses not to pursue this and chooses instead to show Othello as the victim of his biology as well as of Iago. It has been said that Shakespeare adopts the "daring" expedient "of putting the man and the type as it were side by side on the stage" (Jones 87), presenting his audience with "a series of propositions which serve to reverse or disturb their settled notions of black people" (Cowhig 12). In the early acts of the play, despite Iago's racist comments, Othello indeed runs heroically counter to the stereotype in almost every respect. He is not cruel or swayed by passion: he stops the fight between his supporters and those of Brabantio. He is not lustful: he even believes "the young affects" are "defunct" in him (I.iii.263–64). The Othello of the fifth act, however, reinstates some of these stereotypes: we see him as violent, irrational, and jealous, and both he and Emilia accept the traditional association of blackness with the devil, which the rest of the play has so vigorously resisted and has even relocated onto the white devil Iago (V.ii.132, 134, 278). After problematizing issues of both race and gender, Shakespeare, it seems to me, falls back to an essentialist, biology-is-destiny view of both. It is less that he depicts "a black man whose humanity is eroded by the cunning and racism of whites" (Cowhig 7) as that after testing the stereotypes, he ultimately accepts those asserting black credulity, jealousy, violence, and uncontrollable sexuality. Unlike Shakespeare, however, women writers influenced by *Othello* tend to carry further its problematization of stereotypes of difference.

Another aspect of the stereotypical treatment of ethnic otherness in many of these texts is revealed by the fact that it does not matter very much whether the ethnic Other is a non-English European, an African, an Asian, an Arab, or a Native American: all attract similar associations. Indeed, these various ethnic groups tend to be elided by Renaissance and Restoration playwrights. For instance, the unequivocally African Eleazar in the anonymous *Lust's Dominion* is persistently associated with India—or, perhaps, America—and made to swear by "our Indian gods" (W. Carew Hazlitt, e.g., 110, 142, 143, 154). Conversely, Zelide the Aztec princess is referred to as a "Moor," a term that technically denotes African origins (Pix,

False Friend 58). This erasure of the specificity of individual ethnic groups is, of course, demeaning; one of the basic supports of English imperialism is a hierarchical division of the world into the English and everybody else. In light of this, Aphra Behn's insistence in *Oroonoko* on the cultural differences between black Africans and Native Americans, and even between different tribes of Native Americans, is an important way of championing the human individuality of the colonized Other.

In the late sixteenth and early seventeenth centuries black Africans became the sharpest focus of a hierarchical discourse on race. A frequently stated view held that their outward appearance symbolized their inner moral nature. In proverbs and idioms, blackness is routinely associated with night, deception, ugliness, passion, evil, death, the devil, and above all sexuality; the associations of whiteness include day, truth, purity, beauty, reason, goodness, heaven, and chastity. Blackness and whiteness, indeed, reiterated exactly that polarization of women into whores and virgins that women writers of the period were to find so damaging and that some would attempt to dismantle. As a result, one significant alteration made in post-Restoration texts by women is a marked resistance to the stereotypical associations of blackness and whiteness and the reassuringly simple contrasts between Self and Other that they offered to those safely within the dominant culture. Blanket condemnations of blacks as a group tend in these texts to come only from thoughtless characters, from those in the grip of appalling suffering, or from outright villains, like the "gay young courtiers" who call Behn's Abdelazer "Moor! a Devil!" (2:14) or the villain Jaquez in Pix's *Conquest of Spain,* who, in a striking example of the pot calling the kettle, sees the blackness of the Moors as expressing "the innate Malice of their Souls" (21).

Obvious examples of the stereotyped black man in Renaissance drama include Eleazar in *Lust's Dominion,* Aaron in *Titus Andronicus,* and Muly Mumen in Rowley's *All's Lost by Lust.* The facts that two of these play titles contain the word *lust,* and that all three juxtapose the image of the black man with plots that center on the rape or attempted rape of a white woman, reveal the "automatic association" of blacks with threatening, outlaw sexuality (Jones 71). The implicit contradictions here should, however, be recognized. Not one of these black men is the actual rapist: Aaron helps Chiron and Demetrius plot the rape of Lavinia, Eleazar hopes to benefit from the king's rape of his wife, and Muly Mumen turns the circumstances of Jacinta's rape by King Rodericke to his own advantage. But although none are actually rapists, they are implicated all the same, since their blackness presents them as visibly guilty of uncontrollable passion and dark sexuality, so that they are at best symbolic representations of the "blackened" consciences of the white rapists, at worst guilty by proxy. Their blackness proclaims them as morally guilty of rape even as the plot demonstrates that this is not so. If, as modern feminism has suggested, rape is a central act through which patriarchy ensures the subjection and oppression of all women (see, e.g., Brownmiller), this motif of displaced guilt may depict in a confused way the paradoxical role of the black man in a culture defined through binary oppositions: he is superior as a man, inferior as a nonwhite; both within and outside the governing structures of patriarchy; both guilty and not guilty of rape.

If black men in pre-Restoration plays most commonly feature as rapists, black women, like white women, are polarized into images of good passive and bad active females, "passive decorative" queens or "lustful, treacherous" maidservants (Jones 119). The most dramatically effective in the latter category are Zanche in Webster's *The White Devil* and two characters both named Zanthia in Marston's *Sophonisba* and Beaumont and Fletcher's *The Knight of Malta*. The moral nature of the Zanthias contrasts dramatically with that of their virtuous mistresses, while Zanche, the black "devil" (V.i.86), is a living embodiment of the outlaw sexuality and self-assertion of her mistress, the white devil Vittoria Corrombona. The cruelty, lasciviousness, and treachery stereotypically associated with blacks also features in certain female stereotypes, so that black women tend to appear as doubly inferior. Consequently, women writers, in producing more sensitive representations of black characters, were also subtextually presenting more positive representations of themselves.

As Kristina Straub has pointed out, in the late seventeenth and eighteenth centuries ethnic difference tended to be recycled as part of other related discourses of class, sexuality, or gender difference (151–73). Troping your enemy as low status in class, race, and gender can obviously be an effective weapon in the armory of an "establishment" writer defending "high" culture against infiltration by class, racial, and gender outsiders. It is prominent, too, in some Renaissance plays centering on ethnic difference. In Rowley's *All's Lost by Lust* the low-class woman Margaretta, who murders her adulterous upper-class husband, Antonio, identifies herself with the stereotypically lascivious and violent Moors, both by her assertive sexuality—her "unequall" marriage has been "not love, but lust" (III.ii.22)—and by her act of murder. Class, gender, and racial difference combine in a comprehensive vision of violence and evil. (In seventeenth-century law a woman who killed her husband was guilty not only of murder but also of treason, since she had attacked one in lawful authority over her: in this respect Margaretta's act directly paraphrases the uprising of the Spanish Moors under Muly Mumen.) In *Lust's Dominion* the "lascivious [white] Queen" of the subtitle, mistress to Eleazar the Moor and like him lustful and guilty of murder, is also identified with images of blackness: she utters "black curses" against her enemies, and like Eleazar she is identified with lust, darkness, and hell (W. Carew Hazlitt 173; see, e.g., 99). In such cases the implicit and explicit links between women and blacks serve to demonize both.

But very different things might happen when a marginalized low-status group itself accepts the identification with analogous dispossessed aliens and uses this identification to disrupt received stereotypes of class, of race, and of gender. When in *Oroonoko* Behn herself implicitly identifies white women with black slaves and her own white upper-class female narrator with the black slave protagonists, she opens up for questioning all her culture's stereotypes of gender, race, and power (see Pearson, "Gender and Narrative" 184–90). Women's revisions of texts centering on racial difference tend to present these equivalences in different, and more positive, ways. In *Abdelazer,* for instance, black men are shown demonstrating female virtues: even the cruel and Machiavellian Abdelazer can "turn Woman" (88) and show compassion and sympathy. In Pix's *Conquest of Spain,* too, the violated Jacincta identifies herself with the Moors by assuming the disguise of a black woman (34). Doubly marginalized as female and as rape victim, she finds analogies for herself in the black women who also experience a double colonization. Mullymumen, the Moorish king, responds to her plight with emotions that these plays identify as characteristically feminine, "Pity" (75) and "compassion" (76). In the original texts, the identification of women and blacks creates a heavily negative attitude to both; in the work of the female revisionists, it can function more positively to show them sharing oppositional virtues that are potentially dangerous to the values of the ruling patriarchy. In Pix's play these virtues help to bring down the oppressive regime of the white king.

Whereas Aphra Behn is often critical, even confrontational, in her treatment of women's position, Mary Pix generally seems less outspoken and more placatory in tone (see Pearson, *Prostituted Muse* 171–80). And yet when it comes to images of race and nationality, Pix, like Behn, replaces a system of binary opposition with "multiple, heterogeneous *difference,*" especially, I shall argue, in *The False Friend.* Like Behn—and like a number of contemporary dramatists, male and female—she often chooses exotic European and Near Eastern locations not only for tragedies but also for comedies: Turkey in *Ibrahim, the Thirteenth Emperour of the Turks* (1696); Spain in *The Spanish Wives* (1696), *The Conquest of Spain* (1705), and *The Adventures in Madrid* (1706); Venice in *The Deceiver Deceived* (1698); Persepolis in *The Double Distress* (1701); and Russia in *The Czar of Muscovy* (1701). These settings seem to be chosen, however, not only for their superficial exoticism and the opportunities they offer for theatrical spectacle but also for their fruitful images of alienness and specifically of the altered gender relationships possible in plays that feature polarized images of femininity, from confined harem women to the Amazon heroine of *Zelmane; or, The Corinthian Queen* (1704).

Pix is quite capable in her comedies of using ethnic stereotypes as a easy source for jokes and satire. The French, England's oldest and most persistent national enemies and cultural rivals, in particular form an exception to the generalization that Pix presents ethnic difference in a positive light. The French Insulls in *The Deceiver Deceived* (1698) is a ridiculously unsuccessful aspirer to wit and authorship, and Sir John Roverhead and Mrs. Rich in *The Beau Defeated* (1700) are laughed at for their Frenchified language and ways. There is often a serious edge to the comedy, though. Mrs. Rich and Lady Bounce in *The Different Widows* (1703) are criticized for unpatriotically subverting the war effort by smuggling "prohibited" French goods, perfumed gloves or brandy (4; see also *Beau Defeated* 3).

The Beau Defeated is Pix's most coherent play in its use of alienness as a negative quality. The foolish beau Sir John Roverhead is a liminal character in gender, nationality, and even class. Although male, he is seen "Patching, Painting, Powdering like a Woman, and squeaking like an Eunuch" (15), although English he adopts "*French* breeding" (7), and it is finally revealed that although apparently a gentleman, he is really only "a Servant" in the family of the man he pretends to be (46). In this play Pix seems to accept it as axiomatic that the English are superior to the French, as men are to women and the gentry to their servants. The liminal figure is a fool who is inferior and aspires to inferiority.

Nonetheless, Pix does not usually use images of alienness in such negative ways. Like many of her female contemporaries, including Behn and Susannah Centlivre, she often engineers relationships between men and women who are ethnically different, like the French Lovisa and the Spanish Emilius in *The False Friend,* or the English Gaylove and Bellmour and the Spanish Laura and Clarinda in *The Adventures in Madrid*. Ethnic difference has a special erotic excitement: like one latter-day feminist writer of science fiction, Pix creates in her alternative worlds a model for human sexuality, both male and female, that is vigorously "exogamous" (Tiptree 17). In *The Spanish Wives* the governor's wife can resist all sexual temptations except the English colonel Peregrine, and in *The Czar of Muscovy* a forged letter to Marina telling her that her fiancé has married a German woman gains her instant credence (14). In *The Different Widows* Angelica makes the rakish Sir James Bellmont fall in love with her by masquerading as a Spanish lady, "*Dona Angliana Hispaniola Amora*" (24), whose name embodies this exogamous drive by combining England, Spain, and love. Even the relationship between the French fool Insulls and the Venetian Lucinda in *The Deceiver Deceived* is not quite a parody of this convention, since Lucinda seems genuinely fond of him; the relationship seems to anticipate happily her introduction to Versailles. Such alliances serve as a resonant source of theatrical images for the alienness of men and women to each other within patriarchy, an alienness that, in comedy and tragicomedy, can yet lead to successful union and reconciliation.

Indeed, alienness may be the only defense against the most appalling dangers to stable relationships, sometimes imaged as incest. In *The Different Widows* Angelica wins Bellmont by keeping him disoriented about her real identity, pretending to be first a Spanish lady and then his own half sister, thus harmlessly embodying both exogamous and endogamous fantasies. Finally she combines a licit (exogamous) love and an illicit (endogamous) one, since in reality she is both the woman whom Bellmont's family has arranged for him to marry and the woman he has rebelliously chosen of his own accord. More seriously, in *The Double Distress* the Persian Leamira's marriage to the Medean Cleomedon not only represents their personal fulfillment but also exemplifies and facilitates the end of war between their nations. But when Medean Cytheria chooses to marry her fellow Medean Tygranes, she risks the danger of inadvertent incest with her own brother. *The Double Distress,* a distant revision of Beaumont and Fletcher's popular tragicomedy *A King and No King,* ensures a happy ending by revising family, and ethnic, history, so that Cytheria is permitted to marry the man she loves. Heterosexual love is figured as the peaceful meeting of aliens, the end of conflict, political and personal. Difference guarantees safety from incest—and possibly, by implication, from homosexuality—and ethnic difference often serves Pix (as it does Behn) as an image of harmonious heterosexuality. Woman's identification with the racial Other guarantees this harmony and also gives her power within this relationship, as Angelica is empowered by her manipulation of identities as Other.

Pix's full-scale revision of Rowley's *All's Lost by Lust* as *The Conquest of Spain* shows some of the obvious features of post-Restoration alterations of pre-Restoration plays. She simplifies the sprawling multiple plots of Rowley's play and cuts, in accordance with Restoration taste, the interruptions of low comedy in which he specialized. But her alterations to the discourses of gender and race in the original are also marked. In Rowley's play, the general Julianus's daughter Jacinta is raped by the king while Julianus is defending Spain against the invading Moors. The play is decidedly androcentric—sometimes, indeed, as in the fate of Jacinta, sadistically misogynist. It focuses primarily not on the violated woman but on the moral dilemma of her father: Will he revenge his daughter's dishonor, which also dishonors him, or will he consider that his honor depends on remaining faithful to his king, even when that king is guilty of his daughter's rape? In Rowley's play Julianus recruits the Moors to revenge the rape (the influence of *Titus Andronicus* is discernible here, as elsewhere), but they are dangerous allies. The Moor Muly Mumen demonstrates his evil nature by sexually persecuting the violated Jacinta, and when she rejects him he has her tongue cut out and then engineers her death in a typically cruel and devious way, tricking her own father into killing her. He thus proves himself "barbarous" (V.v.13), a "helhound" (20), a "black monster" (186) capable of any "tyranny" (185).

Pix slants attention toward the women and concentrates far more on their feelings and dilemmas. This is particularly noticeable in her wholesale revision of the subplot, the area of the play in which she makes the most sweeping alterations. In fact, she increases one heroine menaced by rape to two, so that Rowley's sexually assertive murderess Margaretta, the opposite of the pure and passive heroine, is rewritten as her double, a character who shares nothing with Rowley's character except the name and is instead a faithful pregnant wife menaced by an Iagoesque villain in her husband's absence. Unlike Jacincta, and unlike her prototype in Rowley's play, Margaretta survives the threat of rape and determines not to surrender to "vain Grief" (76) but to live on peacefully with her beloved husband under the hegemony of the Moors. Harmonious heterosexuality is here not created through the trope of ethnic difference, but ethnic difference, in the form of the Moor's defeat of the corrupt white king, ensures its survival. While Rowley's play eradicates the female altogether, in imaginative and distasteful ways, Pix allows at least one of her heroines to survive and mother the next generation.

Pix not only alters the subplot fundamentally, but she also follows the main plot less closely than, for instance, Behn follows her original in *Abdelazer*. In particular, in *The Conquest of Spain* stereotypes of racial difference are rethought, and terms that are stereotypically attached to blacks by Rowley are redirected by Pix at the truly guilty parties, the white king and his henchmen. It is they, not the Moors, who have proved themselves "Inhuman Monsters, Fiends of Hell . . . this barbarous infernal Race" (19–20). The contrast between black and white, civilization and barbarism, is renegotiated. If white men are associated with culture, and black men, like women, with nature, and if the whites are presented as morally more culpable than the blacks, then one effect of this may be to give a newly positive value to women and to female experience. Margaretta as mother and wife certainly embodies vital female strengths conspicuous in Rowley's play by their absence. Even the rather suffocating central version of female goodness as pure, passive, and persecuted is somewhat modified by the central position taken in the epilogue (not by the playwright) by images of extraordinary female power: the women in the audience are here assigned power over the fate of the play, by implication analogous to that of the British warrior queen, "mighty ANNA."

In her characterization of Mullymumen, Pix retains the barbaric dignity of Rowley's character but reduces stereotypical associations of his blackness with hell and the devil, creating a noble savage motivated by a "thirst of Glory" (32), somewhat on the lines of Dryden's Almanzor, and possibly to be identified with the duke of Marlborough, praised in the epilogue. Mullymumen does not sexually persecute the raped Jacincta: his claim to be the "Rival" (57) of her lover Theomantius seems more a fossil from the old play, or a ploy to demoralize his military opponent, than a genuine motive. Certainly he never approaches Jacincta with his love. Far from engineering her death, he seeks to protect her: she is fatally wounded when a "band of Moors" guarding her is attacked by Spaniards (68)—she is thus a victim not of the ethnic Other but, as in the case of her rape, of her own people—and Mullymumen is overcome with "Pity" (75) and "compassion" (76) at her fate. The evil, lechery, pitiless cruelty, and deviousness assigned to the ethnic Other in *All's Lost by Lust* are here all deflected to where they properly belong—the white autocrat rapist and the corrupt patriarchy that maintains him in power. The woman's identification with the ethnic Other (and his identification with her) here signifies virtue, purity, and kindness, not evil.

When early in the play the king's tools Clothario and Lodovicus try to persuade Jacincta to surrender to the king, they tempt her with images of the racial Other. If she submits, they tell her in a voyeuristic image, she will have all the erotic luxury of "Eastern Queens" (19). Ironically, in a play where all the dangerous and deviant sexuality is displayed by white men, these two villains continue to rely on the trope of the lasciviousness of Oriental women. Jacincta maintains her own dignity by rejecting their insulting version of racial and gender otherness. Later, a victim of rape, she identifies herself with a wholly different version of the Oriental woman, appearing "disguis'd in a Moorish Habit" as a "*Moorish* Lady, who has suffer'd Wrong" (34). (In Rowley's original, the nature of her disguise is not specified.) Pix's Jacincta may adopt such an appearance to symbolize her "blackened" reputation, shame, and loss of "honour" (as a similar disguise does when adopted by the fallen nun Angiolella in Webster's *The Devil's Law-Case* [1623]). But more important than such negative connotations of blackness is Jacincta's identification with the oppressed Moors and with their sexuality taken as an object of scrutiny by white men—in Clothario and Lodovicus's image of "Eastern Queens," for example. *The Conquest of Spain* thus exposes the distorting nature of the conventional associations of blackness, by emphasizing the whites' capacity for transgressive sexuality, by allowing the innocent heroine to identify with the Moors rather than with her own racial group, and by reading rape not as a property of a particular ethnic group but as a political metaphor for the oppression of a particular class and sex. As a result, by interrogating stereotypes of racial otherness, Pix also questions stereotypes of gender and class difference.

Unlike *The Conquest of Spain, The False Friend* does not simply revise a single pre-1660 source. It seems to offer an original—if highly conventionalized—plot. This play might appear to challenge racial stereotypes less than *The Conquest of Spain*. It does not resist, for instance, the identification of the female villain with images of ethnic difference. At the same time, intertextual references to *Othello* are superimposed on the text in a way that problematizes this simple demonization of blackness—and of femaleness. Ethnic difference, although apparently only a peripheral issue in this play, takes on an important symbolic role as a coded way of discussing the paradoxical position within patriarchy of an economically powerful woman, analogous to the position of a militarily powerful black man.

The implicit presence of *Othello* is signaled in some coincidences of nomenclature: a dim tool-villain called Roderigo, for example, takes a similar part in both tragedies. A number of details of plot, theme, and setting, as well as some close verbal echoes, also underline the use of the Shakespearean prototype. Against the will of a Brabantioesque father, the Spanish hero Emilius has, like Othello, secretly married the ethnically different (French) Lovisa, a passive Desdemona-like figure. The play begins with their arrival in Sardinia, rejoicing in their safe passage, in terms more than a little reminiscent of the arrival of Othello and Desdemona in Cyprus. Here Emilius's foster sister Appamia is passionately in love with him herself, and her endogamous desires threaten the stability of his new exogamous relationship. She uses all the Iagoesque tactics she can to make husband and wife suspect each other's fidelity and separate them, and when this fails she poisons both. This sketchy plot summary seems to suggest a fairly simple, though intriguing, use of *Othello* to create a female Iago: an adaptation of Shakespeare's original to allow women roles other than passive suffering, while maintaining the fear that an active woman, who pursues her own sexual desires, must be evil.

But the uses of *Othello* in Pix's play are not, I think, as simple as that. Even Appamia is not simply, as I have suggested, a female Iago. Certainly Pix treats her and her desires with great sympathy and is deeply involved in her dilemma. Appamia is a rich and independent woman with vast estates in the New World, yet all her personal forcefulness and economic power do not alter the fact that as a woman she cannot initiate a relationship with the man she loves but must wait to be chosen. As a result of Pix's sympathy for Appamia—the central emotional pivot, I think, of the play—the character is modeled not only on the evil Iago but also on the heroic Othello.

Indeed, although in the surface story Emilius is equivalent to Othello, it is Appamia who is given most direct quotations from him, as well as from Iago. Like Iago (cf. *Othello* II.iii.341), she seeks the "Subtil Aid of Hell" (46) in her stratagems. Like Iago, she warns her victim that she is an alien who lacks the insider's intuitive grasp of the coded meanings of the behavior of "our *Spanish* Nobles / . . . to Wives" in a society that is foreign to her (29), although she pretends she is not talking about any specific case: "I say not this of our *Emilius*" (31; cf. Iago's "I know our country disposition well . . . / I do not in position / Distinctly speak of her" [III.iii.205, 238–39]). But Appamia also quotes Othello in allusions that heroize her suffering and legitimate her love. In her frustration and sense of grievance she feels a "Wretch" crawled over by "Ingendring Toads" (11; cf. *Othello* IV.ii.62–63, "a cistern, for foul toads / To knot and gender in!"). She also feels plunged in "deep / Unfathomable depths" (46; cf. Othello's images of the "icy current" of the Pontic Sea, III.iii.461), and she invokes "black Revenge" to "Rise" (10; cf. *Othello* III.iii.454, "Arise, black vengeance, from thy hollow cell"). In creating this dramatically compelling amalgam of Othello and Iago, Pix devises an extraordinarily powerful intertextual language for moral ambiguity. Appamia is not simply the traditional demonic woman, not even simply the conventional passionate "darker woman" (see Howe 179). Her association with the Shakespearean hero challenges traditionally negative views of such assertive women and creates a strikingly complex character.

Although not a racial outsider, Appamia is persistently associated not only with Othello but also with America and Native Americans, and she herself certainly identifies her transgressive passions with racial outsiders like Medea (10). As it does for Othello, *black* becomes a crucial word in Appamia's vocabulary of self-reference, and it is much used of her (e.g., "black Revenge," 10, 59; "my Black, and Guilty Annals," 12; "blacker than Hell Creates," 59). Appamia's slave and constant companion, the Aztec princess Zelide, serves, like Webster's Zanche, as a visible embodiment of the "dark" sexual desires of her white mistress. More poignantly, her paradoxical, Oroonokoesque status as slave princess reiterates Appamia's position as a rich plantocrat who is still, because of her gender, in all ways that mean anything to her a slave within her own society.

Stereotypes of black lustfulness and cruelty continue to be articulated around Zelide (e.g., "that Devil Moor" [58]), but they are raised only to be discredited. Appamia reminds us that Zelide appears to be the offspring of hell, but it is only "our Fancy" that imagines that devils look like this, for race and moral status have no necessary connection. Her own white appearance, although apparently "bright as Angels" (46), actually conceals lust and violence. Real and metaphorical blackness are split apart, the one no longer signifying the other. Zelide brews the poison that Appamia uses to kill Lovisa; and yet far from the stereotype, Zelide tries to restrain her mistress's murderous instincts (9). While black maidservants are traditionally lustful and treacherous, the recurrent word used to describe Zelide is *faithful* (12, 27, 29), a word less redolent of irony than *honest* for Iago. Zelide serves Appamia for "Love" (28), and as a result of that love she, like Othello, becomes an innocent murderer. She trembles when Lovisa is given her poison (45), and she feels that she "cou'd weep" for Lovisa's suffering (46). In some respects, the imagery tells us, the white Appamia is more "black," in the discredited metaphorical sense, than Zelide is.

Again, the stereotypical associations of blackness are questioned and reversed: Pix challenges racial stereotypes to make the white woman passionate and violent, the black woman "faithful" and compassionate. But Pix does not simply reverse stereotypes: to do so may maintain their authority. Instead she dissolves them. Appamia combines Iago and Othello in a way that collapses binary oppositions between black and white, male and female, even good and evil. Moreover, the play poignantly implies that Zelide's slavery and (racial) otherness are not deviant but are simply symptomatic of the lot of all women in the play's sterile patriarchy, of the rich and powerful Appamia as well as the vulnerable Lovisa and the literal black slave Zelide.

Appamia is the center of Pix's adaptation—one might almost say interrogation—of *Othello,* but she is by no means the only character who can profitably be read in the light of prototypes in Shakespeare's play. As I have suggested, Lovisa is equivalent to Desdemona, Emilius to Othello, their ethnic difference the possible foundation for a harmonious hetero-sexuality that is never to come to fruition. Pix, however, sometimes abruptly reverses and regenders these identifications. While in *Othello* Iago persuades the protagonist that he has misunderstood his wife's culture and nature, Appamia works at unsettling Lovisa's confidence in her husband. When in act IV Lovisa is wrongly persuaded to suspect Emilius's fidelity, there are moments when he echoes Desdemona ("*Lovisa* might have chid me less Severely," 42; cf. Desdemona's "gentle means, and easy tasks; / He might ha' chid me so," IV.ii.114–15), she Othello ("I / Have a Cause, much Cause," 42; cf. Othello's "It is the cause, it is the cause, my soul," V.ii.1).

Indeed, the play works generally to make the women more active, the men more passive than in the Shakespearean original, a strategy that both locates and resists the dynamic of the Shakespearean tragedy. The hero of Pix's play is named Emilius, a masculine version of the name of Desdemona's maidservant and the wife of Iago, Emilia. Emilius is Othello rebuilt on the lines of a class and gender inferiority, and thus not only purified—he is not guilty of murder—but demystified, stripped of racial stereotyping. Masculinity, especially a traditional model of masculinity as military prowess, is interrogated. In addition to the feminizing of Emilius, the play includes at least one other male Desdemona. Lorenza (oddly given a grammatically feminine name) loves Emilius's sister Adellaida, but she is already married to someone else. When Lorenza discovers that he can never have her, he stabs himself. When asked who is responsible, he quotes Desdemona: "I, my self. Farewel" (49; cf. "I myself, farewell," *Othello* V.ii.125). The play's men, indeed, notably direct their violence not outward, as a traditional concept of masculinity expects, but inward: both · Emilius and Lorenza commit suicide, enacting a role often considered archetypally feminine in Restoration drama (see Pearson, *Prostituted Muse* 45). The passive and self-sacrificing elements that Shakespearean drama considers the core of an essential female nature are reassigned by Pix to male characters, the presentation of two male Desdemonas momentarily suggesting a world where such qualities are not automatically gendered. Again, as in the case of racial stereotypes, binary oppositions are shown in the very process of dissolution.

In fact, Pix produces a play of quite extraordinary "multiple, heterogeneous *difference*" in her revision of *Othello,* as she changes the genders and races of characters in her prototype and blends different and opposing individuals, classes, genders, and races. In particular, Appamia's identification with the racial Other indicates not simple evil but, in the light of the haunting presence of *Othello,* something much more complex. There are suggestions, too, that this identification with the Other in relation to gender and class as well as race might hint at an oppositional analysis of the role of women within a patriarchal society, perpetually marginalized, enslaved, made Other. On the surface an apparently conventional tragedy exhorting obedience to patriarchal imperatives—its subtitle is *The Fate of Disobedience,* and its Brabantioesque patriarch spells out the message that the tragic conclusion is the direct result of disobeying fathers—*The False Friend* uses *Othello* in a subtextual destabilization and subversion of notions of patriarchal authority by inviting a rethinking of stereotypes of class, gender, and race. Possibly this fruitful conflict between levels of meaning was too disguised or too challenging for its first (and as yet only) audience, for the play was not a commercial success. It would be interesting to see whether a modern revival would vindicate Pix's subtle and original dramaturgy.

A number of Restoration women dramatists, then, were attracted to images of racial and ethnic otherness. Mary Pix in particular questions stereotypes of blackness as equivalent to lust, cruelty, and treachery, and even works to dissolve the binary oppositions through which patriarchal culture maintains itself in power. Her heroines often identify with the racial Other: the consequences are in comedy the establishment of the woman as the powerful linchpin of a harmonious heterosexuality, in tragedy the more serious interrogation of hierarchies of gender and class through the image of ethnicity. It is not unfair to say that neither Pix nor Behn was obviously interested in practical improvements in civil rights for black people or campaigned actively against slavery. In fact, they seem to have been more interested in blackness as an image for femininity than for its own sake, and by eroding binary oppositions they hoped to profit personally, as women writers deemed inferior and treated as transgressors within their own culture. Neither Pix nor Behn offers a systematic attack on white racism or imperialism: indeed, Behn feels obliged to give her heroic black Oroonoko a European education and Europeanized features and to make him a dealer in slaves himself. Perhaps we need to wait for the appearance of anglophone black writers like Phyllis Wheatley and Ignatius Sancho for more fundamental disruptions of ethnic stereotypes. All the same, Pix and Behn began a process of questioning such stereotypes that helped lay the foundations that would make the antislavery movement possible, while at the same time by their disruption of binary oppositions they also facilitated the rich and various feminist discourses of the next century.

Notes

1. The term *couch scenes* was coined by Howe (39).
2. All citations and quotations from Pix's plays are taken from volume 1 of Steeves's facsimile edition.
3. For a fuller development of this point, see Pearson, "Romans and Barbarians."

Works Cited

Behn, Aphra. *Abdelazer; or, The Moor's Revenge. The Works of Aphra Behn*. 6 vols. Ed. Montague Summers. London, 1915; New York: Benjamin Blom, 1967. 2:1–98.

Brownmiller, Susan. *Against Our Will: Men, Women, and Rape*. New York: Simon and Schuster, 1975.

Clarke, Charlotte. *The Art of Management; or, Tragedy Expell'd*. London: W. Rayner, 1753.

Cowhig, Ruth. "Blacks in English Renaissance Drama and the Role of Shakespeare's *Othello*." *The Black Presence in English Literature*. Ed. David Dabydeen. Manchester: Manchester UP, 1985. 1–25.

Falkus, Christopher. *The Life and Times of Charles II*. London: Weidenfeld and Nicolson, 1972.

Ferguson, Moira. *Subject to Others: British Writers and Colonial Slavery, 1670–1834*. New York: Routledge, 1992.

Guffey, George. "Aphra Behn's *Oroonoko*: Occasion and Accomplishment." *Two English Novelists: Aphra Behn and Anthony Trollope*. By George Guffey and Andrew Wright. Los Angeles: William Andrews Clark Memorial Library, 1975. 1–76.

Hazlitt, W. Carew, ed. *Dodsley's "A Select Collection of Old English Plays."* Vol. 14. London: Reeves and Turner, 1875.

Hazlitt, William. "Hamlet." *Characters of Shakespeare's Plays. The Complete Works of William Hazlitt.* Ed. P.P. Howe. Vol. 4. n.p., 1930. 23–24.

Hopkins, Charles. *Friendship Improv'd; or, the Female Warrior.* London: J. Tonson, 1700.

Howe, Elizabeth. *The First English Actresses: Women and Drama, 1660–1700.* Cambridge: Cambridge UP, 1992.

Jones, Eldred. *Othello's Countrymen: The African in English Renaissance Drama.* London: Oxford UP, 1965.

Jonson, Ben. *Ben Jonson.* Vol. 7. Ed. C.H. Herford, Percy Simpson, and Evelyn Simpson. Oxford: Clarendon, 1941.

Kabbani, Rana. *Europe's Myths of Orient.* London: Pandora, 1988.

Manley, Delariviere. *The Lost Lover; or, the Jealous Husband.* London: R. Bentley, F. Saunders, J. Knapton, R. Wellington, 1696.

Moi, Toril. *Sexual/Textual Politics.* London: Methuen, 1985.

Odell, George C.D. *Shakespeare from Betterton to Irving.* 2 vols. 1920. New York: Dover, 1966.

Ortner, Sherry B. "Is Female to Male as Nature Is to Culture?" *Woman, Culture, and Society.* Ed. Michelle Zimbalist Rosaldo and Louise Lamphere. Stanford, Calif.: Stanford UP, 1974. 67–87.

Pearson, Jacqueline. "Gender and Narrative in the Fiction of Aphra Behn." *Review of English Studies,* n.s., 42 (1991): 40–56, 179–90.

———. *The Prostituted Muse: Images of Women and Women Dramatists, 1642–1737.* Manchester: Manchester UP, 1988.

———. "Romans and Barbarians: The Structure of Irony in Shakespeare's Roman Tragedies." *Shakespearian Tragedy.* Ed. Malcolm Bradbury and D.J. Palmer. Statford-upon-Avon Studies 20. London: Edward Arnold, 1984. 159–82.

Rowley, William. *The Spanish Gipsies and All's Lost by Lust.* Ed. Edgar C. Morris. Boston: D.C. Heath, 1908.

Shakespeare, William. *Othello.* Ed. M.R. Ridley. London: Methuen, 1965.

———. *Titus Andronicus.* Ed. J.C. Maxwell. London: Methuen, 1953.

Staves, Susan. *Players' Scepters: Fictions of Authority in the Restoration.* Lincoln: U of Nebraska P, 1979.

Steeves, Edna, ed. *The Plays of Mary Pix and Catherine Trotter.* Vol. 1. New York: Garland, 1982.

Straub, Kristina. *Sexual Suspects: Eighteenth-Century Players and Sexual Ideology.* Princeton, N.J.: Princeton UP, 1992.

Taylor, Gary. *Reinventing Shakespeare.* London: Hogarth, 1990.

Tiptree, James, Jr. [pseud. of Alice Sheldon]. "And I awoke and found me here on the cold hill's side." *Ten Thousand Light Years from Home.* New York, 1973. London: Eyre Methuen, 1975. 9–19.

Webster, John. *The White Devil.* Ed. John Russell Brown. London: Methuen, 1960.

Wolfson, Susan J. "Explaining to the Sisters: Mary Lamb's *Tales from Shakespeare.*" *Women's Re-Vision of Shakespeare.* Ed. Marianne Novy. Urbana: U of Illinois P, 1990. 16–40.

Unmanned with Thy Words: Regendering Tragedy in Manley and Trotter

Rebecca Merrens

*R*ecent feminist criticism has made increasingly visible the intersections between the antifeminism of seventeenth-century tragedies and the repressive conditions of women's lives in the early modern period (see, e.g., Brown; Jordan). Several critics have read the escalating violence against women on the Jacobean and Restoration stage as a participant in the ongoing negotiation of women's cultural and economic positions—a process intensified by the sociopolitical instability that dominated the century. Tragedies during this period often construct women as more sinning than sinned against and, thereby, locate them as sources of sociopolitical turmoil. Peter Stallybrass argues, for instance, that female characters function as unstable signs around which political "placements and displacements of the court" are negotiated ("Reading the Body" 129), and Sharon Stockton contends that it is through a process of "scapegoat[ing]" women as always "already corrupted" that Jacobean tragedies "purify, strengthen, and unify" their patriarchal worlds (459, 463).

These readings of tragedy respond to the complex reworkings of women's sociopolitical roles and, as Karen Newman argues, of the construct of "femininity," by foregrounding the unstable and shifting roles of women in seventeenth-century culture.[1] Most analyses of seventeenth-century tragedy, however, fail to acknowledge the ways in which the scapegoating of women as the locus of sociopolitical corruption masks the disorder and fragmentation—indeed, the tragedy—within patrilineal communities in crisis. That is, women are figured as deceitful not only because they do often struggle against the repressive demands of a patriarchal culture that requires their silence, chastity, and obedience but also because, by blaming female characters for the dissolution of putatively

ordered patriarchal communities, those communities are enabled to reconstitute themselves over, against, and through the literal and symbolic dissection of women's bodies. "Unnatural" female characters become the means by which anxiety- and conflict-ridden homosocial networks reestablish themselves as seemingly coherent and by which they mask
the internal divisiveness of the patrilineal system. In this respect, I disagree with the claims of Stockton and others that the final bloody acts
of tragedies in which "unruly" women are often murderously silenced
serve to "purify, strengthen, and unify" the male communities. Instead,
I read these spectacles as hyperbolic displays of male authority that—
in their violence—make visible what these plays try to obscure throughout: the inability of masculine authority to present itself as cohesive and
stable.

By attempting to legitimate an idealized masculine order, these
tragedies participate in one of the dominant discursive and ideological
agendas of the seventeenth century. Throughout the century the seemingly
disparate discourse communities of literature, science, theology, and
political philosophy all worked to create a stable space for patriarchal
authority by variously constraining, rejecting, and dissecting the feminine.
Indeed, the antifeminist premises of such "order" appear to be "natural"
partly because they were produced along a diverse spectrum of cultural
discourses and practices. In this essay I shall argue that the supposedly
distinct discourses of tragedy and science are deeply connected on the
level of ideology. In order to construct and to justify "universal truths" of
cosmic order and knowledge, tragedy and science in the seventeenth
century must violently repress both women and nature, which science
figures as feminine: the principle of order *is* the repression of the feminine,
in a process by which seemingly value-neutral knowledge is constituted by
endlessly scapegoating women and probing nature.[2]

Delariviere Manley's *The Royal Mischief* and Catherine Trotter's
The Fatal Friendship reject this repressive tradition of blaming women
for sociopolitical strife and, instead, locate the source of tragedy explicitly within the contradictions and violence of patrilineal order. Manley's
and Trotter's tragedies have long been ignored or dismissed by literary
critics: one might argue that their absence from the canon and from critical
studies of Restoration drama suggests the extent to which they threaten
patriarchal notions of sociopolitical order and coherence. By offering
alternative conceptions of order not predicated on anatomizing and
torturously punishing women, Manley and Trotter disrupt conventional
associations between women and social disorder. In doing so, they
refashion tragedy to function as a critique of the idealized and yet
perpetually crisis-ridden, agonistic relations among fathers, brothers, and
husbands.

Before considering Manley's and Trotter's tragedies, I shall examine earlier scientific and tragic paradigms—embodied for my purposes here in Francis Bacon's theories of experimentation and in William Congreve's *The Mourning Bride*—in order to suggest the culturally prevalent ideologies against which Manley and Trotter respond. Bacon's theories for inductive methodology and experimentation provide insight into the misogynist logic of masculinist tragedies because, on a fundamental level, both experimentation and tragedy attempt to locate and then to excise feminized corruption in order to shore up masculinist knowledge and authority. What Bacon seeks through the objectifying study of feminized nature, tragedians such as Congreve effect through the torturous and often murderous study of women.

Neither Bacon's nor Congreve's antifeminisms are, of course, "new" or original. Congreve's characterization of gender and gender roles harkens back to gender representation in Jacobean tragedies by Thomas Middleton and John Ford, for example, and as several feminist historians of science have noted, Bacon's belief in the natural inequality between men and women, and his conception of nature as feminine, find countless antecedents in literature and philosophy from antiquity through the seventeenth century.[3] Bacon's antifeminism is significant, however, because it becomes a constitutive component of the inductive methodology that he contends will provide impartial "truths" about the natural world. When Bacon argues that "a true and lawful marriage between the empirical and the rational faculty" allows man to overcome "the fogs and clouds of nature . . . to present these things naked and open," he presents induction as a means to arrive at unbiased knowledge (Preface to *The Great Instauration, Works* 246). Yet as Evelyn Fox Keller notes, Baconian science only "works" if we believe it is " 'natural' to guide, shape, even hound, conquer, and subdue her [nature]—[and that] only in that way is the true 'nature of things' revealed" (*Reflections* 37). While it possesses a long and complex history, antifeminism functions differently in different cultural contexts. In the seventeenth century misogyny informed the logic of powerful new scientific discourses designed to produce ordered knowledge; these, in turn, promoted antifeminism—of the sort Congreve manifests—as crucial to the production of stable, rational order. Indeed, few discourses of the seventeenth century provide as extended a critique of female power, and as complex a methodological justification for the subjection of "unnatural" female roles, as does Baconian science. Science and tragedy in the seventeenth century, in other words, function as mutually constitutive discourses that naturalize and promote repressive practices of vexing the feminine—through experimentation or through female characters—as a means of constructing authoritative meaning and, thus, of representing masculinist power structures as coherent and rational, not fractured and unstable.[4]

F. Hayman inv. et del.　　　　　　　C. Grignion sculp

The Mourning Bride

Almeria fainting into the arms of Leonora, published as the frontispiece to the 1735 edition of *The Mourning Bride*, in *The Works of Mr. Congreve* (1787), vol. 2, iv. By permission of the Department of Special Collections, Stanford University Library.

The pervasive construction of women in most Jacobean and Restoration tragedies either as self-determined, duplicitous, and sexually corrupt or, on the other hand, as male-controlled and virtuous exemplifies and reinscribes prevailing conceptions of gender and nature also found in Bacon's writings. In "Aphorisms on the Composition of the Primary History," Bacon asserts that "nature exists in three states." "Either she is free and develops herself in her own ordinary course," he writes, "or she is forced out of her proper state by the perverseness and insubordination of matter . . . ; or she is constrained and molded by art and human ministry" (403). Bacon then concludes, however, that "the monsters in the several species" are not so unlike the "species themselves," and he contends that these categories—monstrous and "normal"—may be considered as one for the purposes of experimentation. Clearly, for Bacon, all unmediated nature is on some level monstrous. Only "artificial nature," which "takes orders from man, and works under his authority," escapes being demonized and can be made to produce "a new face of bodies, another universe or theater of things" (403). As his "theater" metaphor suggests, crucial to Bacon's theorized mastery over nature is controlling "her" representation. Nature—like female characters on the stage—always threatens to create a new theater of things. Bacon's interest, shared by the homosocial order represented on the stage, lies in finding means of controlling female self-signification—that is, nature "in her own ordinary course"—in order to appropriate unruly feminized representation for masculine ends. As Bacon argues and as tragedies enact, male mastery of the feminine "theater of things"—that is, male mastery of representation—produces the semblance of masculine authority while, in a Foucauldian sense, obscuring the always illusory quality of such domination.[5]

In either case, nature—willing or otherwise—is to be forced into submission by rigorous experiments, which Bacon asserts may "restore" "anything that is of the earth," including man's place in it, "to its perfect and original condition" ("Proemium," *Works* 241). For Bacon, nature denies man access to this prelapsarian world, and he thus constructs "her" as threatening, overpowerful, and duplicitous; this characterization of nature enables him to legitimate violence toward "her" as a means of displaying his mastery. Bacon's attack on feminized nature, then, is twofold: not only does her inherent monstrosity require that she be tortured into acquiescently serving man, but her position as the barrier between man and an edenic world legitimates this violent conquest. In effect, induction provides Bacon with a means of appropriating nature's self-signifying ability for his own ends: nature becomes the natural philosopher's medium over and through which he creates all meaning. Masculine knowledge and authority are primarily constituted as coherent, therefore, through "vexations," "examin[ations]," and "dissect[ions]" of the feminine.

Inductive reasoning and the logic of experimentation have as one of their objectives the reproduction of knowledge—that is, producing "evidence" of nature's corruption and women's fallibility as "new" instances of their fallen status. Plays such as Congreve's *The Mourning Bride* dramatize this discovery of the "truth" of feminine corruption as tragedy. The play articulates profound concerns about the contingency of homosocial bonds and male authority; however, as in Baconian philosophy, Congreve's tragedy displaces male distress by locating the cause of cultural disorder in women with "passions which outstrip the wind" (III.i; 409) and uncontrollable desires. These dual yet intertwined emphases—masculinist anxiety and female "disorder"—are manifest in the dual focuses of the tragic plot. *The Mourning Bride*'s title character, Almeria, mourns for her secret newlywed, Osmyn, a long-standing foe (I.ii) of her father, King Manuel. Almeria believes herself to be the only survivor of the shipwreck in which she presumes Osmyn perished. Unaware that Almeria "in one day, was wedded and a widow" (I.i; 384) to Osmyn, Manuel castigates her for not marrying Garcia, a court favorite whom Manuel chooses for her husband. Manuel exclaims early in the play:

> I tell thee she's to blame not to have feasted
> When my first foe was laid in earth, such enmity,
> Such detestation, bears my blood to his;
> My daughter should have revelled at his death,
> She should have made these palace walls to shake,
> And all this high and ample roof to ring
> With her rejoicings.
>
> [I.ii; 388]

Almeria, "blam[ed]" for not legitimating masculinist warfare and specifically for not "feast[ing]" at her secret husband's presumed death, is doubly damned: if she marries Garcia she betrays her husband, and if she refuses she incurs the wrath of her father.[6] Almeria's stoic response to this conflict, however, emphasizes her moral unassailability: it is precisely because Almeria readily welcomes death rather than remarriage—for which Osmyn praises her as the "Perfection of all faithfulness and love" (II.ii; 397)—and because she consistently articulates repressive conceptions of female virtue that she becomes the exemplary "good" woman throughout the play.

Osmyn, meanwhile, has survived the wreck and is captured by Manuel's forces in the service of Princess Zara, to whom Manuel feels lovingly—yet dangerously—"enslave[d]" (I.ii; 391). Yet Zara herself loves Osmyn. Osmyn and Almeria reunite, but Osmyn continues to conceal their marriage in order to manipulate Zara into using her influence with the king to free his friend, Heli, from Manuel's prison. Osmyn and Heli are by turns imprisoned for each other, due to Zara's alternating bouts of rage at being used and her sympathy for Osmyn's imprisoned plight. Zara is figured, to use Osmyn's explanation to Almeria, as "the reverse of thee" (II.iii; 399). She possesses a "soul / Of godlike mould, intrepid and commanding," but she has "passions which outstrip the wind, as tempests root / The sea" and that cause "fear" within Osmyn's "boding heart" (III.i; 409). In a final complex scheme to fake Osmyn's beheading (and, thus, indelibly to win him over by freeing Heli and him from Manuel), Zara dies by her own poison after the king is mistakenly beheaded. Almeria, Osmyn, and Heli are restored to each other amid political rebellion and regicide in the final bloody scene of the play.

I provide this summary of the plot to call attention to the ways in which female characters function as the cause and locus of patrilineal strife. On one level, Congreve explicitly predicates tragedy in *The Mourning Bride* on agonistic relations among men: when Zara reminds Osmyn, "Was't not for you this war / Commenced?" (II.iii; 401), she clearly locates him as the source of patriarchal discord. Indeed, when Heli recounts to imprisoned Osmyn that "there are disorders ripe for mutiny / Among the troops" and that his subjects "[a]re risen in arms" (III.i; 405) to rebel against Manuel, Osmyn exults, "By Heaven thou'st roused me from my lethargy!" Although aware of his responsibility for having "[c]ommenced" war, Osmyn is nevertheless only "roused" by the prospect of more homosocial strife, which he hopes will bring him greater power and authority. Once he realizes the necessity of his liberty to feed this growing revolt, Osmyn agrees to Heli's politic advice that he "abate of [his] aversion" for the well-connected Zara and, though he "hate her not, nor can dissemble love: / But as I may, I'll do" (III.i; 406). Zara becomes implicated in this tragedy because she provides an expedient means for Osmyn and Heli to regain liberty and to seek "revenge" on male foes: as they "may," they "do," cavalierly abusing her love for Osmyn in the process. The unspoken price that Osmyn and Heli exact for their freedom is violating Zara's trust and placing her in peril with Manuel—whose authority she subverts in order to aid the imprisoned men. We are encouraged to dismiss this cost not only as necessary for the greater male good but also as a legitimate response to overarching female power.

Once Osmyn and Heli involve Zara, however, Congreve shifts his emphasis from exploring male-inspired turmoil to scapegoating women for social strife. He suggests early in the play that tragic "loss . . . melancholy and despair" (I.ii; 391) occur when man inadequately exacts "reveng[e] on his foes" and, thus, makes it clear that male characters rely on violence to ensure order and thereby produce tragedy. While Congreve indicts male factionalism for continually producing tragedy, his analysis of the sources of corruption shifts from identifying ruptures in patriarchal order to attacking Zara's unnatural and corrupt uses of political power. Osmyn and Heli implicate Zara in their plan for "reveng[e]" to free Osmyn, wage war, and protect their privileged friendship; Congreve masks the tragedy of patriarchal factionalism, however, by focusing instead on Zara's unnatural abuse of male political power. Congreve represents as natural the primacy of Osmyn's and Heli's "love" and celebrates their homosocial plans for war against Manuel. To idealize and to naturalize patrilineal order and to mystify the endless production of internal strife and war by and within homosociality, Congreve scapegoats Zara as the unnatural threat to male authority and thus as the source of tragedy in the play. She epitomizes Baconian nature: she is figured as overpowerful and uncontrollable, both the barrier against and the means to Osmyn's and Heli's empowerment and authority. Even as Manuel naively believes himself "much indebted to this fair one," his chief adviser, Gonzalo, comments:

> Her words and action are obscure and double,
> Sometimes concur, and sometimes disagree;
> I like it not.
>
> [IV.i; 420]

These multiple readings of Zara underscore the threat she poses: it is precisely because she refuses, in Bacon's words, to "tak[e] orders from man and wor[k] under his authority" that she is characterized as ambiguously self-signifying, duplicitous, and the locus of "disorder." What Gonzalo "like[s] . . . not" is that, like Baconian nature, Zara's "double"-ness contests male efforts to control female representation and women's generation of meaning.

While Zara is attacked throughout the play as the "reverse of" Almeria, even the "good" Almeria threatens to rupture the bonds among men. Not only does Manuel blame her for resisting male agonistic relations and order, but Osmyn displaces his anxieties about his political impotence onto her. This displacement occurs largely because of the triangular relations between Almeria, Osmyn, and Heli: Osmyn vacillates between privileging his relationship with Almeria—when first reunited with Almeria and Heli, Osmyn comments to Heli that he first saw Almeria "and therefore saw not thee" (II.ii; 399)—and primarily valuing his relationship with Heli, "Whom more than life he loved." Unlike Heli, however, who lovingly supports Osmyn and provides him avenues and encouragement for "revenge," Almeria emphasizes her utter dependence on Osmyn and urges against his desires for autonomous action. She does not want to be "parted" from him and argues that

Mrs. Siddons as Zara in *The Mourning Bride*, in *The Works of Mr. Congreve* (1787), vol. 2, 56. By permission of the Department of Special Collections, Stanford University Library.

> we together
> Feed on each other's heart, devour our woes
> With mutual appetite; and mingling in
> One cup the common stream of both our eyes
> Drink bitter draughts, with never-slaking thirst.
>
> [III.i; 410]

When Osmyn continues to conceal his "dark thought"—his pact with Heli to manipulate Zara (and, implicitly, Almeria)—Almeria urges, "Thy second self should feel each other wound. . . . I am thy wife" (III.i; 411). She pleadingly queries, "am I the bosom-snake, / That sucks thy warm life-blood, and gnaws thy heart?" She repeatedly figures their love and their bond to each other in terms of mutual consumption ("feed," "devour," "mutual appetite," "never-slaking thirst"); dissolution ("mingling in / One cup the common stream"); and death (that which "sucks thy warm life-blood"). Osmyn is reduced by these ominous demands to inarticulate cries—"Oh! Oh!"—and in return figures her as dangerously effeminizing and threatening. He exclaims that "thy excessive love distracts my sense!" (III.i; 410). Then he laments:

> O thou has searched too deep!
> There, there I bleed! there pull the cruel cords,
> That strain my cracking nerves.
>
> [III.i; 411]

Osmyn casts Almeria as not only parasitically devouring him, as her disturbing language suggests, but also destroying and pulling him apart. Indeed, he posits a clear connection between his idealized constitution as a coherent, authoritative male subject—which he actively seeks throughout the play and which his relationship with Heli fosters—and Almeria's fragmenting influence upon him when he bewails, "Why dost thou thus unman me with thy words / And melt me down to mingle with thy weepings?" (III.i; 411). In effect, Congreve legitimates Osmyn's and Heli's bond and their agenda—which asserts Osmyn as aggressively "whole"—by opposing them to his alternative, fractured role defined by Almeria's "unman[ing]" words of "excessive love." While I do not mean to suggest that Almeria functions exactly as Zara does, becoming the means through and against which imprisoned, emasculated men reassert their authority, this scene indicates that even the most "perfect" and beloved woman impinges dangerously upon privileged homosocial bonds and upon the integrity of male subjectivity.[7] Congreve indicates that on a profound level both the whore and the angel threaten male order and authority—a stance that recalls Bacon's ready collapse of the distinction between the "species itself" and "the monsters of the species" into a postlapsarian and feminized nature that is fundamentally dangerous and monstrous.

By representing all women—even the stock "good" woman—as disabling and dissolving male authority and order, Congreve disguises the prevalent conflicts and ruptures among men within the play and powerfully legitimates the violent male relations upon which his tragedy begins and depends. He thus obscures what might have been a social critique of patriarchy by scapegoating women for the problems that patrilineal economies themselves inevitably produce.

Manley's *The Royal Mischief* and Trotter's *The Fatal Friendship* refashion these repressive tragic narratives to celebrate female characters who embody sexual and political prowess and who resist becoming the means by which patriarchal culture violently endeavors to reconstitute itself as "whole" and "naturally" ordered.[8] By the time Manley's and Trotter's tragedies were written in the 1690s, Baconian theories and performances of experimentation, anatomization, and dismemberment of the feminine had become culturally institutionalized. Alvin Snider argues that the Royal Society and late seventeenth-century culture appropriated Baconian theories to "make the issue of his cultural authority ever more explicit" (119) in order to legitimate a variety of scientific and political agendas (see also José). As the Royal Society's claims for the impartiality of scientific knowledge gained acceptance, so did the antifeminist premises upon which seventeenth-century science was based, thereby naturalizing misogyny as an intrinsic component of supposedly "objective" experimental science. Keller demonstrates that a consequence of Reformation theology was the disassociation of feminized nature from God, who was no longer perceived in metonymic relationship with nature but was granted sole sovereignty over "authoring" the world. As Robert Boyle contends, "the vulgar notion of nature" is both "injurious to the glory of God, and a great impediment to the solid and useful study of his works" (4:361). Feminized nature thus becomes not only ontologically separated from God but—like women on the stage—the legitimate site of ongoing exploration. The experimentalist ideology of vexing the feminine to produce order and knowledge that informs earlier antifeminist discourses, then, was more pervasive and more culturally significant by the time Manley and Trotter were writing.

As the theories that Bacon and others developed earlier in the century achieved a cultural prominence (albeit mystified and mythologized, as Snider contends), many writers—and particularly many women writers—began to explore and to critique the antifeminism and partiality of scientific knowledge.[9] Desiree Hellegers argues, for example, that women writers such as Anne Finch challenged medico-scientific antifeminism in the late seventeenth and early eighteenth centuries. Hellegers asserts that

Finch's Pindaric ode, "The Spleen," disputes Thomas Sydenham's writings on women and hysteria and challenges his and the medical establishment's assessment of women's bodies as "inherently disorderly" and chaotic. I contend similarly that Manley's and Trotter's tragedies not only contest the repressive representation of women within seventeenth-century literary tragedies but also critique proliferating cultural discourses—such as scientific writings—that scapegoat the feminine as a means to reassert masculine authority and knowledge. As Manley and Trotter counter masculinist strategies of anatomizing the feminine, they focus our attention on the instability of male-dominated social order, the same instability that Bacon's writing and *The Mourning Bride* attempt to obscure and displace onto women.

In *The Royal Mischief* Manley's heroine, Homais, pursues "the inimitable Prince of Colchis," Levan, in order to escape enforced celibacy and confinement at the hands of her impotent husband, the prince of Libardian, who is also Levan's uncle. Homais then plots with Levan to murder his new wife, Bassima, and Homais's tyrannical husband so that the lovers—Homais and Levan—may evade spousal retribution for their infidelities and consolidate power under their joint rule. The first scenes of *The Royal Mischief* foreground the problem of imposed marriage and unfulfilled female desire: Homais regards her repressive marriage to Libardian and her forbidden love for Levan as a "heavy doom, / Too strong for life to bear" (I.i; 214). While Congreve suggests the complications that arise from the dependence of patrilineal economies on the exchange of women through marriage to unify communities, he blames women, not the patrilineal system itself, for these endemic crises. In contrast, Manley explicitly rejects such demonizing of dynamic, desiring women and explores the culturally produced causes and circumstances of Homais's imposed "heavy doom" as a source of tragedy in the play. The play consistently blames male characters and the oppressive demands of the patrilineal system for tragedy, even for the tragedy that Homais creates.

In a sense *The Royal Mischief* seems similar initially to *The Mourning Bride;* both represent the tragic telos of sexually and politically unruly women. Homais, for example, is characterized by her eunuch, Acmat, as supernaturally powerful and beautiful. Acmat claims that Homais may "Survey the globe, choose where [her] eyes would reign" and that her "courage and . . . beauty must make the universal / World [her] slaves" (I.i; 215). While this describes the very sort of feminized power that Bacon and others represent as threatening to masculine knowledge and empowerment, the spate of infidelities and tragic desires in *The Royal Mischief* depend less on Homais's unparalleled beauty and power than on her imprisonment by her husband. This is no slight distinction; it marks a shift evident in Manley's tragedy away from assuming and then ferreting out feminine corruption and toward exploring the self-divisive patriarchal practices that produce sociopolitical tragedy. In effect, Manley provides an alternative construction of female power because she maintains radically different views of nature and women from those evident in masculinist tragedies. Writers such as Bacon and Congreve blame unnatural, disorderly woman for sociopolitical strife because they assume her to be morally degenerate. Her moral insufficiency legitimates—to use Boyle's word, "allows"—her scrutiny and torment in order to reveal her corruption and to affirm masculine authority and order. Rather than accept the de facto construction of the feminine as morally inferior—a point on which Baconian theories hinge—Manley blames the restrictive, nearly experimental conditions (like a subject of study, Homais is "constantly watched" and controlled) in which Homais is locked away in a marriage that leaves her full of "wants." She is "made Passionate by want of liberty" (I.i; 218).[10] It is not the unnatural heroine whom Manley condemns but the repressive circumstances whereby Homais is "[d]enied . . . to pass the castle-gates" and that "suffer none to have access" to her (I.i; 217). Manley reverses the analytic trajectory away from assuming, anatomizing, and "proving" female corruption to provide a taxonomy of the flawed patrilineal culture that distorts Homais's desires and produces her "heavy doom."

Indeed, even as Homais arranges her love affair, plots murders, and plans political revolt, Manley refuses to (dis)figure her as the sole locus of social disorder. When Levan angrily responds to news of the infidelity of Bassima—his wife—he exclaims:

> Oh, woman fair only to outward show,
> Well have the pens of men and angels
> Been employed to paint your snares!
> Well have the saints and fathers taught us to
> Beware those shining evils, and, as we
> Love our souls, avoid their faithless charms.
> [IV.i; 243]

Levan's antifeminism self-consciously invokes the cautions of centuries of "pens of men" who made this view a commonplace. It also calls to mind reinscriptions of this platitude within contemporary discourses such as science, which predicate male empowerment on being able to discern between "the outer courts of nature, which numbers have trodden" and the "inner chambers" in which nature conceals her secrets (*Great Instauration, Works* 258). Bacon appropriates from standard misogynist thinking a deep suspicion of the rift between the outward beauty of the feminine and the "true nature" she conceals within. By encoding this antifeminist distrust within a supposedly neutral scientific epistemology,

Bacon lends credence to claims such as these by Levan. By articulating a rigid interpretation of female signification, Levan—like Bacon and others—seeks to define the feminine as inherently dangerous and evil and, in this respect, to validate male authority by controlling her. Indeed, Levan's comment that "as we / Love our souls" men must avoid the feminine makes clear that coherent male subjectivity depends entirely upon repressing the feminine.

Homais, however, immediately counters his chronicle of woman's "natural" evil by charging,

> You should not, sure, for one, condemn us all!
> For there are women who have truth and constancy,
> As bright and lasting as the noblest male.
>
> [IV.i; 243]

That Levan accepts Homais's correction indicates Manley's resistance to figuring women as the cause of corruption within the social order and underscores her critique of male hypocrisy that demands female chastity without criticizing male infidelity. The same Levan who rails against female infidelity is, after all, engaged in an affair with Homais.

Throughout the play, male characters similarly—and mistakenly—disparage women in conventionally masculinist terms as "[o]nly exterior beauty, [a form] worn to deceive / The credulous world" (II.i; 221) or laud them as being constituted of "a common softness" (II.i; 227). Homais, however, is more complex than such overdetermined readings of her suggest: in a sense, the play becomes tragic because male characters repeatedly ignore or miscalculate Homais's political desires and cunning and, instead, erroneously (and fatally) attempt to limit her to her "natural" bodily "form." It is precisely because Homais exists outside the dualism of Baconian and tragic categories of the feminine that she both exposes their inadequacy and deceives male characters who continually re-create repressive circumstances whereby women may find agency only through rebellion. Even as Homais dies at Libardian's vengeful hands, she refuses to repent—as her lover Levan does before he kills himself—and instead continues to defy conventional expectations, railing against the ineffectual "effeminate troupe [she had] to deal with" (V.i; 259). In contrast to Levan's contrite lament that he dies with "Extremest detestation of myself," Homais loquaciously imagines her triumphant afterlife in which she will "reign" and experience a "feast at large what we but tasted here" (V.i; 259). These antithetical deaths reinforce Manley's reassessment of tragedy within the play. Levan admits responsibility for political chaos and figures his desires for Homais as his "tragic flaw" for which he attempts to find "forgiveness" through his stoic death. Homais, however, never repents: Manley refuses to mitigate her critique of patrilineal violence by ascribing Homais's actions to an inherent "tragic flaw" that, so the masculinist argument would go, destroys a corrupt woman. Instead, Manley's unrepentant Homais emphasizes—not expiates—the coercive circumstances of women within male-dominated communities.

Just as Manley elevates the conventional "bad" woman to a position of glory, she also mocks the facile "virtue" embodied in the "good" woman, Bassima, Levan's wife, thereby contesting both types of women represented in most Jacobean and Restoration tragedies. Unlike the complex, heroic Homais, Bassima remains flatly idealized as "more than Diana, fair, than Venus, lovely" (II.i; 223) and functions as a mouthpiece for values of "glory," nobility, and virtue—values that ring hollow in a play in which they find no other champions and precious little sympathy (V.i; 255). Set against the sexually and politically dynamic Homais, Bassima claims that "speaking is a crime" and, therefore, that she must remain "fenced about with chastity and glory" (III.i; 237). Her remarks are viewed, even by her lover, Osman, as "empty, notionary sounds" (V.i; 255). Indeed, unlike conventional tragedies, which reward female characters' toeing the patriarchal line, *The Royal Mischief* makes Bassima the first to die by Homais's plan. Osman is punished by being shot alive out of a cannon and "shatter[ed] in a thousand pieces" (V.i; 258), a notorious episode that parodically revises the conventional trope of dismembering the unruly female body as a didactic spectacle.[11] The "smoking relics" of Osman's body that litter the stage graphically demonstrate the play's critique of the men who produce and at least partially perpetuate tragic conflict within the play. Significantly, Osman has been punished and mutilated by men. Whereas, for Congreve, Almeria threatens Osmyn with effeminized fragmentation, Manley represents Osman's wife, Selima, in the final scene

> rang[ing] the fatal plain,
> Gathering the smoking relics of her lord,
> Which singe her as she grasps them.
> [V.i; 260]

While she collects only a "horrid pile" of his dismembered body parts, she reconstitutes his fragmented body. Manley at once exposes and refashions the dominant, pervasive fear that women dissolve male authority and fragment homosocial bonds by representing Selima gathering together what men have put asunder: that her assemblage takes shape as a funeral pyre exemplifies Manley's grim view of the rewards of patrilineal economies.

Yet even as Manley's heroine challenges traditional associations between female characters and natural and social disorder—and, in this

respect, enables us to see male complicity in producing tragic situations—
she remains within a tradition that posits gender antagonism as the source
of tragedy. Although Manley interrogates conventional representations of
gender, she still locates gender as the central issue that produces conflict.
Trotter, like Manley, reworks binary conceptions of gender in *The Fatal
Friendship,* yet she also calls into question the premise that only unconventional female characters promote tragic conflict by locating the source
of strife exclusively within the male community and by refusing to allow
social conflict to be displaced onto female characters.

The significance of *The Fatal Friendship* (1698) offers a feminist recasting of
Congreve's *The Mourning Bride,* performed the previous year.[12] Like
Congreve's tragedy, Trotter's play presents a secret marriage: while
Gramont's father, the Count Roquelaure, urges Gramont to marry the
wealthy widow Lamira, Gramont secretly has married Felicia, whom the
Count himself wishes to marry. *The Fatal Friendship,* as the title suggests,
centers less on intermarital strife, however, and more on Gramont's
relationship with his fellow officer and closest friend, Castalio. Gramont
and Castalio are alternately imprisoned for assisting the other's struggles at
court. Like Osmyn in *The Mourning Bride,* Gramont continues to conceal
knowledge of his marriage with Felicia—and of their kidnapped son—in
order to help his beloved Castalio by marrying Lamira, whose wealth
provides the means for Gramont to secure Castalio's release from prison,
as well as to amass the ransom to rescue his son. Throughout the play
Gramont is motivated almost exclusively by concern for other male
characters: he desires to appease his father, who becomes enraged by
Gramont's initial reluctance to marry Lamira; to free his kidnapped and
ransomed son; and to liberate Castalio from wrongful imprisonment. Yet
Gramont bigamously weds Lamira without realizing that Castalio loves her:
in his most earnest effort to help his friend, Gramont deceives Felicia,
wrongs Lamira, and becomes the means of Castalio's "destruction" (V.i;
205).

The significance of *The Fatal Friendship* lies in Trotter's reworking
of gender relations within the tragedy. While Congreve displaces social
strife onto women in *The Mourning Bride,* Trotter repeatedly affirms her
female characters' desires for "control" and exposes as the source of social
turmoil the duplicity of male characters and the instability of homosocial
bonds. Gramont, for example, bigamously marries Lamira in order to
protect his troubled relationships with his father, son, and male friend. In
doing so, however, he not only damages his relationship with his closest
friend, Castalio, who loves Lamira, but "basely us'[s]" both wives. Notably,
Gramont's trespasses do not go unanswered, nor do women become the
scapegoats for them. When Gramont attempts to be reconciled with
Lamira, he asks how he might "answer to your rage," as though her anger

were unconnected to his deceit. Lamira responds that "thy own upbraiding guilt thou canst not answer" and refuses to minimize her "rage" only to lessen his "guilt" (III.i; 174). Gramont's first wife, Felicia, and Lamira repeatedly decry his "abuse" of them without incurring the retribution conventionally inflicted upon splenetic women and without being (dis)figured as "unnaturally" vengeful. Lamira exposes the injurious nature of the conventional expectations of silence and passivity imposed upon wronged women when she rages, "But think'st thou I will tamely bear my wrongs?" She promises, "Oh, how I'll be revenged! . . . I'll be your plague, anticipate your hell!" (III.i; 173). While Lamira echoes Congreve's famous assessment in *The Mourning Bride* that "Heaven has no rage, like love to hatred turned, / Nor hell a fury, like a woman scorned" (*MB* III.ii; 415), Trotter validates Lamira's anger, and—when her wrath turns against Felicia—even Gramont accepts her rage. Rather than demonize Lamira as unnecessarily tempestuous, Gramont implores her, "On me let all your imprecations fall," and acknowledges, "I alone am guilty" (*FF* III.i; 173). This exchange, like others throughout the play, is critical for its recognition of the "wrongs" inflicted upon female characters by manipulative and financially driven patrilineal marriage practices, and for its emphasis on male "guilt."[13]

Trotter demonstrates that traditional male authority—of the sort that Congreve's Osmyn affects and that Gramont initially seeks in his relationships with Felicia and Lamira—is contingent on rhetorically and physically vexing "unnatural" women. When denied recourse to repressive modes of fabricating sociopolitical order and authority, men are left to acknowledge, "I alone am guilty." While Osmyn, when presented with similar grievances, only further protects his fragile, fragmented self by bemoaning Almeria's "unman[ning]" words, Trotter's Gramont reveals what Bacon and other tragedians obscure: endlessly seeking to produce male empowerment and knowledge by scapegoating the feminine generates "wrongs," "guilt," and ultimately the total dissolution—through death—of male subjectivity. Masculinist tragic paradigms—scientific and dramatic—are predicated on asserting absolute and therefore always unattainable patriarchal authority. Trotter foregrounds the antifeminism and tenuousness of this paradigm by affirming Felicia's and Lamira's grievances, but also by denying male characters the idealized subjectivity and authority that depend on the devaluation of the feminine. Her final description of Gramont as "a most strange example" of "human frailty" (V.i; 207) emphasizes yet again his inability to produce conventional male subjectivity and order.

Trotter extends her critique of patrilineal social order not only by exposing the plight of women within patriarchy but also by describing the demands on them as "unnatural" and by locating tragedy explicitly within networks of self-divisive homosocial obligations. Bellgard, Felicia's meddlesome brother, reports that Gramont's exclusion from court derives from "that fatal quarrel, in which he killed / The general's only son." This event "stopped his [political] progress" (I.i; 148). As in *The Mourning Bride,* conflict derives from "fatal," agonistic relations among men; Trotter, however, maintains these fractured bonds as her focus from the first act through the body-strewn final scene. Tragedy derives from male infighting at court and is perpetuated by male characters' reckless impositions of their always incomplete and divided authority throughout the play. When Gramont, for example, tries to avoid marrying Lamira—because he is secretly married to Felicia—he argues that his father, the Count, would "press a monstrous union / Of things by nature not agreeing" by forcing the marriage (II.i; 160). Unlike conventional tragedies predicated upon inherently chaotic, corrupt, and unruly female characters, *The Fatal Friendship* continually explores the "monstrous" demands of homosocial bonds and the "disorder" that Gramont repeatedly laments "lies within his breast" as a result of his bigamous deceit. By locating tragic "disorder"—a word frequently used within plays and Baconian science to define female characters and feminized nature (Merchant 127–48)—within Gramont, Trotter explicitly rejects the convention that depicts sexually and morally degenerate women as the source of sociopolitical turmoil. In doing so, I argue, she responds not only to precedents within literary tragedies but also to the logic of tragic paradigms such as science that similarly displace strife onto the feminine. Trotter redirects the tragic trajectory toward homosociality, then, through a crucial revision of cultural assumptions concerning the gendering of "chaos" and "order."

Indeed, rather than focusing on excising corruption by the brutal murder of women, the final scene dramatizes the dissolution of homosocial bonds as Bellgard, Castalio, and Gramont blame each other for being "betrayed" by each other's "dissembling, false[ness], and faithless[ness]" (V.i; 204). Trotter appropriates the tropes of revenge and retribution deployed by Congreve and earlier tragedians but provides a resolution that locates blame exclusively among the (self-)destructive male characters.

That the bloody revenge scene is emphatically limited to the three male characters highlights Trotter's relocation of the source of tragedy in patriarchy and conflicts between men. Lamira and Felicia enter only after revenge occurs and the tragedy, in effect, has been resolved. They are as minimally involved in the resolution of the crisis as they were in its production. Instead, the final scene affirms female self-"control" in the face of masculine "disorder." When asked by the Count, "What reparation can be made, Lamira?" she replies:

> The world can make me none. There's nothing here
> But a vicissitude of miseries.

If there is any joy that's permanent,
It must be in that calm, that heavenly state
To which my future days are dedicated.

[V.i; 207]

Felicia, meanwhile, finds her "calm" within the noble family. She is wel-
comed by the Count, her one-time suitor, as "my daughter" who "shall be
dearest to me" (V.i; 206). That these striking female characters are figured
as swiftly absorbed within dominant institutions of patrilineal culture—the
church and the noble family—seems an odd moment of recontainment in
a play that pervasively challenges patriarchy by making visible its institu-
tional fractures and instabilities.[14] It is, however, precisely because this
play critiques patrilineal structures of authority that Felicia's and Lamira's
acceptance of and entrance into them is offered as a hopeful and even a
radical promise.

Having witnessed the fatal consequences of his domineering,
flawed authority and of his attempts to create a stable financial future for
his family by trafficking in women, the Count admits, "I've been to blame."
He promises to demonstrate "my kindness doubled" (V.i; 206). Felicia and
Lamira not only remain alive in the fifth act—no small triumph, given the
misogynist, bloody tropes of conventional tragedies—but they continue to
curtail and to shape patrilineal institutions of authority and order, as they
have throughout the play. In effect, by appropriating and transforming
Baconian and literary tragic paradigms, Trotter blasphemously, parodically
asserts her own "new face of bodies, another universe or theater of
things."[15] Clearly, Bacon's promise of a science that offers a "new"
universal order only works if one accepts as natural the continual
repression of the feminine. Trotter, however, demonstrates that, in resisting
masculinist paradigms that construct knowledge by oppressively controlling the theater of representation, she is enabled to create alternative
representations and possibilities—"another universe" of female representation in which characters such as the Count accept "blame" and in
which women are integrated as vital and valued components of their
refashioned "universe."

Ultimately, Manley and Trotter provide a radical twofold critique
in their tragedies. By forcing us to look beyond the female body for the
source of tragic strife, Manley and Trotter unmask processes of scapegoating women as ideological covers for the inability of patriarchy to assert
itself as unified and ordered. From Manley's and Trotter's tragedies
emerges a new analytic that posits conflict among men for power and
"control"—and not inherent feminized corruption—as a locus of tragedy.
Their analyses argue for plays that are not predicated upon the scrutiny,
vexation, and conquest of the feminine and also for a reassessment of

cultural discourses, such as those of science, that deploy antifeminist tragic strategies. Throughout this essay I have argued that Baconian and Restoration science inform and even legitimate the gendered premises of masculinist tragedies; I also suggest that the tragedies by Manley and Trotter and other "oppositional" voices of the Restoration may be used to complicate and to investigate scientific narratives of misogynist conquest. By understanding, as Trotter writes, the "monstrous" outcome of efforts to reassert an unstable patrilineal authority that is always in need of being shored up, we may be able to recognize the violence contained within conventional associations about women, nature, and the "order" that women and nature are said to threaten.

Notes

I would like to thank Robert Markley for his generous support and comments on this essay.

1. See Newman 15–31 for discussion of Renaissance "method" as used in marriage guidebooks and conduct books for women. See also MacLean.

2. On the construction of the feminine within early modern science, see Keller, *Reflections;* Lloyd; and Schiebinger. For analysis of the relationship between science and early modern discourses, see, for example, Shapiro; Kroll; Markley, *Fallen Languages;* and Reiss.

3. See Middleton and Rowley; and Ford. See also Merchant 164–91; Keller, *Reflections* 33–432; and Lloyd.

4. I am defining the term *experimentation* broadly to suggest discrete experiments upon nature (such as those that Bacon enumerates in *The New Atlantis*) as well as theatrical performances in which women undergo experimental conditions of surveillance, scrutiny, torment, and dismemberment. I read the violence of most tragedies as mutually authorized by (and authorizing) Baconian violence against nature. While I do not read Bacon as originating these attitudes toward nature or women, I argue that his theories for experimentation offered a new means for "vexing" the feminine and thereby bolstered already proliferating antifeminisms of the late sixteenth and seventeenth centuries. See Merrens 179–92.

5. Robert Markley makes a similar point concerning Foucault (*Two-Edg'd Weapons* 42). For more on science as representation, see Golinski.

6. For analysis of how the exchange of women is intended to reinforce homosocial networks, see Rubin. See also Sedgwick.

7. On the construction of the subject and the individual in the seventeenth century, see Stallybrass, "Shakespeare, the Individual, and the Text."

8. These tragedies may also be read as responses to the spate of "she-tragedies" discussed by Laura Brown, which centered on defenseless, victimized female protagonists (64–102).

9. For instance, see Aphra Behn, "The Golden Age," in Rogers and McCarthy 8–14. In addition, recent scholarship examines Margaret Cavendish's

critiques of Restoration science. See, for example, Sarasohn 289–307; Gallagher 24–29; and Mendelson 12–61.

10. Cynthia Lowenthal makes a similar point about the importance of female desire in *The Royal Mischief.* See her forthcoming book, *Performing Identities.*

11. On the inscription of pain on the body as a didactic spectacle, see Foucault 3–69. See also Finke.

12. Trotter's *Fatal Friendship,* Fidelis Morgan notes, also reworks Thomas Otway's tragedies *The Orphan* and *Venice Preserv'd* (Introduction to Trotter's *Fatal Friendship,* 145).

13. The play pervasively comments on the difficult position of women—both the young (presumably) unmarried woman and the wealthy widow—on the marriage market. The fact that marriage becomes contorted into polygamy and verges on endogamy because of male characters' manipulations underscores Trotter's critique of the social practices of patrilineal economies that abuse women in the service of patrilineal authority.

14. The restricted choice between life within the noble family or church presents a historically accurate assessment of the limited options available to Renaissance and, largely, to Restoration women. See King; and Jones.

15. My use of *blasphemy* is informed by Haraway's "Manifesto for Cyborgs."

Works Cited

Bacon, Francis. "Aphorisms on the Composition of the Primary History." 1620. *The Philosophical Works of Francis Bacon.* Ed. John M. Robertson. London: Routledge, 1905. 403–8.

———. *The Great Instauration and The New Organum.* 1620. *The Philosophical Works of Francis Bacon.* Ed. John M. Robertson. London: Routledge, 1905. 241–387.

Boyle, Robert. *The Works of Robert Boyle.* Ed. Thomas Birch. 6 vols. London: A. Millar, 1744.

Brown, Laura. *Ends of Empire: Women and Ideology in Early Eighteenth-Century English Literature.* Ithaca, N.Y.: Cornell UP, 1993.

Congreve, William. *The Mourning Bride.* 1697. *William Congreve: Complete Plays.* Ed. Alexander Charles Ewald. New York: Hill and Wang, 1956. 381–437.

Finke, Laurie. "Painting Women: Images of Femininity in Jacobean Tragedy." *Performing Feminisms: Feminist Critical Theory and Theatre.* Ed. Sue-Ellen Case. Baltimore: Johns Hopkins UP, 1990. 223–36.

Ford, John. '*Tis Pity She's a Whore.* c. 1630. Ed. N.W. Bawcutt. Lincoln: U of Nebraska P, 1966.

Foucault, Michel. *Discipline and Punish: The Birth of the Prison.* Trans. Alan Sheridan. New York: Vintage, 1979.

Gallagher, Catherine. "Embracing the Absolute: The Politics of the Female Subject in Seventeenth-Century England." *Genders* 1 (March 1988): 24–29.

Golinski, Jan. *Science as Public Culture: Chemistry as Enlightenment in Britain.* Cambridge: Cambridge UP, 1992.

Haraway, Donna. "A Manifesto for Cyborgs: Science, Technology, and Socialist

Feminism in the Last Quarter." *Socialist Review* 80 (1985): 65–107. Rpt. in *Women, Class, and the Feminist Imagination: A Socialist Feminist Reader*. Ed. Karen V. Hansen and Ilene J. Philipson. Philadelphia: Temple UP, 1990. 580–617.

Hellegers, Desiree E. " 'The Threatening Angel and the Speaking Ass': The Masculine Mismeasure of Madness in Anne Finch's 'The Spleen.' " *Genre*. Forthcoming.

Jones, Vivien, ed. *Women in the Eighteenth Century*. New York: Routledge, 1990.

Jordan, Constance. *Renaissance Feminism: Literary Texts and Political Models*. Ithaca, N.Y.: Cornell UP, 1990.

José, Nicholas. *Ideas of the Restoration in English Literature, 1660–71*. Cambridge, Mass.: Harvard UP, 1984.

Keller, Evelyn Fox. *Reflections on Gender and Science*. New York: Yale UP, 1985.

———. *Secrets of Life, Secrets of Death: Essays on Language, Gender, and Science*. New York: Routledge, 1992.

Kroll, Richard. *The Material Word: Literate Culture in the Restoration and Early Eighteenth Century*. Baltimore: Johns Hopkins UP, 1991.

Lloyd, Genevieve. *The Man of Reason: "Male" and "Female" in Western Philosophy*. Minneapolis: U of Minnesota P, 1984.

Lowenthal, Cynthia. *Performing Identities*. Forthcoming.

MacLean, Ian. *The Renaissance Notion of Woman*. Cambridge: Cambridge UP, 1980.

Manley, Delariviere. *The Royal Mischief*. 1696. *The Female Wits: Women Playwrights of the Restoration*. Ed. Fidelis Morgan. London: Virago, 1981. 209–61.

Markley, Robert. *Fallen Languages: Crises of Representation in Newtonian England, 1660–1740*. Ithaca, N.Y.: Cornell UP, 1993.

———. *Two-Edg'd Weapons: Style and Ideology in the Comedies of Etherege, Wycherley, and Congreve*. Oxford: Clarendon, 1988.

Mendelson, Sara Heller. *The Mental World of Stuart Women*. Brighton: Harvester, 1987.

Merchant, Carolyn. *The Death of Nature: Women, Ecology, and the Scientific Revolution*. San Francisco: Harper and Row, 1980.

Merrens, Rebecca. "Exchanging Cultural Capital: Troping Woman in Sidney and Bacon." *Genre* 25 (1992): 179–92.

Middleton, Thomas, and William Rowley. *The Changeling*. 1622. Ed. Patricia Thompson. Lincoln: U of Nebraska P, 1966.

Morgan, Fidelis. Introduction to Catherine Trotter's *The Fatal Friendship*. *The Female Wits: Women Playwrights of the Restoration*. Ed. Fidelis Morgan. London: Virago, 1981. 23–31.

Newman, Karen. *Fashioning Femininity and English Renaissance Drama*. Chicago: U of Chicago P, 1991.

Reiss, Timothy. *The Discourse of Modernism*. Ithaca, N.Y.: Cornell UP, 1982.

Rogers, Katharine M., and William McCarthy, eds. *The Meridian Anthology of Early Women Writers*. New York: Meridian, 1987.

Rubin, Gayle. "The Traffic in Women: Notes on the 'Political Economy' of Sex." *Toward an Anthology of Women*. Ed. Rayna Rapp Reiter. New York: Monthly

Review Press, 1976. 157–210. Rpt. in *Women, Class, and the Feminist Imagination: A Socialist Feminist Reader.* Ed. Karen V. Hansen and Ilene J. Philipson. Philadelphia: Temple UP, 1990. 74–113.

Sarasohn, Lisa T. "A Science Turned Upside Down: Feminism and the Natural Philosophy of Margaret Cavendish." *Huntington Library Quarterly* 47 (1984): 289–307.

Schiebinger, Londa. *Nature's Body: Gender in the Making of Modern Science.* Boston: Beacon, 1993.

Sedgwick, Eve Kosofsky. *Between Men: English Literature and Male Homosocial Desire.* New York: Columbia UP, 1985.

Shapiro, Barbara. *Probability and Certainty in Seventeenth-Century England: A Study of the Relationships between Natural Science, Religion, History, Law, and Literature.* Princeton, N.J.: Princeton UP, 1983.

Snider, Alvin. "Bacon, Legitimation, and the 'Origin' of Restoration Science." *The Eighteenth Century: Theory and Interpretation* 32 (1991): 119–38.

Stallybrass, Peter. "Reading the Body: *The Revenger's Tragedy* and the Jacobean Theater of Consumption." *Renaissance Drama* 18 (1987): 121–48.

———. "Shakespeare, the Individual, and the Text." *Cultural Studies.* Ed. Lawrence Grossberg, Cary Nelson, and Paula Treichler. New York: Routledge, 1992. 593–610.

Stockton, Sharon. "The 'Broken Rib of Mankind': The Sociopolitical Function of the Scapegoat in *The Changeling.*" *Papers on Language and Literature* 26 (1990): 459–77.

Trotter, Catherine. *The Fatal Friendship.* 1698. *The Female Wits: Women Playwrights of the Restoration.* Ed. Fidelis Morgan. London: Virago, 1981. 147–207.

In the Carnival World of Adam's Garden: Roving and Rape in Behn's *Rover*

Dagny Boebel

*G*ayatri Spivak represents the development of language as a "fall." In language, which is binarily structured, she notes, "the superior term belongs to presence and the logos; the inferior serves to define its status and mark a fall" (lxix). The task, Spivak writes, is to "revers[e] and displac[e] the binaries, which constitute a violent hierarchy. . . . To deconstruct the oppositions is first . . . to overthrow the hierarchy" (lxxvii). This analysis of binaries serves as grounds for the liberation of discourse in Aphra Behn's *The Rover*. Behn in 1677 transformed the setting of Thomas Killigrew's 1654 closet drama *Thomaso* from Spanish Inquisition to Neapolitan carnival. The carnival setting serves as a metaphor for Behn's deconstruction of patriarchal privilege. Behn dissolves binarily structured discourse, effecting such chaos through liberative disguise in the form of carnivalesque circumstance and subverted political phallicism. In the carnival world of *The Rover* signifiers break free from their former moorings in phallic discourse, as Behn liberates the female characters to signify solely themselves. Thus they escape the domination maintained by that "signification [that] serves to sustain relations of domination" (Thompson 146).

Behn's shift of setting, while it provides a locus of genuine chaotic liberation, also makes it possible for her to satirize masculine notions of carnival liberty. For while the Puritan commonwealth was viewed by Royalists like Behn as an oppressive regime, not unlike the Spanish Inquisition, Behn makes it clear that carnivalesque freedom, as it was understood by the Cavaliers, locked women into a sexual double bind as oppressive, in its way, as the moral and spiritual double bind that Puritan preachers inflicted on women under the guise of liberating them (Jardine 49–50).

To his Royalist supporters, the return of Charles II, who over-turned the oppressive Puritan ban on festivity and carnality, was associated with a celebration of physical delight and with a dissolution of hierarchy. The Restoration was even imaged in terms referring to Adam's prelapsarian garden. Graham Perry cites Abraham Cowley's Restoration Ode as an example of Cavalier confidence that the reign of Charles II had restored the Golden Age: "the very ground / Ought with a face of Paradise be found" (107–8). The diary of Samuel Pepys also abounds in such imagery. Perry notes a "sense of the freshness of life" and of social leveling, in images of a king who "might be encountered at the playhouse, or riding down the street, stopping to chat with acquaintances," or "overhead making love" (113). Charles II seemed to live a common life with the people.

Descriptions of the enthusiastic followers of Charles II abound with images of carnival as it was manifested in the old British festive culture, "the 'heathenish' and popish revellings [and] sinful merry-making" (Under-down 47) that the Puritan preachers and writers had striven, as early as the reign of Elizabeth I, to wipe out. David Underdown contends that Puritan-ism had gradually evolved into an ideology of discipline, bent on maintain-ing patriarchal order. He writes, "Anxieties about collapsing familial disci-plines were central to the whole crisis of order. Revels were an obvious scape-goat. They permitted women an unacceptable degree of sexual freedom" (48).

Although the carnivalesque revels had been adapted to the church calendar, Mikhail Bakhtin notes that reveling had roots in the "early stages of pre-class and pre-political social order" (7). It is this egalitarian order, conceptualized as Saturn's Golden Age, that is celebrated in the Roman Saturnalia (9). According to Bakhtin, carnival has a radically dehierarchiz-ing effect, for "all the symbols . . . are filled with . . . the sense of the gay relativity of prevailing truths and authorities. We find here a characteristic logic, the peculiar logic of the 'inside out,' of the 'turnabout,' of a continual shifting from top to bottom, from front to rear" (11). Robert Weimann refers to the same phenomenon as "topsy-turvydom" and notes that "as early as the Roman Saturnalia such topsy-turvydom was associated with a utopian dream of the Golden Age" (20–21). The effect of carnival, as Bakhtin and Weimann describe it, and as Behn represents it, is deconstructive.

When Aphra Behn returned to England from Surinam in 1663, she must have been struck by the changes that the decline of the Protectorate and the restoration of the Stuart king had wrought. Behn had left England at a time when "the Cromwellian dictatorship was still unchallenged, and the iron rule of the Saints and Major-generals was absolute. . . . theaters were closed [and] adultery and fornication were punishable by death" (Woodcock 26). Underdown observes that the "Restoration was a vic-tory . . . for adherents of traditional festive culture" (275), most of whom were Royalists and many of whom were female. But for Behn, as an analysis of *The Rover* reveals, disillusionment followed this initial euphoria.

Behn's attraction to carnival is consistent with what some have claimed is her radical feminist outlook, and thus it significantly differs from Cavalier festive practices. George Woodcock contends that she had been radicalized by her experiences in Surinam, which made her critical of law, religion, slavery, racism, and the institution of marriage and led her to assert that women should have equal opportunities with men (150). This trend of proposing the removal of male demarcation from the public sphere found, as Janet Todd summarizes, an echo over one hundred years later through Wollstonecraft, who went one step further to confirm that "in the revolutionary decade of the 1790's . . . femininity was a cultural construction and . . . writing was an act of self-assertion for women" (4). Unlike Wollstonecraft, however, Behn had a strongly positive view of female sexuality and a taste for wit and bawdiness. This taste put her at odds with those who were promoting what Todd calls "a sentimental construction of femininity, a state associated with modesty, passivity, chastity, moral elevation and suffering" (4). Behn harshly satirized the predominantly Whig promoters of this construction, associating them with the Puritan oppressors. She was not alone in making such an association. Underdown notes that after the Restoration "the terms—'Roundhead,' 'Cavalier,' 'the people of God,' 'the Presbyterian crew'—were . . . swamped by the more enduring 'Whig' and 'Tory' " (289). But the deconstruction Behn performs in *The Rover* reveals her as a critic not only of repressive Whig prudery but also of Cavalier carnival, which elevated male bodies and masculine sexual desire but denied women rights to their own bodies and their own desire.

The carnival world of *The Rover* inverts the violent hierarchy in at least three ways:

First, Behn privileges women's speech. In her opening scene, she gives her female characters both the power to construct masculinity according to their desires and the power to signify themselves. In doing this, she reveals how arbitrary, how unmoored in any metaphysical reality, are the definitions, classifications, and uses men have created for the feminine.

Second, echoing the ancient British festive tradition of mumming, Behn does away with textual signification altogether, replacing it with the silent language of bodily symbol.

Third, Behn deconstructs both the moral code and masculine, carnivalesque deconstructions of this code, unmasking the phallic violence of both. Angellica, with whose proper name Behn displaces the phallic unangelic meaning of "prostitute," has her sign attacked both by the Whiggish prude Blunt and by the Cavalier Willmore. Willmore represents himself as a spokesman of feminine sexual liberation, but his brand of carnivalesque liberty merely reasserts, and even intensifies, the culture's dominant male authority structures. It is a mask behind which he seeks violently to reassert masculine authority. As a rapist, for whom feminine desire has no significance, he is as hypocritical as Blunt, whose collaborator he eventually becomes in a proposed gang rape.

In the epilogue to *The Rover* Behn attacks the Whigs, who were strongly challenging Royalist power in the 1670s, by associating them with the repressive Commonwealth:

> With canting rule you would the stage refine,
> And to dull method all our sense confine,
> With th' insolence of the commonwealths you rule.
> [14–16]

Cant is mechanical, predictable, monotonous discourse, unlike the fluid, unpredictable, transgressive, and dehierarchizing language of carnival. Against "canting rule" Behn sets

> A popish carnival! A masquerade!
> The devil's in't if this will please the nation
> In these our blessed times of reformation.
> [2–4]

The language of carnival is, in its multiplicity, in its fluidity, and in its absence of hierarchy, not "popish"—that is, not representative of masculine dominance and authority—but rather suggestive of the joyful expression of feminine pleasure and desire that French feminists, in an adaptation of Roland Barthes's concept, call *jouissance,* "an archaic form of expressivity originating in the body of the mother" (Rose 54). Given the revolutionary character of carnival as understood by Behn, the problem with male revelers is that, fixated in their phallicism, they do not carry the revolution of carnival far enough.

It is not surprising, then, that in *The Rover* Behn is not content to undermine only Whig pretensions. Her carnival setting provides her with an opportunity to create her own carnivalesque displacements, exposing how arbitrary the male system of signification is. Virginia Woolf has likened the pen in the hand of a woman writer to a pickax, breaking apart the male-constructed narrative, in which, Woolf observes, women play no part except in relationship to men. Woolf asks her readers to consider the oddity of an Other narrative, in which men are represented only in relationships with women—as lovers, husbands, fathers, brothers. Behn creates such a narrative, defined by the Other, in the first scene of *The*

Rover. The play opens with female characters wittily deconstructing patriarchy and discussing men solely with respect to feminine desire. Hellena praises Belvile, Florinda's lover, because he is "gay and so handsome" (I.i. 30–31). Hellena, whose convent upbringing seems only to have strengthened her libido, wishes for "some mad companion or other that will spoil my devotion" (37–38). Hellena's tongue is not silenced later by the arrival of her brother Don Pedro and his train. Even Florinda, who is less outspoken than her sister, bravely condemns the marriage that has been arranged for her by her father: "I hate Vincentio, sir, and I would not have a man so dear to me as my brother follow the ill customs of our country and make a slave of his sister" (66–68). With similar boldness, Hellena transgresses the boundaries between religious and carnal discourse and displaces the one/Other, soul/body, and male/female hierarchy. *Saint* becomes her signifier for *lover,* *prayer* for *seduction,* and the female, not the male, becomes the sexually active party: "You may chance to be mistaken in my way of devotion. A nun! Yes, I am like to make a fine nun! I have an excellent humor for a grate! No, I'll have a saint of my own to pray to shortly, if I like any that dares venture on me" (149–52). Such outspoken challenges to masculine and ecclesiastical authority lead their brother Don Pedro to declare both of them "mad!" (98). The women, however, rightly associate madness with carnival *jouissance.* Despite Don Pedro's order, "Take her hence and lock her up all this Carnival" (143), they escape, disguised as gypsies, Europe's dark rovers, to "be as mad as the rest" (181–82). Outside the logical syntax of patriarchal discourse that Luce Irigaray views as "a means of masculine . . . self-production" is *madness,* that is, an "other" (carnival) syntax, which is "lacking, repressed, censured" (132) but which rescues the feminine from destruction.

In carnival the bodily element is "deeply positive." Indecent, bawdy expressions are "so many sparks of the carnival bonfire which renews the world" (Bakhtin 19, 17). The carnivalesque elevation of carnality in general and of feminine sexuality in particular is illustrated in *The Rover* by two processions, the first composed of female carnival celebrants, the second of men. Both the women, who wear and carry roses, and the men, whose bodies are covered with horns, symbolize the displacement of phallic discourse by a body language that dissolves the hierarchical male/female binary and privileges feminine *jouissance.*

The Rover is set during the Puritan Interregnum, and the male protagonists, banished English Cavaliers, have come ashore at Naples, as Willmore says, "to enjoy myself a little this Carnival . . . [in] a warm climate, where the kind sun has its godlike power" (I.ii.69–75). He comes upon women, dressed like courtesans, carrying baskets of roses and wearing papers that say "Roses for every month" (I.ii.83). Reading the "rose" as a feminine genital symbol, Willmore enthusiastically suggests, "I might but strew such roses over me and under me. Fair one, would you would give me leave to gather at your bush this idle month; I would go near to make somebody smell of it all the year after" (I.ii.91–95). Willmore's apparently enthusiastic support for feminine sexual liberation is reaffirmed a few minutes later when he is approached by a group of "men dressed all over with horns of several sorts, making grimaces at one another" (I.ii, stage directions). While Belvile disapproves of their obscene flaunting of a symbol of masculine humiliation, Willmore approves: "This is a gardener of Adam's own breeding. . . . I like their sober grave way; 'tis a kind of legal authorized fornication, where the men are not chid for 't, nor the women despised, as amongst our dull English" (I.ii.116–21).

Behn's procession of horned men recalls the English mummers' pageants, a carnival form with which Behn was doubtless familiar and whose origins Alan Brody traces to pre-Christian agricultural rituals (117) based, as Marija Gimbutas and others have noted, in the worship of the Great Goddess. Brody notes that the custom of horn dancing has continued in England into modern times and that being selected to dance wearing horns is considered an honor. Horned animals were sacred to the Goddess, and an ancient Sumerian myth suggests that both the rose and the horn may be female genital symbols. The vulva of Inanna, Queen of Heaven and Earth, was referred to as "the horn" (Wolkstein and Kramer 37). Weimann also traces in mummers' plays, which are marked by topsy-turvy elements both in language and in structure, "the dim reflections of a more primitive society still fairly homogeneous in its property and class structure" (19).

Willmore seems to revive these ancient associations when he denies that the rose and the horn, both signifiers of female sexual desire and power, signify disgrace. He replaces the pejorative meanings with more ancient, honorable, and religious meanings. In "The Laugh of the Medusa" Hélène Cixous attributes the power to effect such revolutionary shifts to the "feminine text [that] cannot fail to be more than subversive. It is volcanic; as it is written it brings about an upheaval of the old property crust, carrier of masculine investments" (888). Unfortunately, Willmore's later actions with respect to Angellica and Florinda make it clear that his promising displacement of the pejorative meaning of horns does not displace the male/female hierarchy, nor does it liberate women from a moral code designed to deny them desire and to keep them in their places. In fact, Willmore and Blunt think and act in nearly identical ways. Behn's text, however, *is* subversive: it performs a carnivalesque displacement by exposing both Whigs and Tories, Puritans and Cavaliers, as upholders of a violent, hierarchical gender ideology.

The kind of upheaval to which Cixous refers occurred when women began playing roles that had formerly been played by boys. Elaine Showalter argues that during the Restoration, the depiction of Ophelia's madness took on a subversive dimension (82). For Ophelia, as for the women in *The Rover,* madness was defined as resistance to the erasure of feminine sexuality in phallic discourse, a resistance diagnosed by seventeenth- and eighteenth-century physicians as "erotomania." In *Madness and Civilization* Michel Foucault shows how Philippe Pinel cured a girl of seventeen who "suffered a loss of reason as a result of a forbidden romantic attachment." Assuming the authority of the father, Pinel induced her to confess and so " 'brought an end to her continual agitation' " (273). As was the case with Pinel's patient, Ophelia's madness took on "subversive" dimensions. Showalter writes, "Ophelia's bawdy songs and verbal license . . . give her access to 'an entirely different range of experience' from what she is allowed as the dutiful daughter [and] seem to be her one sanctioned form of self-assertion as a woman" (81).

While Ophelia's "self-assertion" is "quickly followed," Showalter notes, "as if in retribution, by her death" (81), the self-assertions by the women in *The Rover* are validated. Although Hellena's and Florinda's bold assertions lead their brother to declare them "mad" and in need of confinement, the women manage to escape to the "divertissements of Carnival" and "be as mad as the rest" (I.i.178, 181). Indeed, Behn may be consciously using *Hamlet* as a subtext for *The Rover.* Willmore, for example, may be echoing Hamlet's reference to Jeptha's sacrifice of his daughter when he warns Hellena to avoid the fate of "Jeptha's daughter" (I.ii.179), that is, to avoid dying with her virginity intact. Hellena has fled from her own "Jeptha," a brother intent on locking her away in a convent so that he can appropriate her fortune. It is her strong sexual desire (erotomania) that leads her to resist his authority. Unlike *Hamlet,* where Ophelia is a lonely and doomed "mad" female voice, however, in *The Rover* Hellena and her "mad" sisters challenge the dominant discourse and deconstruct its "truths."

One of these "truths" is that women, unlike men, are either angels or whores, a binary that Hamlet may be deconstructing when he advises Ophelia, "Get thee to a nunnery." Behn carries Hamlet's deconstruction much further. Through her self-signifying nun, Hellena, and her self-signifying prostitute, Angellica Bianca, Behn unites the two extremes of sexual possibilities for women. Behn gives Hellena, Jones DeRitter notes, some lines that in *Thomaso* were spoken by prostitutes. Hellena declares adultery preferable to forced marriage (I.i.131), and she rejects constancy as an ideal. She tells Willmore, "When I begin, I fancy I shall love like anything" and "have a new man to seek" (I.ii.194, 193). The prostitute Angellica Bianca, on the other hand, signifies herself a virgin, for, despite her lack of chastity from a masculine, physical point of view, she views herself as spiritually intact. She has never given her "virgin heart" to anyone (IV.ii.151).

One of Behn's most interesting reversals is Angellica Bianca's assumption of the role of chaste redeemer. In *A Letter of Genteel and Moral Advice to a Young Lady* (1740), Wetenhall Wilkes presents the middle-class view of the aristocracy as marked by self-indulgence and excess, imaged by the licentious rake, "who must be subjected to a feminized, virtuous, 'heroic passion' by female chastity" (Jones 15). By permitting Angellica to signify herself as no man would signify her—that is, as redemptive female—Behn makes her, as Janet Todd suggests, a symbol for the female writer in general and for Aphra Behn, whose initials also were A.B., in particular. Both Angellica Bianca and Aphra Behn had their "signs" attacked. In 1684 a Whig wrote of Behn:

> Then let her from the next inconstant Lover,
> Take a new copy for a second Rover,
> Describe the Cunning of a jilting Whore
> From the ill Arts herself has us'd before.
> [cited in Woodcock 173]

In *The Rover* a contemptuous Willmore, behaving in this instance like a Whig, tears down Angellica's sign, claiming to act in the interests of public morality:

> The posture's loose and negligent;
> The sight on't would beget a warm desire
> In souls whom impotence and age had chilled.
> [II.i.221–23]

Willmore's physical assault on the sign is paralleled by Blunt's verbal attack. Upon seeing Angellica's advertisement of herself and learning that she is a "famous courtesan, that's to be sold" (II.i.102), Blunt responds bluntly, with appropriate Whiggish (and Protestant) prudery: "How! To be sold? Nay, then I have nothing to say to her. Sold? What impudence is practiced in this country; with what order and decency whoring's established here by virtue of the Inquisition! Come, let's be gone; I'm sure we're no chapmen for this commodity" (II.i.103–7).

As Todd and others have noted, female signification, that is, women's public speaking and writing, was often metaphorically represented as prostitution. Women who wrote for the public were "public women." The assaults of Willmore the Cavalier and of Blunt the Whig on the sign of Angellica symbolically represent, or foreshadow, their later sexual assaults on Florinda, who, by "loosing" herself from a home in which she has been imprisoned, has signified herself, they reason, a "loose" woman.

In 1685 Behn published, as the opening poem in *Poems upon Several Occasions,* a long poem on the Golden Age, picturing it as a time without war, government, religion, private property, or rape. Behn's view of rape strikingly contrasts with that of an eighteenth-century barrister, who wrote that rape is "the 'artless sincerity of natural passion' " (cited in Clark, *Women's Silence* 34). In alliance with the barrister, the earl of Rochester, a close friend of Behn's, represents rape as part of the normal activity in the nightly "carnival" atmosphere in St. James's Park. The park's foliage equally attracts and shelters "Great ladies, chambermaids, and drudges, / The ragpicker, and heiress," none of whom, it seems, consider sexual assault an infringement of their rights (cited in Goreau 167). But unlike her male friends and colleagues, Behn refuses to view rape as an inevitable and natural part of carnival. Her condemnation of rape sounds radical, given the fact that there was an element of rape in most sexual encounters of the period, as Sara F. Matthews Grieco notes. "It would seem," she observes, "that most sexual relations were short and frequently brutal. Men apparently made little attempt to ensure the enjoyment of their partner, and foreplay was so rare as to be practically nonexistent. The stock description, 'he threw me on the ground, stuck a handkerchief in my mouth, and lifted my skirts,' is a constant of both legitimate and illegitimate relations, and even if force was not used, the threat of violence was always present" (79).

Given the common belief of the period that female orgasm was necessary for conception, it can be argued that concern for female pleasure was more common than Grieco claims. However, as Nazife Bashar points out, force and violence were not necessarily viewed as inconsistent with female consent and pleasure. Bashar quotes Sir Henry Finch's *Law; or, A Discourse Thereof:* "Rape is the forcible ravishment of a woman, but if she conceive it is not rape, for she cannot conceive unless she consent" (36). Anna Clark cites a judge in a trial for rape and murder who asked the jury "to consider 'if though violence was used, it was with her consent.' " Clark writes that "violence was merely one means of seduction" ("Rape or Seduction?" 17, 18). The notion that female consent was necessary for conception was one of the factors that contributed to the lowering of the rate of conviction for rape in the seventeenth century. Bashar notes "a significant decrease, both in the number of rape cases coming to court and in the rate of conviction between 1558 and 1700, when conviction rates decreased from one in four to one in eight." Given these odds, Bashar concludes that "women would have become more reluctant to charge a man with rape when the probability of his conviction was decreasing" (35).

Angellica Bianca seems to have internalized the commonly held view that violence was an acceptable means of seduction. Accompanying herself with a lute, she sings a song that functions as a "sign." It tells the story of Damon, a shepherd, who had been languishing in a "soft desire" for Caelia (II.i.176). He is lying in the shade, weaving a flower for her hair when she suddenly appears with her flock. Looking at her, he sees "guilty smiles and blushes" and

> the bashful youth all transport grew,
> And with *kind force* he taught the virgin how
> To yield what all his sighs could never do.
> [III.i.189–91; italics mine]

This "sign" in song, doubtless sung to arouse potential customers, supports the male-constructed narrative, or myth, of the naturalness of rape. According to this myth, men, led on by the beauty of women, fall prey to the "artless sincerity of natural passion." The myth, "that rape is a crime of passion touched off by female beauty," Susan Brownmiller contends, "is given great credence, and women are influenced to believe that to be raped . . . is a testament to beauty" (333–41). The myth also supports the notion that such force is a kindness to women, for it gives them pleasure they would otherwise be denied.

Angellica Bianca accepts what Brownmiller calls the male-constructed narrative of rape. She seeks to have Willmore re-create the "kind force" of her musical sign. Her "virgin heart" (IV.ii.151) must be taken by force. She exhorts Willmore,

> Why art thou soft?
> Thy looks are bravely rough and meant for war.
> Could'st thou not storm on still?
> I then perhaps had been as free as thou.
> [II.ii.137–40]

But while Angellica seems to desire that Willmore take her body as violently and as forcefully as he has attacked her sign by pulling it down, this scene with Willmore turns the rape-narrative, if not topsy-turvy, at least ninety degrees. Angellica is the aggressor, but still she must, in order to fit her concept of herself as modest virgin, be the victim of male violence.

It is illuminating to compare Angellica's inversion of the rape narrative with Hellena's earlier displacement of the male/female binary in her saint-prayer speech. While Hellena gives the redemptive role to the masculine term, Angellica reserves it for the feminine. While, for Angellica, the chaste, redeeming female must be taken by force, Hellena gives the aggressive role to the feminine term. Her planned assault, however, is verbal. In both cases, Behn employs carnivalesque displacement. For although, as Todd acknowledges, Angellica Bianca's construction seems sentimental and traditional, she is, in fact, radically reconstructing the meanings of *prostitute* and *virgin*. As a prostitute, Angellica is constructed in phallic discourse as carnal and, therefore, as fallen or low. She resignifies herself as spiritual and redemptive and is bitterly disappointed that Willmore remains unredeemed after she has given him

> a heart entire
> Which I had pride enough to think when'er I gave,
> It would have raised the man above the vulgar,
> Made him all soul.
>
> [III.i.170–73]

Willmore is unmoved by Angellica's attempts at resignification. She remains for him "the kind baggage" (III.vi.42–43).

Angellica's signification of rape, her song and her theatrical plea to her lover to "storm on still," differ strikingly from actual sexual assaults in *The Rover,* which negate and silence women. Behn's female-constructed rape narratives challenge the male-constructed myth. In *The Rover* virtually all of the male characters are rapists or potential rapists. Behn's rapists are not aroused by the beauty of their victim; drunken, in the dark, they may not even see her very clearly. And rape, far from being an expression of uncontrollable sexual desire, may be an act of violence to punish, for the crime of being female, whatever woman happens to be in the rapist's clutches.

The victim of both "actual" sexual assaults in *The Rover* is Florinda, who fits more closely than Hellena the sentimental construction of womanhood. Internalizing such an ideal, Behn might be saying, makes one the perfect victim. The repeated attacks on Florinda correspond to a recent study that suggests that a woman who has earlier been assaulted is at greater risk of being raped again (see "Rape Risk"). In fact, Florinda's first sexual assault occurred during the siege of Pamplona, when, as she reminds her brother, "I was exposed to such dangers as the licensed lust of common soldiers threatened when rage and conquest flew through the city, then Belvile . . . threw himself into all dangers to save my honor" (I.i.74–78).

In Naples the first assault upon Florinda occurs at night, while she waits in her garden for a visit from Belvile. She is nervous because her lover is late. Willmore, flushed from drink and from his successful seduction of

Angellica, in the dark garden can see only that Florinda is "a female." Had there been more light, and had he been less drunk, he would have recognized her as his friend's mistress, because he has seen her picture. In the darkness he sees only "a woman . . . a very wench!" (III.v.16–17). In the patriarchal system of signs, once she is loosed from her signification as Belvile's mistress, Florinda becomes a sign of generalized "woman," equated only with her biological essence, thus "a very wench." Willmore first tries seduction: "Come, come kiss me. . . . Thou mayst be free with me; I'll be very secret" (23–31), but Florinda calls him a "filthy beast" (33). He becomes more forceful, telling her, "Thou art . . . obliged . . . to deny me nothing" (40–42). It is, after all, carnival. Sexual license, as he understands it, must prevail; his freedom is her obligation. Finally he grabs her, and she begs him, "Sir, let me go, I conjure you, or I'll call out" (49). He is so certain that he is in the right that he tells her, "You were best to call witness to see how finely you treat me. Do!" (50). When she threatens, "I'll cry . . . rape . . . if you do not instantly let me go" (52), he insists that this is not rape but consensual sex: "A rape! Come come, you lie, you baggage, you lie. What! I'll warrant you would fain have the world believe now that you are not so forward as I. No, not you. Why at this time of night was your cobweb door set open, dear spider, but to catch flies? Ha! Come, or I shall be damnably angry" (54–58). Rape is as he—and the discourse of dominance—define it, not as she experiences it.

Willmore decides that she is holding out because she wants payment: "[H]ere's a pistole for you" (62). When Florinda continues to struggle, he asks, "Why, how now, mistress, are you so high i' th' mouth a pistole won't down with you?" (68–69). Finally Belvile arrives and stops the assault when he hears her cries.

From Willmore's point of view, his behavior was correct. He was simply the victim of mistaken identity. "How the devil," he asks, "should I know Florinda?" (III.vi.1). His violation was that he attacked the "property" of his friend. But since he did not actually penetrate her, that is, "ruin" her, forgiveness comes rather easily. Clark notes that in the late seventeenth and eighteenth centuries, discourse structured the definition of rape around the opposition of chastity and unchastity, so that a rapist would only be punished if he assaulted a chaste woman. Bashar supports Clark's observation, noting that virtually all convictions for rape between 1650 and 1700 were assaults on children:

> When ordinary women of little or no property in any form ap-
> peared as victims in rape cases at Assizes and Quarter Sessions
> rape was not treated very seriously. . . . The only convictions that
> were imposed were on men accused of raping young girls. Per-
> haps the contemporary connection between virginity and property

explains this phenomenon. . . . Rape of a virgin, a young
woman, was regarded as the theft of her virginity, the property
of her father to be used in procuring an advantageous marriage.
Only the rapes that had in them some element of property, in the
form of virginity, ended in the conviction of the accused. [Bashar 42]

Because the law was more concerned with property than with a woman's
rights, "society regarded the distinction between rape and seduction as
unimportant: a woman was damaged property in either case" (Clark, *Women's
Silence* 8). And, Clark continues, "British justice was overwhelmingly
concerned with property. . . . in the eyes of the law sexual assault was
only significant when it involved the 'property' of a man—a virginal
daughter or a wife. The law of rape, in fact, had evolved to protect the theft
of female sexual property, not to protect women themselves" (46–47).

Through Florinda's experience, Behn deconstructs the prevailing
code of morality and sexual politics, in which rape was viewed as either the
"natural" expression of passions or as possessive appropriation. Such a
view is inconsistent both with Behn's construction of carnivalesque
egalitarianism and with Willmore's publicly professed notion of carnivalesque libertarianism, which emphasized sexual freedom for women as
well as for men. In truth, however, Willmore shares the attitude, noted by
Clark, that rape is a crime against property. Only a "woman of quality," a
virginal daughter or a wife of a propertied man, is subject to rape. Other
women are common property. Carnival masquerade, of course, makes it
impossible to tell a gypsy or a prostitute from an aristocrat. Therefore,
Willmore's praise of carnival, with its dissolution of normal social identity, is exposed as a reiteration of paternal authority over women and
the negation of female desire. Florinda's carnival "undress" gives Willmore a "right" to have her: "By this light, I took her for an errant harlot"
(III.vi.21).

Ugly as Willmore's attack on Florinda is, Willmore is not so sinister
as Blunt, who is motivated by a desire to do violence to women in general.
Florinda presents him with his first opportunity in a scene that soon
degenerates into a proposed gang rape, in which not only Willmore but
also Belvile and Don Pedro, Florinda's brother, vie for the right to be the
first to assault her. First, however, they interrupt Blunt before he has been
able to carry out his threat to rape and torture Florinda:

Cruel? Yes, I will kiss and beat thee all over, kiss and see thee all
over; thou shalt lie with me too, not that I care for the enjoyment, but to let thee see I have ta'en deliberated malice to thee,
and will be revenged on one whore for the sins of another. I will

smile and deceive thee; flatter thee, and beat thee; embrace thee and rob thee, as she did me; fawn on thee, and strip thee stark naked; then hang thee out at my window by the heels, with a paper of scurvy verses fastened to thy breast in praise of damnable women. [IV.v.53–62]

Even this brute, however, considers forcible penetration "kind force." He tells her, "I am resolved to make up my loss here on thy body; I'll take it out in *kindness* and in beating" (IV.v.84–86; italics mine). His friends arrive—including Belvile, whom he calls "a cormorant at whore . . . he'd have a limb or two of thee, my virgin pullet" (IV.v.118–19)—and an individual assault threatens to become a gang rape. Willmore says, "We must enter and partake. No resistance" (V.28–29). While Florinda remains hidden from view, Blunt, Frederick, Willmore, Belvile, and Florinda's brother Don Pedro argue about who will go first and, in a scene with obvious phallic symbolism, decide to "draw cuts. . . . the longest sword carries her" (V.98–100). That would give her brother Don Pedro the right to rape her first because, as a Spaniard, he has the longest sword. Behn opens her play with one kind of brotherly "kindness" and threatens to end it with another—incestuous rape—thus exposing both as different aspects of the same arbitrary patriarchal domination.

Before Don Pedro discovers that his intended victim is his own sister, however, he is drawn away on some pretext, and Florinda is exposed first as a "woman of quality" and, finally, as Belvile's mistress and Don Pedro's sister.

Although the women in *The Rover* are given voice and courage and their desires are validated, the assaults on Florinda silence her. She does not confront Belvile about his participation in the prospective gang rape, and she does not tell Hellena about Willmore's assault. Florinda has doubtless internalized the prevailing view of sexual assault at the time: "No harm, no punishment" (Staves 104). It was not until the next century, Susan Staves notes, that a law of attempted rape slowly developed (103). Florinda's silence may represent the stifling of carnivalesque communication, that is, the limits of *jouissance*. She experiences a violent reassertion of phallic hierarchy and prerogatives.

Other female figures in the final act, however, challenge this hierarchy. In a curious instance of carnivalesque topsy-turvydom, the prostitute Angellica Bianca again plays a double role. Speaking with the voice of outraged feminine virtue, she becomes the phallic enforcer of chastity. Thrusting a pistol, the image of violent phallic power, into Willmore's breast, Angellica Bianca tells him, "I have vowed thy death by all that's sacred" (V.234–35). Willmore rejects constancy but makes the following offer:

nature never meant me [to be constant]
· · · · · · · · · · · · · ·
I must, like cheerful birds, sing in all groves
And perch on every bough.
Yet, after all, [I] could build my nest with thee,
Thither repairing when I'd loved my round,
And still reserve a tributary flame
To gain your credit, I'll pay you back your charity,
And be obliged for nothing but love.

[V.299–307]

The reader or spectator recalls that Willmore has earlier displayed a confused, or perhaps cynical, view of female sexuality. He has rejected the sexual double standard by elevating horns as a mark of honor and by expressing a distaste for "virtuous women." However, his delight at Hellena's vocation—"A nun! Oh, now I love thee for't" (I.ii.176)—and his opposite response to Angellica's—"It quenches all manner of fire in me" (I.ii.333)—represent a retreat from his enthusiastic endorsement of female *jouissance*. Willmore's true political nature is revealed when an insulted and outraged Angellica declares that he must die "for the public safety of our sex" (V.312), exposing under his carnival libertinism his fundamental role as rapist and proponent of male domination.

Willmore escapes, however, when Antonio enters and disarms Angellica. Angellica's pistol remains silent. But the "mad" voice of carnival *jouissance,* and its inversion of the gender hierarchy, is not stilled. It is Hellena who is left to restore carnival. Shortly after Willmore escapes Angellica's pistol, he is faced with another "deadly" threat. Hellena threatens to leave. Willmore's reply is an inverted echo of his earlier bird-bough speech to Angellica: "If we part so, let me die like a bird upon a bough" (V.467). The final promises of Willmore and Hellena to each other invert the sexual double standard. He tells her, "I am called Robert the Constant" (V.482). She replies, "I am called Hellena the Inconstant" (488).

Behn lets Willmore escape both prosecution as a rapist and death at the hands of Angellica. He has no choice, however, but to inhabit the topsy-turvy world—Adam's garden—he had earlier idealized. Whereas Willmore had planned to be the gardener—the planter of horns, the "flowers of every night" (I.ii.114–15)—he will be, in fact, if we are to take Hellena's taunt and his proclamation of constancy seriously, the ground in which they are planted. As earth, he is in the female position. Hellena is on top. Willmore is metaphorically where Blunt has been literally after Lucetta robs him and drops him into the sewer. Naked and humiliated, Blunt wallows in the night soil while, comfortably above ground, Lucetta glories in the spoils of her conquest, all emblems of male privilege, property, and power: "A rich coat; sword and hat; these breeches . . . a gold watch! A purse—Ha! Gold . . . A bunch of diamond rings . . . the family arms!" (III.iii.37–40).

In *The Rover,* through reversals like these, through challenging and exposing patriarchal systems of signification and their underpinnings in an ethos of oppressive dominance, Aphra Behn accomplishes the task Gayatri Spivak has handed to the female writer: she undoes the "fall" by overthrowing the "violent hierarchy."

Works Cited

Bakhtin, Mikhail. *Rabelais and His World.* Trans. Hélène Iswolsky. 1968. Bloomington: Indiana UP, 1984.

Bashar, Nazife. "Rape in England between 1550 and 1700." *The Sexual Dynamics of History: Men's Power, Women's Resistance.* Ed. London Feminist History Group. London: Pluto, 1983. 28–42.

Behn, Aphra. *The Rover; or, The Banished Cavaliers.* 1677. Ed. Frederick M. Link. Lincoln: U of Nebraska P, 1967.

Brody, Alan. *The English Mummers and Their Plays.* Philadelphia: U of Pennsylvania P, 1969.

Brownmiller, Susan. *Against Our Will: Men, Women, and Rape.* New York: Simon and Schuster, 1975.

Cixous, Hélène. "The Laugh of the Medusa." *Signs* (Summer 1976): 875–91.

Cixous, Hélène, and Catherine Clement. *The Newly Born Woman.* Trans. Betsy Wing. Minneapolis: U of Minnesota P, 1986.

Clark, Anna. "Rape or Seduction? A Controversy over Sexual Violence in the Nineteenth Century." *The Sexual Dynamics of History: Men's Power, Women's Resistance.* Ed. London Feminist History Group. London: Pluto, 1983. 13–27.

———. *Women's Silence, Men's Violence: Sexual Assault in England, 1770–1845.* New York: Pandora, 1987.

DeRitter, Jones. "The Gypsy, *The Rover,* and the Wanderer: Aphra Behn's Revision of Thomas Killigrew." *Restoration* 10.2 (Fall 1986): 82–92.

Foucault, Michel. *Madness and Civilization.* Trans. Richard Howard. New York: Pantheon, 1965.

Gimbutas, Marija. *The Language of the Goddess: Unearthing Hidden Symbols of Western Civilization.* San Francisco: Harper, 1989.

Goreau, Angeline. *Reconstructing Aphra.* New York: Dial, 1980.

Grieco, Sara F. Matthews. "The Body, Appearance, and Sexuality." *A History of Women.* Vol. 3. Ed. Georges Duby and Michelle Perrot. Cambridge, Mass.: Belknap, 1993. 46–48.

Irigaray, Luce. *This Sex Which Is Not One.* Trans. Catherine Porter. Ithaca, N.Y.: Cornell UP, 1985.

Jardine, Lisa. *Still Harping on Daughters.* Totowa, N.J.: Barnes and Noble, 1983.

Jones, Vivien, ed. *Women in the Eighteenth Century.* New York: Routledge, 1990.

Lerner, Gerda. *The Creation of Patriarchy*. New York: Oxford UP, 1986.

Perry, Graham. *The Seventeenth Century*. New York: Longman, 1989.

"Rape Risk Linked to Earlier Assaults." *Fort Wayne Journal Gazette*. 17 Aug. 1992. 5A.

Rose, Jacqueline. "Introduction—II." *Feminine Sexuality*. By Jacques Lacan. Ed. Juliett Mitchell and Jacqueline Rose. Trans. Jacqueline Rose. New York: Norton, 1982. 27–57.

Shakespeare, William. *The Complete Works*. Ed. Stanley Wells and Gary Taylor. Oxford: Clarendon, 1988.

Showalter, Elaine. "Representing Ophelia: Women, Madness, and the Responsibilities of Feminist Criticism." *Shakespeare and the Question of Theory*. Ed. Patricia Parker and Geoffrey Hartman. New York: Methuen, 1985. 77–94.

Spivak, Gayatri. Translator's Preface. *Of Grammatology*. By Jacques Derrida. Trans. Gayatri Spivak. Baltimore: Johns Hopkins UP, 1976. ix–lxxxvii.

Staves, Susan. "Fielding and the Comedy of Attempted Rape." *History, Gender, and Eighteenth-Century Literature*. Ed. Beth Fowkes Tobin. Athens: U of Georgia P, 1994. 86–112.

Thompson, J. *Studies in the Theory of Ideology*. Berkeley: U of California P, 1984.

Todd, Janet. *The Sign of Angellica*. New York: Columbia UP, 1989.

Underdown, David. *Revel, Riot, and Rebellion*. New York: Oxford UP, 1985.

Weimann, Robert. *Shakespeare and the Popular Tradition in the Theater*. Ed. Robert Schwartz. Baltimore: Johns Hopkins UP, 1978.

Wolkstein, Diane, and Samuel Noah Kramer. *Inanna, Queen of Heaven and Earth*. New York: Harper and Row, 1983.

Woodcock, George. *The English Sappho*. New York: Black Rose, 1989.

Woolf, Virginia. *A Room of One's Own*. New York: Harcourt Brace Jovanovich, 1929.

Closure and Subversion in Behn's Comedies

Peggy Thompson

*E*arly in her monumental struggle with Lovelace, Samuel Richardson's Clarissa wonders "how it will end." For the rest of the novel, she and her tormentor fight to control the conclusion of their drama. Clarissa, who is greatly moved while viewing *Venice Preserved,* insists that all violations of the human spirit and body be taken seriously, that their destructive effects be recognized. Lovelace, who must feign being touched by Thomas Otway's tragedy, prefers and expects an "end" to their struggle more typical of romantic comedy, an end in which all conflicts are simply erased by marriage. "And what is that injury which a *church rite* will at any time repair?" he wonders as he contemplates continued manipulation and deceit even after he has raped Clarissa. "Is not *the catastrophe of every story that ends in wedlock accounted happy,* be the difficulty in the progress to it ever so great?" (944). The reliance of a depraved character like Lovelace on this kind of resolution should warn women of the insidious potential of romantic comedy, a genre long thought to champion strong and spirited female characters. Such characters do regularly inhabit the radically disordered environments of romantic comedy. But the revolutionary promise of Shakespeare's "green world" or Philip Barry's "holiday" fades when these women are typically subsumed back into an essentially conservative vision (Carlson 21–23; Rose 88–89). It is the emphatically "old-fashioned" Mr. Hardcastle who proclaims that "the Mistakes of the Night shall be crowned with a merry morning" (Goldsmith 216), and the morning is "merry" not simply because his daughter will wed the man she loves but also because she will wed a socially and economically suitable suitor. Indeed, by ensuring social stability, economic security, and familial harmony, as well, presumably, as emotional fulfillment, the weddings that typically conclude romantic comedy seem indeed to resolve all significant conflicts. But as seventeenth-century playwright

Aphra Behn was increasingly to acknowledge, the gratifying closure that results is an illusion—especially for women.

Many students of comedy, including Northrop Frye, would undoubtedly quarrel with the word *illusion*. The conclusions of romantic comedy, Frye argues, mark the advent of a new golden age in which the ills of a society are not masked, but exposed and corrected, the final festivity (very often a wedding) a communal celebration of social regeneration (163–71). Nevertheless, the dramatist's and the audience's idealistic, sometimes revolutionary vision must work against the sociological and anthropological observation that in almost all cultures marriage is an essentially conservative institution (Boone 36). By regulating the passage of property from one "legitimate" owner to the next, marriage reinforces existing notions of legitimacy, so that even in plays such as *A Midsummer Night's Dream,* where authority adapts to young love, the conflict occurs within very conservative parameters, and the result is still a solidifying of current social structure. When Behn wrote, that structure was decidedly patriarchal, figuring inheritance and descent exclusively in the male line. Legal provisions for married women's separate property were extremely limited and often unenforced (Staves, *Separate Property* 221–30).

Moreover, as David Ogg has succinctly observed, "in giving up her personalty," or personal property, a seventeenth-century bride "gave up her personality, two words which originally meant the same thing" (71). She was a possession for which her husband was responsible. He was to control and direct her; she was to obey first and love, if at all, second. Significantly, one of the few Restoration comedies that seriously questions the value of marriage, Dryden's *Marriage A-la-Mode* (see Hume, "Myth" 29), eventually reaffirms the institution precisely because it defines women as property rather than property holders. Deciding against infidelity, Palamede and Rhodophil make "a firm League, not to invade each others propriety" (V.i.359–60). P.F. Vernon argues that this attitude is exceptional in Restoration comedy because "it lumps together marriage of convenience and marriage of free choice almost without distinction" (377). But the distinction, as Vernon later admits, exists only in drama; in seventeenth- and eighteenth-century life "money came first" (386), which is largely why marriage as dramatic closure is so problematic, especially for women who not only were denied love matches but were also treated as part of the property that always "came first."

One might have expected the increasingly popular approach to marriage as a contract between two consenting adults to have mitigated the objectification of wives in the late seventeenth century, but in fact the reverse was largely true. Most women were ill prepared to bargain on their own behalf, either because of ignorance or because of social and religious pressure not to detract from the proper attitude of love and respect toward their future husbands.[1] What is worse, the male relations who often negotiated for their daughters, sisters, and nieces did so, not to protect their wards' autonomy and property, but to enhance familial and dynastic interests, a motive to which judges did not object (Staves, *Separate Property* 116–17). Restoration comedy does object consistently and seriously to mercenary marriages (see Vernon), but as Robert Hume has made indisputably clear, marriage as an institution is never seriously attacked ("Myth" 29). Instead, the contractual approach itself is idealized in some of the dramatic proviso scenes that culminate in agreements to wed.[2] These scenes have little to do with actual contemporary prenuptial arrangements, because marriage was never contractual "in the sense that the two parties could negotiate whatever provisions were dictated by their individual wills" (Staves, *Separate Property* 168). Thus, the sort of autonomous agreement reached by Congreve's Mirabel and Millamant is part of the larger illusion that marriage can bring complete and happy closure.

Predictably, a double sexual standard accompanied patriarchal marriage. Men could sow their wild oats, but nonmonogamous women would be harshly condemned because they blurred the lines of inheritance and descent. In Restoration comedy this inequity was underscored by ubiquitous marriages between virginal brides and rakish grooms.[3] Like the eighteenth-century fictional heroines whose femininity is coded in "paradigms of sexual vulnerability" (Miller xi), the heroines of Restoration comedy must preserve their virginity to sustain their status as heroines. Referring to George Etherege's Loveit, John Traugott brutally explicates the distinctly nonheroic fate that awaits a woman who succumbs to her seducer: "She is as good as on the street" (401). But despite Traugott's harsh prognosis, the distinction between a fallen woman like Loveit and a steadfast virgin like Harriet Woodvill is not as clear as it may appear. The pressure on Restoration heroines to resist seduction by men who eventually could become their husbands foregrounds the sexist oppression implicit in the "romantic courtship" leading to marriage. Joseph Allen Boone's remarks about fiction are helpful here: "The objectification and subjugation of woman inherent in idealized versions of romantic love are simply carried to their logical extreme in the pure seduction narrative: by reducing women to anonymous objects of sexual conquest, the seducer no less than the legitimate suitor attempts to erase those signs of female autonomy and otherness that threaten his own identity as the superior and more powerful sex" (100). As we have seen, female ownership of property was prominent among those threatening "signs of female autonomy and otherness," but so was sexual desire, a usurpation of male power that must be controlled—either through marriage or seduction (and subsequent ostracism). Thus, like the distinction between wife and mistress, that between husband and seducer is blurred by the common effects of containment and control.

One type of female character in Restoration comedy who may seem to get away with infidelity is the wife of the mercenary cit. But her fate, in fact, summarizes and caricatures the various ways women in Restoration marriages are objectified. First, she is married to a man who self-consciously and unapologetically views his bride as a possession and who, like Wycherley's Pinchwife, "only marry'd to keep a Whore to [him]self" (I.i.425). Next, she is seduced by a man who punishes the deserving husband by violating his "property" and who, in the 1670s especially, may be motivated as much by egotistic aggression as he is by a desire to liberate or gratify (Underwood 27–28; Traugott 385–87; Thompson 109–14). Finally, she is denied a sympathetic reaction to her fate by the dramatist, who uses her character as a satiric device functioning merely to expose the foolish husband. Thus, the formulaic conventionality that Hume has insisted we recognize in the apparently libertine action of many Restoration comedies ("Myth" 36; *Development* 144–48) has serious implications insofar as it desensitizes us to the pain not only of the unhappy wife but of female characters generally. Because it focuses on the suffering wife's dilemma without offering a facile solution, Southerne's *The Wives' Excuse* is a striking (and notably unpopular) exception to this pattern, as, as we will see, are many of Behn's later comedies.

Even when Restoration comedy subdues and domesticates its male protagonists, the dynamic of their reform oppresses the women it would seem to reward. In order to transform the wild boy into the virtuous man, Restoration heroines must remain chaste.[4] In contrast, the male role of redeemer in Restoration comedy requires only that our heroes are thoughtful enough to provide a screen for the women they have seduced. Like his more famous counterpart, Congreve's Mirabel, James Howard's Welbred in *The English Monsieur* arranges marriage for the woman he seduced with another, less deserving man and is admired for it. Thomas Shadwell's Belfond Jr. in *The Squire of Alsatia* needs simply to proclaim his former mistress's "purity" to redeem her, thus graphically demonstrating male power to define female worth. In a very few cases, the seducer (as in *The Debauchee* and Thomas D'Urfey's *The Campaigners*) or the rapist (in Charles Sedley's *Bellamira*) will offer himself as husband to the woman whose weakness he has exposed, but here too he controls the situation and her fate—as Lovelace knew all too well. Just as it was the man's prerogative to parcel out assets or freedom within marriage, so it was his to offer marriage in the first place. In this context, the distinction Norman Holland makes so emphatically in his groundbreaking work on Etherege, Wycherley, and Congreve is collapsed: "Every one of the eleven plays we have considered deals with the reform of the hero, not his reward. His initiation into true love at the end—his 'reward'—marks his reclamation to virtue" (203). In effect, both the male's "reward" and his "reform"—not to mention his "true love" and his "virtue"—take the shape of a marriage in which he can control virtually all property and behavior.

The restrictive, profoundly unfair implications of the marriages concluding many romantic comedies must have been particularly uncongenial to Behn, a woman noted for her repeated attacks on double sexual standards and on marriages between any but freely chosen, mutually affectionate partners. But Behn was a professional playwright who, scholars agree, catered to public taste (Hume, *Development* 284–85; Kavenik 186–90; Payne 110–11). In fact, all but two of her seventeen extant dramas are resolved by marriage or romantic unions, many between rakes and virgins. As her career progressed, however, Behn subverted this sexist convention in increasingly radical ways. Like her poetry, her comedies variously and powerfully question the assumptions that happiness resides in marriage and that marriage should be denied to sexually experienced women. But Behn cannot rewrite the political and economic structures that reserve power and wealth for men. Therefore, her latest and most challenging plays simply resist closure for central female characters, thus evading the trap of romantic union while simultaneously acknowledging the absence of alternatives for women.

Behn's earliest comedy, *The Amorous Prince* (1671), resists neither marriage as closure nor many of the sexist conventions that accompany such resolutions.[5] This early work concludes with five agreements to marry, including one between a seducer and a grateful victim. Behn seems to excuse both Prince Frederick's seduction and abandonment of Cloris and his attempted rape of Laura, by having several characters rationalize his sexual aggression paradoxically as both weakness, the "Frailties of [his] Sex" (4:166), and strength, his "Youth and Vigor" (4:164).[6] Cloris's brother Curtis muses on the Prince's ability to hurt others without redress:

> when I call upon my Wrongs,
> Something within me pleads so kindly for him,
> As would persuade me that he could not err.
> [4:183]

Behn thus distracts us from the Prince's obvious social and political power, an exaggerated instance of men's more general power over women, by granting him a more enigmatic control over others, perhaps as a mark of his ultimate worth. But social and political power is an explicit concern when Prince Frederick repents upon discovering Cloris's high social standing. Cloris describes her subsequent pardon of Prince Frederick as "my Duty and my Glory" (4:206), thus affirming the Prince's authority as well, perhaps, as her responsibility to domesticate the vigorous male. In the epilogue, Behn assumes without question that her audiences will be much more judgmental of the woman who succumbs to sexual, social, and political pressure than they will of the man who exerts it. Cloris tries to explain her "hasty condescension":

> 'Twas want of Art, not Virtue, was my Crime;
> And that's, I vow, the Author's Fault, not mine.
> She might have made the Women pitiless,
> But that had harder been to me than this:
> She might have made our Lovers constant too,
> A Work which Heaven it self can scarcely do;
> But simple Nature never taught the way
> To hide those Passions which she must obey.
> [4:212–13]

Ostensibly blaming "the Author," Cloris ultimately appeals to nature and heaven to explain men who cannot be constant and women who cannot resist. Thus, Behn's final words on sexual desire and experience in this play implicitly attack the social expectation that women "hide [their] passions," but the epilogue also reinscribes as "natural" the distinction between the lusting, blameless male and the weak but responsible female.

Like her first comedy, Behn's second, *The Dutch Lover* (1673), concludes with multiple marriages—in this instance seven. Two unite men with women they have considered raping, and in both cases Behn stresses the women's supposed culpability. Silvio, in love with Cleonte, whom he believes to be his sister, warns her that his passion will drive him either to kill or to rape her (1:282). Later, when he is falsely informed that Cleonte is willing to quench his desire, he is outraged because she has "out-sinn'd" him, and he plans to murder her (1:317). He soon learns, however, both that Cleonte is "chaste as Angels are" and that she is not his sister (1:319). In the wedding that is to result, Behn presents without question a revealingly absurd instance of marriage as closure: the woman "out-sins" the man by apparently acceding to his wishes and then is redeemed, all complications resolved, by her newly affirmed chastity and the sudden availability of that happy ending, wedlock. The case of another female character in this play, Hippolyta, also illustrates the extremely precarious position of women who cross the line into sexual experience. Seduced by Antonio, Hippolyta is the shame of her brother Marcel, who longs to "take them in their foul Embraces, / And send their Souls to Hell" (1:235). When

Antonio steps between Hippolyta and her brother's murderous shame, the play gives image to the fallen woman's absolute dependence on her seducer to ward off other, more vengeful male action against her. Because Antonio is now willing to call her wife, Marcel is willing to take her back into her father's house. Hippolyta responds to both men with "humble Thanks" (1:307).

Though Behn thus egregiously reinforces the most insidious implications of comic closure in this early work, she does indicate some awareness of the problems involved. For example, unlike so many other brothers in Restoration comedy, including Behn's own plays, Hippolyta's brother Marcel acknowledges the irony in his eagerness to seduce one woman while seeking to murder his sister because she has been seduced: "To fair *Clarinda* such a Siege I lay, / As did that Traitor to *Hippolyta*" (1:243). Through Marcel, then, Behn constructs sexually experienced women as pathetic victims as well as shameful failures. (Other more positive constructions appear only in her later comedies.)

Also in *The Dutch Lover,* Behn brings to the surface the malicious motives of the seducer. Antonio explains viciously and at length that he seduced Hippolyta, led her from town to town spreading her shame, and finally advertised her as a prostitute—all to avenge himself on her brother, who had ruined his hopes with another woman (1:275–76). By foregrounding the nonsexual dynamics of this relationship, Behn questions the assumption that such men are acting on natural libidinous energy, which women are responsible for controlling, and thus further critiques the simplistic illusion that the stories of comic heroines should be determined exclusively by their sexual innocence or experience and by the relative "generosity" of male response.

Three years later, in *The Town Fop; or, Sir Timothy Tawdry* (1676), Behn's conclusion raises questions focused less on a double sexual standard measuring one's eligibility for marriage than on the assumption that marriage is a happy "catastrophe" for any story. Early in the play, Lord Plotwell forces his nephew Bellmour to marry Diana, who loves Bellmour and is maddened by his continued devotion to Celinda. By the end of the play Bellmour is released from the marriage by a suddenly gracious, sympathetic, and generous Lord Plotwell, and Diana—foiled in attempts to revenge herself on Bellmour—simply resolves to love Friendlove, the man who loves her (3:88). The quick acceptance of substitute partners in a play like *Twelfth Night* may underscore the irrationality of love, but this is not the case in *The Town Fop,* where impassioned scenes focus on the pain of Diana's first, unrequited love:

> O, what a Defeat is here!
> The only Man, who from all Nature's store

> I found most charming, fit for my Desires;
> And now after a thousand Expectations,
> Such as all Maids that love like me do hope,
> Just ready for the highest Joys of Love!
> Then to be met thus cold—nay, worse, with scorn.
>
> [3:48]

Such scenes prepare us to see Diana's final "resolution" to accept another man not as blissful closure but as bittersweet compromise.

Phillis ends this play married to a man who promises her even less fulfillment than Friendlove does Diana. After her uncle disowns her simply for being a sibling of the rebellious Bellmour, Phillis marries the patently repulsive and brutal Sir Timothy, only to be subsequently reconciled with her family. Lord Plotwell's sudden tenderness toward his niece and nephews is as improbable personally as the resulting divorce between Bellmour and Diana is legally (Staves, *Players' Scepters* 173–74). Both exemplify the generic convention of comic revocability; unlike tragedy, in which the downward trajectory of the hero is irreversible, comedy never lets us lose hope. But here the convention is cruelly ironic for Phillis, whose father has a change of heart too late for her to escape a new husband who plans to visit his whore within two days. Phillis's last pathetic speech gloomily recounts her victimization. "Sir," she tells Bellmour, "you deny'd me my Portion, and my Uncle design'd to turn me out of doors, and in my Despair I accepted of him" (3:92). Marriages to fools like Sir Timothy in other Restoration comedies (including Behn's *The Amorous Prince* and *The Dutch Lover*) rarely evoke sympathy because they usually involve women who have no identity other than the wish to be married and who, because of their servant class or sexual experience, exist only as punishment for the fools. But in Phillis's case we uneasily anticipate her life with a man who has threatened to rape her (3:80–81), who planned to trick her into submission with a sham marriage, and who insists to Bellmour: "[S]ince you say I shall not have your Sister, by Fortune, I will have your Sister, and love your Sister, and lie with your Sister, in spite of you" (3:93). Thus Behn's celebrated attacks on unwanted marriages do not always end happily. Indeed, by marking the conclusion of a play, such marriages—once we are made to recognize their emotional and physical consequences—are more haunting critiques than those that are ultimately avoided or annulled, and they provide none but the bitterest "sense of an ending."

Behn's humanization of Diana and Phillis in *The Town Fop* is recapitulated in Laura Lucretia of *The Feign'd Curtizans* (1679) and Ariadne of *The Second Part of the Rover* (1681), two more women who must accept partners other than those to whom they are most powerfully drawn. But the most fascinating and famous of Behn's disappointed women appears just a year after *The Town Fop;* she is, of course, Angelica Bianca of *The Rover; or, The Banish't Cavaliers* (1677). Angelica's fate reiterates the formula that happiness is reserved for virgins; she loses the man she loves to the wild—but not so wild as to be unchaste—Hellena. Angelica's counterpart in Behn's source, *Thomaso* by Thomas Killigrew, admits before her seduction that " 'once a whore and ever' is the world's adage." Behn's Angelica initially rejects this binary perspective, showing no shame of her sexual experience, only of her prostitution, as Nancy Copeland points out (24). But by act IV Angelica admits that only one plot is available to the sexually experienced woman, no matter what other qualities she may have:

> Nice Reputation, tho it leave behind
> More Virtues than inhabit where that dwells,
> Yet that once gone, those virtues shine no more.
> [1:78]

Copeland observes that Angelica's language becomes conventional here (25). But in the context created by Angelica's total, generally unconventional characterization, the speech takes on new poignancy and perspective. In other words, Angelica's recognition of this principle, which denies her full humanity, is ironically part of the powerful and moving characterization that will not let us dismiss her as a whore.

Behn further complicates Angelica's fate with her portrayal of the man who, according to social and literary convention, is justified in abandoning the courtesan. On the one hand, Willmore is the roving political expatriate whose "cavalier" attitude toward love is admirably consistent with his resistance to bourgeois economic values (Brown 60–61). On the other, he is strikingly similar to the sadistic Blunt, who freely admits that he intends to rape Florinda as an act of vengeful domination: "Cruel, yes, I will kiss and beat thee all over; kiss, and see thee all over; thou shalt lie with me too, not that I care for the Injoyment, but to let thee see I have ta'en deliberated Malice to thee, and will be revenged on one Whore for the Sins of another" (1:83). Behn thus uses Blunt to draw attention to the power relations between men and women, particularly the vicious sexual power hiding behind claims of libertine freedom and pleasure. Significantly, she consistently identifies this revolting character with Willmore, as Jones DeRitter has demonstrated: "Willmore's attempt to rape Florinda occurs immediately after Blunt's misadventure with Lucetta; when Florinda discovers that the intruder in her garden is not Belvile, her description of Willmore as 'a filthy beast' (B:III.v.33) reminds the audience of Blunt, who has just fallen through a trap door into a sewer. On a more circumstantial level, Blunt agrees with and supports Willmore in instances where Killigrew's Edwardo and Thomaso [their counterparts in Behn's source] are clearly at odds (see B:II.i.290–91; Kl:II.iii.336)" (87).

Never repentant of his attacks on Florinda and notably unappreciative of her forgiveness, Willmore is, as DeRitter notes, excluded from the comic community of Belville's wedding (90). He is also forced to endure Angelica's final denunciation, the most famous of many scenes in which Behn insists that we do not facilely dismiss her female characters—especially those who have transgressed onto the male territory of desire. The pistol that Angelica points at Willmore while she upbraids him is both a visual measure of the emotional distress he has caused and a substitute for the sexual and economic power he has convinced her to exchange for love, as she reminds him:

> Had I remain'd in innocent Security,
> I shou'd have thought all Men were born my Slaves;
> And worn my Pow'r like Lightning in my Eyes,
> To have destroy'd at Pleasure when offended.
>
> [1:95]

Made otherwise impotent by faithless love, Angelica must resort to the gun to neutralize the political and social power on which even an expatriate male can rely to legitimate his sexual potency. With a single pull of the trigger, then, Angelica could symbolically explode male power as it has been inscribed in romantic comedy. But Behn is simply not ready to condemn her Tory cavalier. Rather than murder Willmore as she planned, Angelica saves him from a jealous rival, and he is eventually granted the happy ending Lovelace understandably assumes is available to him— marriage to a desirable and wealthy virgin.

Four years later, however, Behn renounces the conventional, sexist conclusion of *The Rover* in one of the most explicit ways possible: she writes a sequel in which she not only humanizes her whore but also rewards her. *The Second Part of the Rover* (1681) echoes the first part in its emphasis on the distinction between women "of quality" and those who deserve no respect, but it does so from an entirely different perspective. In *The Rover* it is Florinda's "quality" that saves her from gang rape, the distinction serving to whitewash the horrible intentions of Willmore and his friends as a case of mistaken identity. Thus, though Behn may be critical elsewhere of the polarization of women into those with and without "quality," she must rely on the dichotomy here in order to save Willmore his status even as problematic hero and the play its status as comedy. In *The Second Part of the Rover,* however, Behn explicitly and frequently attacks "quality" as a determinant of male-female relations, often by calling attention to the economic and social nature of this supposedly moral distinction. For example, two "monsters" (a giantess and a dwarf) are courted as "Ladies of Quality" exclusively because of their wealth. Such mockery of "quality" adumbrates the unconventional conclusion of this play, in which the widowed Willmore chooses the prostitute La Nuche over the attractive and wealthy virgin Ariadne. Hero and whore pledge love to each other, without "the formal Foppery of Marriage" (1:208). The degree to which this conclusion is revolutionary is reflected in critical response. A disbelieving Katharine Rogers, for example, assumes that La Nuche "must realize that he will use and discard her" (22), while Peter Holland sees the resolution, not as an affirmation of La Nuche, but as a degradation of Willmore: "No rake marries a whore and remains hero" (68). Can there be any doubt about the strength of the conventions within—and against—which Behn is working?

In *The City Heiress; or, Sir Timothy Treat-All* (1682), Behn seems to accept Holland's judgment. The Tory hero Wilding is loved by three women: his current mistress, Diana; Lady Galliard, a young widow he seduces during the play; and the virginal heiress Charlot. He finally agrees to marry Charlot. But again this apparently conventional conclusion is offered in the context of eloquent scenes that acknowledge the emotional pain engendered by Wilding's formulaic actions. The seduction of Lady Galliard, for example, is preceded by a magnificent extended argument in which she reveals the depth of her love and fear: "Let my Heart break with Love, / I cannot be that wretched thing you'd have me" (2:265). After the seduction, she is as wretched as she predicted she would be:

> What have I done? Ah, whither shall I fly? [*Weeps*]
> ·　·　·　·　·　·　·　·　·　·　·　·　·
> Shall I survive this Shame? No, if I do,
> Eternal Blushes dwell upon my Cheeks,
> To tell the World my Crime.
>
> [2:270–71]

Her shame and despair are understandable reactions to the condemnation and powerlessness Galliard knows her sexual experience will cost her if she is not able to cover her transgression with marriage. She ends this "comedy" gazing and sighing on Wilding, as she gives her hand to another suitor and bids "fond Love" to "be gone" (2:298).

In the same play, Wilding's other former mistress, Diana, bluntly examines the unattractive options left to her: poverty and disrepute or marriage to Wilding's uncle, the despicable Sir Timothy. "Ah," she sighs to her maid, Betty,

> when I find the difference of their Embraces,
> The soft dear Arms of *Wilding* round my Neck.
> From those cold feeble ones of this old Dotard;
> When I shall meet, instead of *Tom's* warm kisses,
> A hollow Pair of thin blue wither'd Lips,
> Trembling with Palsy, stinking with Disease,
> By Age and Nature barricado'd up
> With a kind Nose and Chin;
> What Fancy or what Thought can make my Hours supportable?
>   [2:286]

Betty's ready answer, "six thousand Pounds a Year," reminds us of the economic forces that converge with the desire for social acceptance to reinforce the institution of marriage both in and out of comedy. Behn's plays often succumb to those pressures, but only after reminding us of their emotional and psychic toll.

We have already seen, however, that Behn goes far beyond eliciting sympathy for unhappy women in her critique of the sexist assumptions informing comic closure. Indeed, in a play as early as *Sir Patient Fancy* (1678), she seems deliberately to eschew sympathy for Lady, or Lucia, Fancy. At the end of this play Lady Fancy and Wittmore bluntly explain to Sir Patient that they were lovers before the marriage, which they plotted for money (4:114). Sir Patient announces plans to divorce her, and she looks forward to life with her beloved Wittmore and the eight thousand pounds Sir Patient has put in her control. Here, a happy ending is granted, not simply to the long-suffering wife of an unbearable old cit, but to an unfaithful wife who chose to marry for admittedly mercenary ends. Behn thus provides her heroine with romantic love and economic security without concern for social respectability, without apology, and without sentiment. Of course, Behn is not alone in writing such plays. Citing Otway's *The Soldiers Fortune* and *The Atheist* as examples, Susan Staves points to a whole group of "cynical" plays written between 1675 and 1687. These plays, she argues, are marked by an unprecedented representation onstage of old, but heretofore unacknowledged attitudes and behaviors, including "adulterous wives showing contempt for their husbands" (*Players' Scepters* 168). *Sir Patient Fancy* is part of this group, but it is also part of a significant pattern of subversion and resistance in Behn's own canon, a pattern culminating in her last two comedies.

By resisting all closure for the major female character in *The Lucky Chance; or, An Alderman's Bargain* (1686), Behn reveals a more overt and desperate frustration with the sexist implications of conventional comic endings. The play foregrounds such implications in the fate of two secondary characters, Leticia and Diana. The first is tricked into marrying the baby-talking Sir Feeble Fainwou'd, but she avoids consummation by agilely running around her bedchamber until rescued by what appears to be a frightening ghost. Leticia's improbable salvation calls attention to the social and literary demand that she remain a virgin. Diana struggles similarly to avoid an arranged marriage. As Catherine Gallagher puts it, "The plots of Diana and Leticia rely on the idea that there is an irreversible moment of matrimonial exchange after which the woman is 'given' and cannot be given again" (32). We have already seen Behn challenge this idea and the concomitant romantic ideal of a "heroine's virgin union with her beloved" in earlier plays like *Sir Patient Fancy* and *The Second Part of the Rover,* plays in which nonvirgins are "given again"—to the men they most desire.[7] But in *The Lucky Chance* Behn includes a heroine who rejects not only double sexual standards and patriarchal marriage but also romantic union as an ideal marking closure. Married to the greedy Sir Fulbank, Julia has two sexual liaisons with the man she loves, Gayman. In the first, he knows her only as his anonymous benefactor, whom he later describes to an angry Julia as a worse bedfellow than "a Canvas Bag of wooden Ladles" (3:246). In the second, he secretly replaces her husband in her bed as a result of a gambling bet; she is again furious and banishes Sir Fulbank from her bed forever. He, in turn, admits (as does Sir Feeble Fainwou'd) how foolish he has been to marry a woman who could not love him and bequeaths both his estate and his wife to Gayman. Julia responds scornfully, however, reminding Gayman of his earlier insults. In short, we have no idea what Julia's future holds. Will she remain chaste until Fulbank dies? Will she and Gayman resume their affair before she is a widow? Will she ever forgive Gayman his insults and deception? Will she ever accept being passed from one man to another as if part of an estate? Note that the answers to all questions rest with Julia. And she, like her creator, Behn, resists giving up her power by coming to closure.[8]

Behn's last play, *The Younger Brother; or, The Amorous Jilt* (1696), insistently reminds us of the narrow confines within which such resistance by a woman can take place.[9] Behn puts the resisting character, "the amorous jilt" of the subtitle, in the context of an extremely conventional romantic comedy. The old but wealthy Lady Youthly is to marry the impoverished younger brother, George, while George's father, Sir Rowland, plans to marry Youthly's granddaughter Teresia, who offers a sizable income as well as physical beauty. In its symmetry, the "fair swap," as Sir Rowland terms it, caricatures the formulaic romantic comedy: youth and love are to be sacrificed for money and lust (4:340). Predictably, the play concludes with a wedding between George and Teresia, one of three marriages marking the familiar circumvention of blocking elders and then forgiveness by them in *The Younger Brother.*

The conventionality of this comedy both highlights and minimizes the unconventional behavior of "the amorous jilt," Mirtilla. When the play opens, Mirtilla has already jilted George for a rich husband, Sir Morgan Blunder. She has an affair with George's friend the Prince. And she is infatuated with the young page "Endimion" (George's sister Olivia disguised as a boy). When George and the Prince catch Mirtilla pursuing Endimion, she defiantly refuses to repent and announces that she will take back no former lover (4:392). Mirtilla seems to get away with her indifference to the desires and demands of others—even her illicit lovers, for the Prince gives her an alibi as he returns her to Sir Morgan, claiming he rescued her from a fire her husband thought had killed her. When a grateful Sir Morgan offers to let the Prince "visit her" in the future (4:397), it appears that Mirtilla is concluding the play with both a profitable, respectable marriage and continued amorous freedom. But by having one man return a now silent Mirtilla to another, as the two of them discuss their rights to her, Behn graphically reminds us of the severe limits within which Mirtilla can exercise her will and keep her options "open." The play ends with a celebratory dance, a visual image of the triumph of love and youth. But the final lines remind us that the weddings in this play also mark the triumph of a patriarchal, objectifying system: George gloats that his "younger Brother's share" is "one that's Rich, Witty, Young, and Fair" (4:397). Stage directions do not describe Mirtilla's response, but Lady Youthly weeps; most narrowly her tears are those of frustrated lust, but they might justifiably be shed for all women in Behn's final bleak vision.

"The great principle which every woman is taught is to keep her legs together. When she has given up that principle, she has given up every notion of female honour and virtue, which are all included in chastity" (cited in Boswell 156). Thus Samuel Johnson crudely summarizes the extraordinarily harsh and narrow confines within which women of his day and Behn's had to live. Behn seems increasingly to have recognized that as long as women's stories, and only women's stories, are written primarily as tales of sexual vulnerability, all resolution means defeat. Gallagher has noted that in her prologue to *The Forced Marriage,* Behn characterizes her writing as a response to this dilemma, as a means to sustain her erotic power, to "keep as well as gain the Victory" (25). But of course the profession of writing, especially the writing of sexually frank plays, is itself another kind of experience unacceptable for women. "Modesty is the distinguishing virtue of that sex," Jeremy Collier insists, "and that it might be always at hand, 'tis wrought into the mechanism of the body" (391).[10] In the conclusions of her comedies, however, Behn increasingly resists the opposition between sexual experience and an essential, biological construction of woman. She works to "keep as well as gain the Victory," by simultaneously affirming female sexuality (as part of the strength and vitality of her comic heroines) and denying the assumption of men like Collier, Johnson, and Lovelace that women's sexual experience must determine their destinies.

But if Behn's comic endings restore power to women, especially to those who are not virgins, it is only the very limited power available to women within seventeenth-century economic and social structures, from which the dramatist never fantasizes an escape. Martine Brownley has related the irresolution of many feminist works to the absence of viable endings for women like Virginia Woolf's Judith Shakespeare. The same can be said of another of Woolf's heroines, Aphra Behn. Like many of her own dramatic characters, Behn struggled all her life against the restraints of a culture that frequently balked at her entrance into public economic, political, and literary exchanges while attempting to define and condemn her on the basis of her sexual experience. The revolution of 1688 would have reinforced Behn's sense as a Tory that a happy ending was not possible for her, but her despair as a woman appears to have been equally strong. The dramatist's growing resistance to clear closure for her heroines marks her growing resistance to sexual and biological definition. It also acknowledges the social and economic forces that allow no alternatives.

Notes

1. Despite Protestant idealization of marriage in the late sixteenth and seventeenth centuries (Boone 49; Rose 2–4, 29–32), religious conduct books continued to dictate subservience in wives. *Of Domesticall Duties* (1622), for example, claims that "where they [man and woman] are linked together in one yoake, it is given by nature that he should governe, she obey" (cited in Boone 49–50), while *The Whole Duty of Man* (1658) cautions, "Nor let . . . wives think that any faults or provocations of the husband can justify their forwardness" (cited in Root 4).

2. This is not to imply that dramatic proviso scenes were exclusively or even primarily the result of a contractual approach to marriage. Maximillian Novak, for example, points out a literary source, "French romances or the comedies based on them" (26).

3. Hume, "Myth" 34–36. Hume would probably quarrel with my term *rakish,* but he supports my point, that extramarital sexual activity by men is taken for granted in these plays while "heroines of comedies are invariably spotless and pure" (34). Similarly, Robert L. Root Jr. observes: "Chastity is important in most plays; women who are not virgins (or widows) do not win the chief male characters in seventeenth century plays" (14).

4. For more on the redeeming function of women in seventeenth-century life and literature, see Hume, "Myth" 48–53; Berkeley; Boone 60–61; and Hagstrum 163–65. In addition, Rita Goldberg explains how *Clarissa* divides

sinners and saviors along gender lines, thus implying Clarissa's responsibility for Lovelace's reformation (111–22).

5. Dates given are those of first production, as noted in Rogers 14–15.

6. I am indebted to Frances M. Kavenik (180) for this point. For additional exculpatory references to the Prince's sexual aggression, see Behn 4:146, 169. All citations from Behn's plays are from Summers's edition of the *Works*.

7. The quoted phrase is from Root's discussion of yet another comedy by Behn that refuses to satisfy this convention, *The False Count* (1682). Here Julia consummates her marriage with Francisco before uniting with her lover (10).

8. The resemblance between the questions remaining about Julia and the often ridiculed questions linking one episode of a soap opera with another is significant. In her recent book, *No End to Her,* Martha Nochimson demonstrates how congenial the soap opera's lack of closure is to a female perspective.

9. Two others apparently had a hand in authoring this play, Charles Gildon and an unidentified G.J. We do not yet know what their contributions were (see Coakley).

10. Given such a view, it is little wonder that Behn eventually abandons her persona as author-lover and fashions a public self out of the "royalist/patronal/male dynamic," as Deborah C. Payne points out (116). But Payne's observation applies only to Behn's prefatory writing; it does not deny the feminist subversion of Behn's comic conclusions.

Works Cited

Behn, Aphra. *The Works of Aphra Behn.* 6 vols. Ed. Montague Summers. London, 1915; New York: Benjamim Blom, 1967.

Berkeley, David S. "The Penitent Rake in Restoration Comedy." *Modern Philology* 49 (1951–52): 109–28.

Boone, Joseph Allen. *Tradition Counter Tradition: Love and the Form of Fiction.* Chicago: U of Chicago P, 1987.

Boswell, James. *Boswell in Search of a Wife, 1766–1769.* Ed. Frank Brady and Frederick A. Pottle. New York: McGraw-Hill, 1956.

Brown, Laura. *English Dramatic Form, 1660–1760: An Essay in Generic History.* New Haven, Conn.: Yale UP, 1981.

Brownley, Martine W. "Where Is Shakespeare's Sister?" Paper presented at the Phi Beta Kappa Convocation, Agnes Scott College, Decatur, Ga. 11 April 1990.

Carlson, Susan. *Women and Comedy: Rewriting the British Theatrical Tradition.* Ann Arbor: U·of Michigan P, 1991.

Coakley, Jean. "Substantiating Aphra: The Role of Statistical Analysis." Paper presented at the annual meeting of the American Society for Eighteenth-Century Studies, New Orleans. 30 March 1989.

Collier, Jeremy. Selections from "A Short View of the Immorality and Profaneness of the English Stage, Together with the Sense of Antiquity upon This Argument." *British Dramatists from Dryden to Sheridan.* 2d ed. Ed. George H. Nettleton and Arthur E. Case. Rev. George Winchester Stone Jr. New York: Houghton Mifflin, 1969. 389–91.

Copeland, Nancy. "Once a Whore and Ever?: Whore and Virgin in *The Rover* and Its Antecedents." *Restoration* 16 (1992): 20–27.

DeRitter, Jones. "The Gypsy, *The Rover*, and the Wanderer: Aphra Behn's Revision of Thomas Killigrew." *Restoration* 10 (1986): 82–92.

Dryden, John. *Marriage A-la-Mode*. 1673. *The Works of John Dryden*. Vol. 11. Ed. John Loftis and David Stuart Rodes et al. Berkeley: U of California P, 1978. 219–316.

Frye, Northrop. *The Anatomy of Criticism*. Princeton, N.J.: Princeton UP, 1957.

Gallagher, Catherine. "Who Was That Masked Woman?: The Prostitute and the Playwright in the Comedies of Aphra Behn." *Women's Studies* 15 (1988): 23–42.

Goldberg, Rita. *Sex and Enlightenment: Women in Richardson and Diderot*. Cambridge: Cambridge UP, 1984.

Goldsmith, Oliver. *She Stoops to Conquer. Collected Works of Oliver Goldsmith*. Vol. 5. Ed. Arthur Friedman. Oxford: Clarendon, 1966. 99–217.

Hagstrum, Jean H. *Sex and Sensibility: Ideal and Erotic Love from Milton to Mozart*. Chicago: U of Chicago P, 1980.

Holland, Norman N. *The First Modern Comedies: The Significance of Etherege, Wycherley, and Congreve*. Cambridge, Mass.: Harvard UP, 1959.

Holland, Peter. *The Ornament of Action: Text and Performance in Restoration Comedy*. Cambridge: Cambridge UP, 1979.

Hume, Robert D. *The Development of English Drama in the Late Seventeenth Century*. Oxford: Clarendon, 1976.

———. "The Myth of the Rake in 'Restoration' Comedy." *Studies in the Literary Imagination* 10 (1977): 25–55.

Kavenik, Frances M. "Aphra Behn: The Playwright as 'Breeches Part.' " *Curtain Calls: British and American Women and the Theater, 1660–1820*. Ed. Mary Anne Schofield and Cecilia Macheski. Athens: Ohio UP, 1991. 177–92.

Miller, Nancy K. *The Heroine's Text: Readings in the French and English Novel, 1722–1782*. New York: Columbia UP, 1980.

Nochimson, Martha. *No End to Her: Soap Opera and the Female Subject*. Berkeley: U of California P, 1993.

Novak, Maximillian E. "Love, Scandal, and the Moral Milieu of Congreve's Comedies." *Congreve Consider'd*. Ed. Maximillian E. Novak and Aubrey Williams. Los Angeles: William Andrews Clark Memorial Library, 1971. 24–50.

Ogg, David. *England in the Reigns of James II and William III*. Oxford: Clarendon P, 1955.

Payne, Deborah C. " 'And Poets Shall by Patron Princes Live': Aphra Behn and Patronage." *Curtain Calls: British and American Women and the Theater, 1660–1820*. Ed. Mary Anne Schofield and Cecilia Macheski. Athens: Ohio UP, 1991. 105–19.

Richardson, Samuel. *Clarissa; or, The History of a Young Lady*. Ed. Angus Ross. New York: Penguin, 1985.

Rogers, Katherine M. "Aphra Behn (1640?–16 April 1689)." *Restoration and Eighteenth-Century Dramatists*. 1st ser. Ed. Paula R. Backsheider. *Dictionary of Literary Biography* 80. Detroit: Gale, 1989. 14–28.

Root, Robert L., Jr. "Aphra Behn, Arranged Marriage, and Restoration Comedy." *Women and Literature* 5 (1978): 3–14.

Rose, Mary Beth. *The Expense of Spirit: Love and Sexuality in English Renaissance Drama.* Ithaca, N.Y.: Cornell UP, 1988.

Staves, Susan. *Married Women's Separate Property in England, 1660–1833.* Cambridge, Mass.: Harvard UP, 1990.

———. *Players' Scepters: Fictions of Authority in the Restoration.* Lincoln: U of Nebraska P, 1979.

Thompson, Peggy. "The Limits of Parody in *The Country Wife.*" *Studies in Philology* 89 (1991): 100–114.

Traugott, John. "The Rake's Progress from Court to Comedy: A Study of Comic Form." *Studies in English Literature* 6 (1966): 381–407.

Underwood, Dale. *Etherege and the Seventeenth-Century Comedy of Manners.* New Haven, Conn.: Yale UP, 1957.

Vernon, P.F. "Marriage of Convenience and the Moral Code of Restoration Comedy." *Essays in Criticism* 12 (1962): 370–87.

Wycherley, William. *The Country-Wife. The Plays of William Wycherley.* Ed. Arthur Friedman. Oxford: Clarendon, 1979. 239–355.

Lady Fulbank and the Poet's Dream in Behn's *Lucky Chance*

Robert A. Erickson

*T*he development of English drama in the seventeenth century may be seen as the gradual opening and *emergence* of a female space of performance. From the Elizabethan "inner stage," used for intimate, often secret or sexual representations, to the whole intricate and colorful within-doors elaboration of the masque in which aristocratic women were performing long before 1660, to the final consolidation of the enclosed Restoration stage housed within a theater, women came out of the darkness into fullness of theatrical being. Put another way, as the Elizabethan open theater contracted to the more intimate enclosed space of the Restoration theater, the spectacle of women's voices, gestures, and writings expanded and flourished. Aphra Behn, more than any other woman playwright, created a permanent female space—for herself, for other women, and for dramatic culture—in the Restoration theater world of London. Her most important female character, Lady Julia Fulbank, is her dramatic surrogate, the playwright and producer within Behn's late comedy, *The Lucky Chance.*

Lady Fulbank is, in Behn's introductory adjectives in the dramatis personae, "honest and generous" (*Five Plays* 10).[1] She is a young woman of honor, she is virtuous, and she is bountiful, befitting her position as a "lady." She was played by Elizabeth Barry, the most famous actress of her time, a woman who, like Aphra Behn, her friend, overcame great obstacles to achieve success and stability in the precarious theatrical world of Restoration London. The second description of Lady Fulbank in the play is by Charles Gayman, the man with whom she is "In love," as the dramatis personae tells us. When the naive idealist Harry Bellmour asks plaintively, "Whether is Honour, Truth and Friendship fled?" Gayman, the worldly young cynic and libertine rake, replies, "Why, there ne're was such a Vertue, / 'Tis all a Poets Dream," and goes on to reinforce this observation by confessing that he is still in love with a "dear jilting Gypsy," the "faithless

Portrait of Aphra Behn, in *The Dramatick Works of his Grace George Villiers, late Duke of Buckingham* (1715), vol. 2, 204. By permission of the Department of Special Collections, Stanford University Libraries.

Julia . . . the Old Alderman's Wife" (13 [3]). After having been apparently forced into marriage with old Sir Cautious Fulbank, Julia has fashioned her own independence and her own "name." She has her own space within the house, her "apartment," a suite of rooms including her own bedroom; she has access to her husband's considerable wealth; she has her own servants; and she has freedom to act out her own self-chosen roles and to direct her own cast of characters in a play she has written for her own special purposes, one that will affirm the "Poets Dream" of both Eros and Virtue as a reality.

Having outlived her fellow poet and friend, John Wilmot, second earl of Rochester, who died an old man at thirty-three, Aphra Behn was an old woman at forty-six. She lived a life full of physical strain and frequent illness, and in 1686 she was in declining health and fortune, writing furiously with a sense that she did not have much time left. (She died two years later.) I shall argue that in *The Lucky Chance* Behn creates a version of herself as playwright in the character of Lady Fulbank, and that she re-creates, elegiacally, in the character of Charles Gayman—the quintessentially inconstant male "rover" protagonist of many of her works—several of the men she had known most intimately, especially Wilmot, John Hoyle, Thomas Otway, and Charles II. *The Lucky Chance* is Behn's last dramatic testament, her gospel of Eros, embodied in the virtuous artistic libertinism of Lady Fulbank, one of the few women "writers" in Restoration drama to create a successful script within the authorial script and a character who, like Behn, takes on the world of men and achieves highly ambivalent results. *The Lucky Chance* is a female author's response to the founding fathers of Restoration comedy, the male playwrights and their protagonists. Lady Fulbank is Behn's female libertine hero counterpoised against the great male libertine heroes of the roaring '70s, epitomized by Wycherley's Harry Horner of *The Country Wife* and Etherege's Dorimant of *The Man of Mode.*

For introductory purposes, I will take Horner as the prototypical Restoration rake-hero. The Horner ethos might be characterized as the religion of a modern Dionysus, replete with wine, women, and sexual masques and feasts. In the first act, after the Quack confers upon him the title of "Doctor" or teacher, Horner as a mock-Jesus reiterating the paradoxical "Verily, I tell you" formula begins to preach an ironic new masculinist gospel of "wine" in place of "love": "I tell you, 'tis as hard to be a good Fellow, a good Friend, and a Lover of Women, as 'tis to be a good Fellow, a good Friend, and a Lover of Money: You cannot follow both, then choose your side; Wine gives you liberty, Love takes it away. . . . Wine gives you joy, Love grief and tortures. . . . Wine makes us witty; Love only Sots: Wine makes us sleep, Love breaks it" (Wycherley 9 [6, 7]).[2] He immediately makes a "convert" of his libertine friend, Dorilant. Horner's ironic gospel of wine is a cover-up for his new project of whoring "Women of Quality" (7 [6]) under the mask of impotence. His new doctrine culminates in the final act, when his Bacchantes, the wine-bearing "virtuous gang" of Lady Fidget, Mrs. Dainty Fidget, and Mrs. Squeamish, the "unbelieving Sisters" of act I (5 [3]), confess in a mock-religious catechism of Horner to being "Sister Sharers" of his sexual gifts (71 [94]).

Horner is not only a new kind of Dissenting preacher; he is also a new kind of "writer" and satirist. A large part of his satiric Dionysus project, the conversion of women and men into his sexual disciples and unwitting gulls, depends on the power of phallic inscription. As his name suggests, he "horns" husbands' heads; with his phallus he creates "cuckolds" and "whores." Pinchwife tells his fellow dupe and cuckold Sir Jasper, in outraged impotence at the end of the play, when he finally divines the truth, that "he has whor'd my Wife, and yours too" (75 [98]).

In *The Lucky Chance* Behn implicitly sets her gospel of Eros against Horner's gospel of Dionysus. She adopts the satiric paradigm—first introduced into English literature by that archetypal romance satirist, the Wife of Bath—of the failed male hero who is redeemed by the power of a woman's creative love, and she turns it into a more intractable and problematic fable of gender conflict and the fate of the female artist. Behn divides her own experience as a woman of the world between the polarized representations of two "ladies": the old, ugly, poor "landlady," Gammer Grime, wife of a City blacksmith, and the beautiful, young, wealthy Lady Fulbank, wife of a successful City banker. Within Lady Fulbank's orbit are two other important women characters, Diana and Leticia, whose names signify modesty and gladness. These three women constitute a triadic female community of feeling and morality within the play, a relationship characterized most memorably by Lady Fulbank's commiserating with Leticia, her younger counterpart in an unequal marriage, about the young wife's wedding night: "I was sick to know with what Christian Patience you bore the Martyrdom of this Night" (71 [48]).

The action of the play traces the intertwined progress of Lady Fulbank as playwright and of the young rake Gayman (alias Wasteall), who has spent his small fortune on gifts to Lady Fulbank and at the outset is doomed to "moyl on in the damn'd dirty Road" (35 [20]) of male prostitution as Gammer Grime's favorite boarder in one of the most squalid parts of Restoration London. Lady Fulbank redeems the unwitting Gayman from the dirty realm of "Old Nasty" with a gift of five hundred pounds, and she has him conducted to her own London townhouse, where, in an elaborate masque of her devising, he is made to go through a solemn quasi–marriage ceremony. The play ends with Gayman winning a wager with Sir Cautious Fulbank to have his wife for one night; Lady Fulbank is tricked into sleeping with the unregenerate rake, and she vows never again to enter her husband's bed. We are left with the expectation that Gayman and Lady Fulbank will reunite after her husband's death.

We first meet Lady Fulbank as we move from the public street of the City, the world of grime and noise, into a private townhouse interior, a dramaturgic repetition of the playgoer entering the candlelit phantasmagoria of the Theater Royal from the hubbub of Covent Garden's streets. Bredwell hands her a letter from Gayman, and she reads it aloud. Her first action in the play is to speak Gayman's plight into being, into her own and the spectators' experience. As the stage phenomenon "Lady Fulbank," she is the vivid, authentic, and authoritative oral-visual being created by the imaginative interplay of the actress and her audience. She is Gayman's author-within-the-play as she enacts and performs him out of his written words. She utters him and is thus his living fate; she speaks him into birth and is thus his dramatic mother. Here Behn, the beleaguered, heroic woman playwright with fifteen plays to her credit and a richly lived experience of the twenty or so years of Restoration theatrical history, puts her heroine in the authoritative position usually reserved for the libertine male hero. In this she reverses the normal pattern of male-authored plays, which tend to introduce the leading female character through accounts by the male protagonist or his close male associates.

Lady Fulbank here both recalls and reverses the prototypical figure of Dorimant (Etherege's version of Rochester) at his birth on the stage as both reader and writer. In *The Man of Mode* Dorimant enters reciting the verses of Edmund Waller, the godfather to male and female poets of the Restoration; then he reads from the billet-doux he has written to Loveit "in cold blood" (Etherege 82).[3] Dorimant enters reading like a murderer; Lady Fulbank enters reading like a life-giver, as Behn reverses the convention of the man reading the woman and dismissing her. Lady Fulbank welcomes her fallen lover; Dorimant is merely disgusted by his. For Dorimant writing is a death act, an act of fatigue and disgust, like "hanging an arse" in the mechanical operations of the spirit portrayed in pornographic Restoration satire. He enters as the malevolent satirist, Rochester in his self-loathing poetic mode, facing the world with weary contempt as he asks, "What vermin are those chattering without?" (82). Like him, many male writing characters in Restoration comedy—Pinchwife and Sir Feeble come to mind in this context—use the act of writing for hostile, constrictive, defacing, deceptive, manipulative, and self-engrossing ends.

Gayman writes Lady Fulbank's name, Julia, three times in his letter and laments his "separation" from her. He knows, but does not acknowledge, that his life depends on her. The name Julia, like Astraea, Behn's nom de plume, has Augustan overtones. Derived from the Roman gens name Julius, it suggests nobility and honor: Julia was the granddaughter of Augustus Caesar and the legendary mistress of Ovid; as the feminine counterpart of the seventh month of the year, the name suggests high summer, the peak of ripeness. Julia is the fruitful summer redeemer of Gayman, the "winter Fly" (15 [5]) who languishes in the claustrophobic realm of Gammer Grime. Behn makes her a kind of mythic goddess as well as a highly individualized character representing a powerful female social type.

As Behn knowingly nears the end of her productive life as a literary artist, she creates a metaphor of the woman writer in the world by making Lady Fulbank the woman writer-in-the-play. We may instructively examine this submerged motif in Restoration comedy by first contrasting Lady Fulbank with Wycherley's brilliant characterization of Margery Pinchwife, the "country wife," as a writer of love letters. Margery's brutal and foolish husband, like Sir Cautious, equates women and money throughout the play and, in an indelible formulation that applies as aptly to *The Lucky Chance* as to *The Country Wife,* sees them both as objects that must be controlled by men at all times: "Our sisters and daughters, like usurers' money, are safest when put out; but our wives, like their writings, are never safe but in our closets under lock and key" (Wycherley 65 [85]). Sisters and daughters are best "put out" on the marriage market. "Put out" suggests the Latin derivation of *prostitute* from "to stand before" or "stand out" for sale, and the term reinforces Pinchwife's view of all women as whores, or commodities.[4] An old usurer like Sir Cautious Fulbank is not at all averse to arranging the marriage for sale of his foppish nephew, Bearjest, to Sir Feeble's daughter, Diana, and Sir Cautious will eventually preside over the prostitution of his own wife to Gayman for one night. The "writings" to which Pinchwife refers are the usurer's legal and monetary documents, which are safest in the bank. These writings are equated with women. Marriage settlements and documents fixed women, as long as they were married, into the status of legal nonentities. Margery breaks out of this status of being fixed and "written" when she literally comes out of the "closet" after *writing* her own letter to Horner, and Aphra Behn—whose first name, according to Angeline Goreau, was derived from a third-century Christian martyr converted from sacred prostitution—first broke that barrier by putting herself out as a "published" writer in 1670.

As everyone now knows, when she chose to make her fortune in the world by taking up her female pen—by writing for money—Behn crossed the line from respectable seventeenth-century womanhood into a more dangerous and disreputable realm. The ideal woman in early modern England was a silent text—fixed, written, layered, covered (the wife as *femme couvert,* in legal terminology), effaced, veiled, or ornamented. She was a text in the literal sense of *textus* as a "woven fabric," a web, a clothed figure pictured in Nathan Bailey's later definitive derivation of *woman* from the Welsh *wan,* a *"Web* and *Man, q.d.* a weaving person" (*Dictionnarium Britannicum,* entry for "woman"). Woman is also "womb-man," and the womb was often imaged as spinning or sewing the child into being (see Erickson, *Mother Midnight* 16).[5] Bailey's stress on a "weaving" rather than a "woven" person suggests woman's active ability to weave herself, and Behn—a country woman herself from the county of Kent—made the momentous transition from the realm of woman defined as a silent text through the phase of woman as a weaver-of-texts to the achievement of an individual woman putting together and putting forward her own fictional texts.

In a curious way, the experience of Margery Pinchwife in act IV, scene 2, of *The Country Wife* recapitulates that entire process, as does the experience of Richardson's Pamela in a far more complex novelistic movement.[6] Pinchwife and Margery are here pitted against each other in a writing contest, and the lowly Margery wins. Early in the writing scene Pinchwife laments how the force of "Love" (or Cupid-Eros) gives women "first their craft, their art of deluding; out of natures hands, they came plain, open, silly and fit for slaves, as she and Heaven intended 'em" (Wycherley 46 [59]). He equates women's "craft" with their fiction-making power, and he believes he can strangle "the little Monster," Cupid, by forcing Margery to write a letter to Horner terminating their relationship. The killing of Cupid is paralleled by the defacing of Margery: if she does not write as she is directed, Pinchwife "will write Whore with this Penknife in [her] Face" (47 [61]). For him, writing is the phallic assertion of violence and domination, fixing and defining woman as "whore" while defacing her. Margery will continue to be only a "written" wife—not simply effaced but destroyed, a state Pinchwife comes close to effecting later in the play, when his penknife is replaced by his sword and he twice draws on her.

At this point, Margery, who "can't do't very well," evades her husband's commands and, while he exits—after telling her Horner's name—she makes the transition from "written" woman to "writing" woman in a brilliant solo tour de force for the actress. Stage direction: *"She writes, and repeats what she hath writ"* (49 [62]). The writing and the oral repetition of the writing in the authority of Margery's stage presence seal her new independence. As she acts out with her body the writing of her true passion for Horner, she enacts her own growing mastery of self-presentation, the assertion of her own freedom: "[N]ow he has taught me to write Letters: You shall have longer ones from me" (49 [63]). She substitutes her own letter for the one Pinchwife made her write, and her husband becomes her unwitting go-between. The movement in this scene of woman learning to write her own feelings under threat of physical injury is a schematic for woman learning to live independently in a dangerous world, one of the earliest representations of the underlying dynamic of Richardson's *Clarissa,* the culminating novelistic expression of the implied proposition "I write, therefore I am."[7]

When we next see Margery, in scene 4, Pinchwife has locked her in the chamber. She is sitting alone in the classic writer's posture, *"leaning on her elbow, A table, Pen, Ink, and Paper."* In the grip of "the *London* disease they call Love," she is about to finish her second letter to Horner when her husband surprises her and *"snatches the paper from her"* (59 [77]). Again he threatens her with bodily harm and forces her to finish the letter. She signs her sister-in-law Alithea's name to the letter, fools Pinchwife, disguises herself as Alithea, and emerges from captivity just as Pinchwife thinks he is locking her up, when he and "Alithea" leave for Horner's. Here Margery exchanges *herself* for Alithea as easily as she exchanged her own letter for Pinchwife's. She thus engineers two adroit self-inscriptions, her own letter and her reinscription of herself, via the "text" of woman's clothing, as her sister-in-law. She becomes her own letter in a way similar to Pamela's becoming her own written text woven around her body in Richardson's novel; she is "written" now by herself, not by her husband or the patriarchal marriage system. Furthermore, she has fashioned a scenario in which both Pinchwife and Horner will take the roles she has assigned them. By the end of the play, however, Margery's self-emancipation from virtual slavery into the status of an independent woman who *makes her own proposal of marriage* to Horner is abruptly extinguished when her declaration of love for him is effectively suppressed, and Lucy and the Quack preserve Horner's masquerade of impotence, a lie that everyone consents to believe, even Margery under enormous duress. So ends Mrs. Pinchwife's career as the woman writer-within-the-play.

Eleven years later Behn created Lady Fulbank as a far more sophisticated woman writer, yet one who meets a similar fate. The ungendered word *playwright* as a constructor, or maker, of plays came into general use during the Restoration (*OED,* quotation from 1687: "Play-wright"). A "wright" is a worker and shaper of materials for a specific functional purpose (a wheelwright, a shipwright), and the term calls attention to the hard physical work of writing plays, a new kind of woman's work. And Lady Fulbank is not only a playwright but also a producer of her own play, with all the work that such production entails. Whereas Margery is always foregrounded onstage in the process of learning to "write" and learning to live in London society, Lady Fulbank is quietly at work behind the idle, elegant surface of her appearance and station in life.

First she constructs a scenario for releasing Gayman from the clutches of one of the most vividly realized female grotesques in Restoration drama, Gayman's landlady, Gammer Grime. Behn takes great pains to show how far her soiled phallic hero has fallen, and into what sort of abyss. Young Bredwell (whose wholesome-sounding name also evokes the women's prison, Bridewell), working for Lady Fulbank as well as being an apprentice to her banker husband, sets the scene in the descriptive idiom of the chroniclers of London lowlife, Tom Brown or Ned Ward, in an astonishingly novelistic anticipation of the Dickensian grotesque that emerges from the darkest London underclass.[8] Bredwell tells how on his visit to Wasteall in "a nasty Place, called *Alsatia*" (21 [9]) he encountered at the door

> the beastly thing he calls a Landlady; who lookt as if she'ad been of her own Husband's making, compos'd of moulded Smith's Dust. I ask'd for Mr. *Wastall,* and she began to open— and did so rail at him, that what with her *Billingsgate,* and her Husband's Hammers, I was both deaf and dumb—at last the Hammers ceas'd, and she grew weary, and call'd down Mr. *Was-tall;* but he not answering—I was sent up a Ladder rather than a pair of Stairs; at last I scal'd the top, and enter'd the inchanted Castle; there did I find him, spight of the Noise below, drowning his Cares in Sleep. [21 (9)]

Part of Behn's satiric project with Gayman is to put him through the experience of what a destitute woman might suffer, much as the Wife of Bath puts the graceless young knight of her tale through a series of passive roles in which he is acted upon by women (see Martin). Gayman, like the proverbial young female prostitute, is "driven to the last degree of Poverty" (22 [10]), and he lives in the kind of garret apartment memorialized by Swift as the abode of his mentally unstable Grub Street projector in *A Tale of a Tub* as well as that of "A Beautiful Young Nymph Going to Bed." Bredwell continues:

> Had you but seen his Lodgings, Madam! . . . 'Tis a pretty convenient Tub. . . . He may lie along in't, there's just room for an old Joyn'd Stool besides the Bed, which one cannot call a Cabin, about the largeness of a Pantry Bin, or a Usurer's Trunk, there had been Dornex [silk] Curtains to't in the days of *Yore;* but they were now annihilated, and nothing left to save his Eyes from the Light, but my Land-ladies Blew Apron, ty'd by the strings before the Window, in which stood a broken six-penny Looking-Glass, that show'd as many Faces, as the Scene in *Henry* the Eighth, which could but just stand upright, and then the Comb-Case fill'd it. [22 (10)]

Lady Fulbank replies, "What a lewd Description hast thou made of his Chamber"; the "tub" recalls the sweating tub cure for venereal disease (see Coakley). Like the old wicked witch who imprisons the maiden in her enchanted castle, Gammer—the vulgar name for an old wife, grandmother, or godmother—keeps Gayman in the dark, bound by her apron strings. She has pawned her best petticoat and " 'postle Spoons" to maintain Gayman and possess his "Manhood." She is also the major constraining figure of the play, the insatiable female counterpart of the grasping, superannuated Sir Feeble Fainwoud, the impotent husband of Leticia, Bredwell's sister and Bellmour's true love.

In "The Disappointment" Aphra Behn (with the help of some French antecedents) wrote the greatest poem in the Restoration about male impotence as seen from a woman's point of view, and the theme of temporary impotence and the recovery of male sexual potency occurs in *The Lucky Chance* and in her other works.[9] When Gammer tells Gayman that his good clothes have dwindled to an old campaign coat and a pair of "Piss-burned shammy Breeches," and that his "very Badg of Manhood's gone too" he seems abjectly to agree with her when he replies, "[I]-Faith no Wonder if you rail so." Her virulent tongue seems to hold him in impotent abjection as, with a touch of pity, she undeceives him: "Your Silver Sword I mean—transmogrified to this two-handed Basket Hilt—this old Sir *Guy* of *Warwick*—which will sell for nothing but old Iron" (31–32 [18]). Gayman has pawned his silver sword for an old-fashioned Guy of Warwick. Behn's superb metaphor emblematizes Gayman's sexual decline in the world from a promiscuous and well-to-do gay blade to "the dull drudging" workhorse in her employ.

Behn was probably intimately familiar with the kind of environment in which Gayman finds himself mired, because her debt-ridden friend Thomas Otway, the failed actor turned playwright, had retreated to "Alsatia" (Whitefriars) and died there in destitution a year before this play was written. Named after Alsace, the disputed territory between France and Germany, this area in the City of London claimed to be exempt from City jurisdiction, a special status confirmed by a charter of James I in 1608. The area became a haven for debtors and a seething matrix of crime and violence. Shadwell's *Squire of Alsatia* (1688) offers a definitive literary representation of the area, particularly its criminal argot. As late as 1747, long after the exempt status of Alsatia had been abolished, Hogarth pictured his idle apprentice being arrested in Alsatia's Blood Bowl House after having been betrayed by his whore (Weinreb and Hibbert 20–21). It is fitting, then, that Behn should—before Shadwell—choose this liminal, fluctuating, transitional territory as her setting for Gayman's decline in the world and as the milieu for her own great termagant, Gammer Grime.

Gammer's domain is an "old Iron" world of pounding hammers, dirt, and din. She seems an emblem of the Iron Age in which the mythic Roman goddess of justice in the Age of Gold, Astraea, was driven to heaven by the wickedness and impiety of mankind to be constellated as Virgo. Gammer's realm is an image of the new world of mechanism displacing the old vitalist world of the alchemist-hermeticist tradition, arguably the major paradigm shift in the representation of nature in early modern discourse, as outlined and documented in Carolyn Merchant's pioneering study. *The Lucky Chance* dramatizes this metamorphosis in the literary activities of Lady Fulbank, a reincarnation of Astraea, the Golden Age, and Aphra Behn herself, redeeming Gayman-Everyman from the mechanistic world of Gammer Grime into the Golden World of her creative imagination in her own Masque of Eros.

To follow this redemptive movement, we must note further what Gammer Grime and Lady Fulbank have in common. They are both unhappily married and "in love" with Gayman; they each give him gifts to "redeem" him from debt (22 [10], 33 [18]), and they conceal their gifts from their husbands; they are both "City wives," though far removed from each other in social status; they are both "full" (one "fulsome" (30), the other full of vitality); and they are both metonymically bonded to the earth, Gammer in a mechanical sense, through the grime and dust of her husband's iron hammers, and Julia in an organic, natural sense, through her association with river "Banks." The words *banks, flowers,* and *bliss* recur so often together in Behn's erotic poetry that they have the status of a sexual motif or archetype. The point of the similarities between the two characters is that they are the secret sharers of Gayman and, more important, the secret sharers of each other. Together they represent two sides of the same woman, much as the Loathly Lady and the beautiful young wife in Alison's Tale are the two projected halves of the phenomenon of the Wife of Bath, woman in her total lived experience from nubile maiden to post-menopausal crone, a phenomenon recalling the most ancient of all myths of womanhood, that of Kore and Demeter, a motif Behn plays out in her last two major fictions, here and in *Oroonoko*.[10] The differences between Gammer Grime and Lady Fulbank are most significant in Lady Fulbank's power as an artist of Virtue and Eros to overcome Gammer's hold on Gayman and restore him to his rightful place in her own affections, while at the same time testing his constancy.

In order to bring about this project, Lady Fulbank constructs a masquerade-masque, the Masque of Eros, for Gayman's benefit, and with his full but unwitting participation. As creator of the Masque of Eros, she assembles and directs a cast of singers, dancers, and musicians, constructs an elaborate set with all the latest effects that stage machinery can produce—"a Pavilion all form'd of gilded Clouds which hung by

Geometry" (65 [44])—and writes her own scenario in the riddling idiom of magic, pastoral, and romance, the language (in Gayman's own words) of a "Poets Dream." Gayman reads, *"Receive what Love and Fortune present you with, be grateful and be silent, or 'twill vanish like a Dream, and leave you more wretched than it found you"* (34 [20]). The young rake will be taken to an elegant London townhouse where a masque with dancing nymphs and shepherds is performed. The dance vanishes, a ring is put on his finger, and he is put in bed with a woman whom he later says he finds old and ugly. Now, anticipating this scenario, Bredwell, the benevolent red devil following the careful stage directions of his dramatic manager for his most important speech (of which she is the author), assumes a different voice to invoke the erotic theatrical world of sensual magic, signaled by the word *Curtains,* opposing Gammer's blue apron over the garret window. He will conduct Gayman to this world of Eros, if Gayman dare trust him:

> If you have Courage, Youth, or Love, you'll follow me,
> *(In feign'd Heroick Tone.)*
> When Nights black Curtains drawn around the World,
> And mortal's Eyes are safely lockt in Sleep,
> And no bold Spy dares view when Gods caress:
> Then I'll conduct thee to the Banks of Bliss.
>
> [35 (20)]

Lady Fulbank has subverted her own assigned identity in the patriarchal order by appropriating her husband's commercial appellation and converting it into a name of rich and subtle female erotic power, signaled by the play on her own name in "the Banks of Bliss." The term suggests two riverbanks with a stream running through them, an obvious sexual metaphor drawn from nature. In Jane Sharp's *Midwives Book,* another attempt by a Restoration woman writer to create her own space in a predominantly male discourse, the female genitals are described in images that evoke an edenic natural world: "At the bottom of the woman's belly is a little bank called a mountain of pleasure near the well-spring. . . . under this hill is the springhead" (33–34). This image of the mons veneris will reach its definitive expression in eighteenth-century fiction in the name of the protagonist of Cleland's *Memoirs of a Woman of Pleasure,* but for Behn the significant word is *bank*. The joining of "Lady" to "Fulbank" creates a metonymy for the mons veneris and a verbal image of readiness for fully active sex. Behn's friend the earl of Rochester had already used an epithet for the female genitals similar to hers, in "The Imperfect Enjoyment," perhaps the most famous poem ever written about premature ejaculation:

My flutt'ring Soul, sprung with the pointed kiss,
Hangs hov'ring o're her Balmy Brinks of Bliss.
But whilst her busie hand, wou'd guide that part,
Which shou'd convey my Soul up to her Heart,
In liquid Raptures, I dissove all o're,
Melt into Sperme, and spend at ev'ry Pore.

[Wilmot 30–31]

Gayman the libertine as cynical naturalist—an image of Rochester at his most sensually materialistic—of course dismisses the "Spirits, Ghosts, Hobgoblins, Furys, Fiends, and Devils" with which he has heard "old Wives" frighten fools and children. He constructs a more plausible (and entirely erroneous) scenario for the devil's visit: an old "Female Devil" full of lust has invented this ruse to hire him for her sexual satisfaction, and he is only too willing to oblige until he can *"purchase new and fresh Delight"* (35 [20]). Gayman is clearly the kind of libertine who beds anything "in Petticoats that ever dared" him (51 [33]). What seems to redeem this despicable rake for Aphra Behn–Lady Fulbank is his apparently sincere adherence to the notion of the reviving power of Eros. Gayman opens act II with a curse on his birth, his fortune, and his stars almost identical to that of Behn's Lysander at the end of "The Disappointment," or of Chaucer's Troilus, a curse that turns into a hymn to "Love," that "charming Sin" of Eros:

But let me hold thee, thou soft smiling God,
Close to my heart while Life continues there.
Till the last pantings of my vital Blood,
Nay, the last spark of Life and Fire be Love's!

[29 (16)]

Gayman's effusion is amplified by Lady Fulbank's hymn to Eros, which opens the masque scene just after Pert, her waiting maid, disguised as an ancient crone, leads Gayman into a dark chamber of her mistress's apartment, accompanied by soft music. A singer appears and renders a complex expression of the power of Eros in verses written by Lady Fulbank, as prologue to her miniature masque-within-the-masquerade (51–52 [33]). The song virtually sums up in three stanzas most of the basic tenets of Restoration libertinism: an antirationalist skepticism, the promotion of a varied sensualism, the predominance of nature over custom, freedom of thought and expression, the revolt against conventional arranged marriage, and the return to a golden age of natural innocence (Underwood 14).

All these elements can be found in Behn's gospel of Eros, but the philosophical point of the song is that Eros represents a force of spiritual and intellectual renewal beyond the gross delights of the sensual body, beyond the rake's self-gratifying phallicism, beyond Horner's witty masculinist gospel of wine and Dionysus, beyond the defacing and controlling acts of male writing in Restoration comedy. Here and in nearly all of her erotic poetry, Behn, "the female Apollo," constructs a life-enhancing, feminized version of sexual libertinism in opposition to the pervasive masculine model of aggressive, invasive bisexuality described by Randolph Trumbach and others. Hers is a doctrine of the virtues of erotic love close in some respects to the hermeticists' vision of the loving androgynous figure of the male and female principles of nature fused in harmonious and gentle copulation (Merchant 22). The song characterizes Eros as a *"Pleasing Delusion,"* a divine witchery *"stronger than Wine,"* a *"Disease that has more Joys than Health,"* a force that "betters" its subject. Eros gives benefits that "Reason never can bestow," wakes the dull senses, teaches the arts of pleasing, liberates misers and emboldens cowards, reforms drunkards and incites even air-headed fops to think. When *"full brute Appetite"* is satisfied, Eros suffuses *"new Spirits"* into the body, teaching *"the roveing Mind,"* like that of Behn's "rover" or of Gayman, to know the limits of a self-renewing form of desire. Such a force approximates a state of *"Heaven"* on earth for those blest with its power (52 [33]). The hymn is thus close in conception to Rochester's revisionist version of Miltonic "right reason" as the true government of thought by action, of reason by "sense," in his great *Satyr* (1679):

> Thus, whilst against false reas'ning I inveigh,
> I own right *Reason,* which I would obey:
> That *Reason* that distinguishes by sense,
> And gives us *Rules* of good, and ill from thence:
> That bounds desires with a reforming Will,
> To keep' em more in vigour, not to kill.
> [Wilmot 94]

Both Rochester and Behn emphasize the bounds of "just Desire," but Behn characteristically stresses the all-pervading power and necessity of Eros that leads to an exalted state of virtue and pleasure. Rochester's "action" is Behn's more creative and liberating erotic "Love." The poem expresses her doctrine of virtuous female *and* male libertinism. Just after the song is sung, nymphs and shepherds initiate the masque with a dance: *"Then two dance alone"* (52 [33]). That dance of a nymph and a shepherd, however it was staged, is another evocative image of Behn's later vision, articulated in *Oroonoko* and in her plays and poems, of creative erotic and spiritual harmony between man and woman.

In the first act Lady Fulbank lamented to Bredwell and Pert having broken her "sacred Vows to Gayman" (20 [8]):

Oh how fatal are forc'd Marriages
How many Ruines one such Match pulls on—
Had I but kept my sacred Vows to Gayman
How happy had I been—how prosperous he!
Whilst now I languish in a loath'd Embrace,
Pine out my Life with Age—Consumptious Coughs.
[20 (8–9)]

Apparently she and Gayman had performed between them a "contract" marriage. In the seventeenth century and well into the eighteenth, before the Marriage Act of 1754, the authenticity of such a marriage was recognized by canon law: "A spousal or betrothal *in words of the present tense (sponsalia per verba de praesenti),* and *not* the ceremony in which the priest blessed the spousal, made the marriage. . . . [After 1600] though the Church of England required the presence of a priest at the ceremony, and prescribed the details of that ceremony by prayer book and canon . . . it retained the medieval doctrine that consent made marriage" (Alleman 7–8; cf. Stone 67–95; Coakley 91–94, 235). Such a marriage could be an oral or written contract (with or without witnesses) was usually accompanied by an exchange of rings, and did not require physical consummation. If the contract was oral, then witnesses were more important. One of the best brief accounts of an oral contract marriage among the many allusions to it in Restoration comedy occurs in the following exchange between Bellmour and Leticia:

BELLMOUR. And Want compell'd thee to this wretched
Marriage—did it?
LETICIA. 'Tis not a Marriage, since my *Belmour* lives:
The Consummation were Adultery.
I was thy Wife before, wo't thou deny me?
BELLMOUR. No by those Powers that heard our mutual Vows,
Those Vows that tye us faster than dull Priests.
(37 [22])

The vow that passes the lips and cannot be revoked—as in the all-important oath, blessing, or curse in biblical literature—is the crucial element in sealing the contract, and the spoken consent of both partners is necessary. (Note here the contrast to *written* marriage settlements, which associate the woman with property.) Such a contract (or "precontract") was considered irrevocable. It had the binding power of fate as utterance, a fatal bond. For a woman playwright of the Restoration, the oral, present- or future-tense contract would seem to have special appeal as a dramatic construct. In her imaginative works, Behn seems to favor the authenticity of immediate contact through the mouth, voice, breath, and bodily presence of her male and female protagonists over written, textual, formal contact. And the binding nature of oral, present-tense contact seems to be associated more with "feminine" than with "masculine" experience in Restoration drama. It is superseded by male experience and definition, which saw the written contract as superior. The actual oral contract conditions for marriage in this era, however, tended to the advantage of the male who "promised" marriage and who then reneged on the promise, a situation played out over and over again in the literature related to courtship and marriage, particularly the drama and the emerging novel.

Returning now to the masque scene in act III, we see that Lady Fulbank's masque is an elaborate scenario devised to negate the former breaking of her "Vows" (20 [8]) to Gayman and to reaffirm them through the magic of *spoken* verse, with the crucial difference that she keeps her physical self outside the scene and acts through her intermediaries, her troupe of masquers. At the end of the play she confirms to Bredwell, as witness for her "Honour," that in producing the masquerade scenario she "had no Design on [Gayman's] Person, but that of trying of his Constancy" (97 [69]). It is the old "trial of constancy" motif, but now the woman tries the man, in an inversion of the patristic or Petrarchan conventions of the man trying the woman. As act IV opens, Gayman-Wasteall says he is wasting his youth in vain pursuit of Lady Fulbank, neglecting his own best interests and despising other beauties. "Why at your Feet are all my Fortunes laid, / And why does all my Fate depend on you?" (64 [43]). His facile command of the rhetoric of love conceals a real truth: she is literally his "Fate," his "invisible Mistress" (68 [45-46]). As we have seen, she speaks him into dramatic being early in the play, and she writes the script that redeems him from the mechanistic hell of Gammer Grime, testing his love and constancy. She arranges the terms of their reenacted marriage in the masque, but it is all done indirectly, putting upon him the responsibility of finding his way back to her.

When he faithlessly gives her the very ring she had arranged for Pert to give him in the masque ceremony, she has become not only his invisible but also his epistemological "Mistress." She *knows* all about him: "No more dissembling, I know your Land is gone—I know each Circumstance of all your wants" (64 [43]). She cross-examines him as he evades and lies in a remarkable novelistic anticipation of Clarissa's verbal duels with Lovelace. He finally submits to her will and admits that he has been tempted with large sums of gold, perhaps by the devil, and he then describes how he was led to an "inchanted Palace in the Clouds" (65 [44])—the counterpart to the ironic "inchanted Castle" of Gammer Grime described by Bredwell (21 [9])—where he was attended by "Young Dancing-singing Fiends innumerable" and an "old *Proserpine* . . . a silent Devil—but she was laid in a Pavillion, all form'd of gilded Clouds, which hung by Geometry, whither I was convey'd, after much Ceremony, and laid in Bed with her" (65 [44]). Apparently Pert as the old crone led him to the bed where Lady Fulbank lay silent, wondering how he would behave. He forced his arms around her, but he is either lying or he seems to have been so obsessed with the image of the old woman who wanted him for sex that he remembers her as a "Carcase . . . so rivell'd, lean, and rough—a Canvass Bag of wooden Ladles were a better Bed-fellow." Here the old fable of the old Loathly Lady who contains within her the beautiful young wife reaches its comic climax. Lady Fulbank takes him at his word and is deeply offended: " 'S'life after all to seem deform'd, old, ugly . . . [*Walking in a fret*]" (66 [44]).

This scene and the entire fourth act, with Gayman's "lucky chance" and the bargain scene, take place in Sir Feeble's house, away from Lady Fulbank's theatrical scene of operations and influence. The final movement in Lady Fulbank's progress as a writer and producer of her own fantasy of redemption, her Masque of Eros, takes place in her "Antichamber" bedroom where the masque was performed, and it concludes unhappily with her victimization in a crude scenario hastily devised by her lover and her collaborative husband—a male-authored parody of her own seductive masque, which makes both woman and Eros into objects of barter. After Gayman gets his revenge, with his own troupe of devils, on Bearjest and Noisy for abusing him to Sir Cautious, Lady Fulbank has a last extended dialogue with her husband. Her self-representation here as a woman who has created herself out of her own definition of "Honour" and "Virtue" is a kind of last testament of her independence (and of Behn's) before her inevitable fall (and Behn's imminent death). The entire play is replete with echoes of Shakespeare, Behn's master playwright and guide, and here Lady Fulbank plays upon her husband's impotence in recalling Hotspur to Glendower (*1 Henry IV* III.i.53–54): Sir Cautious says that "a Wedding is a sort of an Alarm to Love; it calls up every Mans Courage," and she replies, "Ay but will it come when 'tis call'd?" (86 [60]). But it is Sir Cautious's moral, not physical, impotence that Behn satirizes here, in contrast to Lady Fulbank's authentic virtue. She will not flatter him; she will not "simper—look demure, and justify [her] Honour when none questions it" (87 [60]), as do the "virtuous Gang" of Lady Fidget and her friends in *The Country Wife*. Lady Fulbank admits,

We can not help our Inclinations Sir,
No more than Time, or Light from coming on—
But I can keep my Vertue Sir intire.

[87 (61)]

She says she can control her body even though she is inclined toward a younger man. She can love discreetly, love as she ought, love honestly. When Sir Cautious hints that he might look the other way if she were unfaithful, she takes him up short. She could only hate him if he tamely suffered cuckoldom. Far more than his age, infirmity, and greed, what is satirized here goes to the heart of Behn's ethic of constancy in this play and in her other works. It is Sir Cautious's hateful vacillation between seeming to condone her infidelity for his own gain and then weakly pretending he was only trying her virtue that the satirist Aphra Behn, through Lady Fulbank, finds most reprehensible.

At the end, we see a fusion of the random inconstancy of Sir Cautious with that of Gayman, the "winter Fly" who has "got a Fly" (75) or a familiar spirit who gives him his lucky streak with the dice. And Lady Fulbank, who in this scene emerges as a virtuous Desdemona in the guise of a Restoration female libertine, echoes at the end the tragic tones of an Emilia when she realizes at last that it was her husband who not only left her "Honour" unguarded but actively promoted his own cuckolding and her undoing:

> GAYMAN. Base as he is 'twas he exposed this Treasure
>   Like silly *Indians* barter'd thee for Trifles.
> SIR CAUTIOUS. Oh treacherous Villain!—
> LADY FULBANK. Hah . . . my Husband do this?
> GAYMAN. He, by Love, he was the kind Procurer,
>   Contriv'd the means, and brought me to thy Bed.
> LADY FULBANK. My Husband! My wise Husband!
>
> [92–93 (66)][11]

Lady Fulbank, however, is not a heroine devoted to death. In the historical context of the sanctity of verbal contracts in marriage, her defiant *unmarriage* "Vow" in her husband's presence, an irrevocable oath she takes on her knees "by all things Just and sacred, / To separate for ever from his Bed . . . I've sworn, nor are the Stars more fixt than I" (93 [66]), is a moment as memorable in the history of women's declarations of independence in European letters as Clarissa's vow, after the rape, never to have Lovelace, as Mary Wollstonecraft's epistle dedicatory to Talleyrand in *A Vindication of the Rights of Woman,* or as Nora's slamming the door on her husband in *A Doll's House* almost two centuries after the appearance of this most serious of Behn's satiric comedies.

Lady Fulbank's hymn to Eros in act III and her defense of her "Vertue" here are the two main elements in Behn's gospel of Eros, the disguised "Morality" of the play. *The Lucky Chance* was written after a four-year dramatic hiatus by its author. She had had four years to mature this dramatic project, and in the preface she offers her famous apologia as a female playwright (7 [3]). As a female satirist, Behn seems to want her drama to express, indirectly, her own unique view of enduring virtue (on classical models), alongside that of her male contemporaries. When she considers "how Ancient and Honourable a Date Plays have born, how they have been the peculiar Care of the most Illustrious Persons of *Greece* and *Rome*," she dedicates the play to the "new" Rochester, the eminent statesman Laurence Hyde, and she reminds him of the heuristic wisdom of another great statesman, Cardinal Richelieu: "That there was no surer Testimony to be given of the flourishing Greatness of a State, than publick Pleasures and Divertisements—for they are, says he—the Schools of Vertue, where Vice is always either punish't, or disdain'd. They are secret Instructions to the People, in things that 'tis impossible to insinuate into them any other Way. 'Tis Example that prevails above Reason or DIVINE PRECEPTS.... 'tis Example alone that inspires Morality, and best establishes Vertue" (3, Epistle Dedicatory; italics reversed). The playwright wishes to leave us with the "Example" of Lady Fulbank, the female poet.

Notes

1. All quotations from *The Lucky Chance* are from *Five Plays,* a reprint of the Montague Summers edition of 1915. I have corrected this edition against the first edition in the British Library (shelfmark 644 g 16); page numbers of the British Library edition are in brackets—or parentheses when the citation itself is in brackets. Behn's use of the long dash is significant as a cue to the actors. The subtitle of the play is *The Alderman's Bargain,* referring primarily to Sir Cautious's arrangement with Gayman, but the word *bargain* is played upon at several points, and Lady Fulbank makes her own "bargain" with Gayman: "[I]f you can afford me a Lease of your Love, / Till the old Gentleman my Husband depart this wicked World, / I'm for the Bargain" (42 [24]). An "alderman" in the City of London during the Restoration was a magistrate next in dignity to the mayor, the chief officer of one of the City's twenty-six wards (*OED,* quotation from 1667). In its etymology, the word literally means "old man" and is related to "elder." It is the perfect term for Sir Cautious Fulbank and Sir Feeble Fainwoud, the two representatives of the controlling patriarchy of the world of this play.

Despite its deficiencies as a scholarly edition, Jean A. Coakley's *Aphra Behn's "The Luckey Chance" (1687): A Critical Edition* contains much useful material from contemporary sources.

Of recent criticism (besides that cited elsewhere), I would like to note the articles by Munns and Zimbardo as the most relevant to my concerns in this essay. I wish also to express my gratitude to several of my recent students in Restoration drama courses, especially Sharon Kay Randolph, Sabrina Lobdell, and Kirsten Edmondson, for their perceptive comments on this play.

2. All citations from *The Country Wife* are from the edition of Wycherley edited by Scott McMillin, which I have corrected for accidentals against the first edition in the British Library (shelfmark C 34 1 26). Page numbers of the British Library edition are in brackets.

3. All citations from *The Man of Mode* are from the edition of Etherege edited by Scott McMillin.

4. See Gallagher 26. I disagree at many points with this provocative article (*The Lucky Chance* is the only one of Behn's "comedies" discussed in it), especially with the notion that "by flaunting her self-sale, Aphra Behn embraced the title of whore" (29). Aphra Behn as a published woman writer is a much more complex phenomenon than this epithet suggests, as Gallagher herself notes.

5. A crucial (and neglected) stage in the transition from woman as one who sews to woman as one who writes was the making of samplers, the often complex and skillfully artistic exercises in embroidery by girls and women containing the alphabet and quotations or mottoes worked in ornamental characters and patterns. It should be noted that the womb-weaving trope suggests that writing—the weaving of texts—is life-giving rather than restrictive and defining.

6. I have discussed this process in *Mother Midnight* (71–102, 108–9).

7. See Erickson, *Mother Midnight* 108–9, 159–83, 186–92; and idem, " 'Written in the Heart' " 18–53.

8. See Zimbardo for a discussion of Behn's anticipation of the novel in her drama. For particular reference to this scene, see 378–79.

9. See *A Voyage to the Isle of Love,* Behn's free translation of Paul Tallemant's French original (1663). Referring to himself, the male protagonist says, "And as the Tide of Love flow'd in, so fast / My Low, my Ebbing Vigor out did hast. / But 'twas not long, thus idly, and undone / I lay, before vast Seas came rowling on, / Spring-tides of Joy, that the rich neighboring shoar / And down the fragrant Banks it proudly bore, / O're-flow'd and ravisht all great Natures store" (Behn, *Works* 6:287).

Compare these lines from *The Lucky Chance:*

PERT (disguised as an Old Woman). . . . A Woman's Passion is like the Tide, it stays for no man, when the hour is come.

GAYMAN. I'm sorry I have took it as it's Turning; I'm sure mine's ebbing out as fast. [50–51 (33)]

10. See Erickson, "Mrs. A. Behn and the Myth of Oroonoko-Imoinda" 206, 208–10, and, for a fuller discussion of the mythology of mother-daughter relationships in the context of fate, *Mother Midnight,* esp. 1–50.

11. Compare:

> *OTHELLO*. Cassio did top her; ask thy husband else.
>
> · · · · · · · · · · · · · · · · · ·
>
>   . . . . Thy husband knew it all.
> *EMILIA*. My husband?
> *OTHELLO*. Thy husband.
> *EMILIA*. That she was false to wedlock.
> *OTHELLO*. Ay, with Cassio.
>
>   · · · · · · · · · · · · · · · · ·
>
> EMILIA. My husband?
> *OTHELLO*. Ay, 'twas he that told me on her first.
>
> · · · · · · · · · · · · · · · · · ·
>
> *EMILIA*. . . . . My husband?
> *OTHELLO*. What needs this iterance, woman? I say thy husband.
>
> *EMILIA*. O mistress, villainy hath made mocks with love!
>   My husband say she was false?
> *OTHELLO*. . . . . He, woman:
>   I say, thy husband; dost understand the word?
> My friend, thy husband, honest, honest Iago.
>
> · · · · · · · · · · · · · · · · · ·
>
>   . . . . Then must you speak
> Of one that lov'd not wisely but too well;
>   . . . of one whose hand,
> (Like the base Indian) threw a pearl away
> Richer than all his tribe.
>   [V.ii.136, 139–43, 147–48, 149–54, 343–44, 346–48]

Works Cited

Alleman, Gellert Spencer. *Matrimonial Law and the Materials of Restoration Comedy*. Wallingford, Pa., n.d.

Bailey, Nathan. *Dictionnarium Britannicum: Or a more Compleat Universal Etymological English Dictionary than any Extant*. 2d ed. London, 1736.

Behn, Aphra. *Aphra Behn: Five Plays Selected and Introduced by Maureen Duffy*. Ed. Maureen Duffy. London: Methuen, 1990.

———. *The Works of Aphra Behn*. 6 vols. Ed. Montague Summers. London, 1915; New York: Benjamin Blom, 1967.

Coakley, Jean A., ed. *Aphra Behn's "The Luckey Chance" (1687): A Critical Edition*. New York: Garland, 1987.

Duffy, Maureen. *The Passionate Shepherdess: Aphra Behn, 1640–89*. London: Cape, 1977.

Erickson, Robert A. *Mother Midnight: Birth, Sex, and Fate in Eighteenth-Century Fiction*. New York: AMS, 1986.

———. "Mrs. A. Behn and the Myth of Oroonoko-Imoinda," *Eighteenth-Century Fiction* 5.3 (April 1993): 201–16.

————. " 'Written in the Heart': *Clarissa* and Scripture." *Eighteenth-Century Fiction* 2.1 (Oct. 1986): 17–52.

Etherege, George. *The Man of Mode; or, Sir Fopling Flutter.* 1676. *Restoration and Eighteenth-Century Comedy.* Ed. Scott McMillin. New York: Norton, 1973. 79–151.

Gallagher, Catherine. "Who Was That Masked Woman?: The Prostitute and the Playwright in the Comedies of Aphra Behn." *Women's Studies* 15 (1988): 23–42.

Goreau, Angeline. *Reconstructing Aphra.* New York: Dial, 1980.

Martin, Priscilla. *Chaucer's Women.* London: Macmillan, n.d.

Merchant, Carolyn. *The Death of Nature: Women, Ecology, and the Scientific Revolution.* San Francisco: Harper and Row, 1980.

Munns, Jessica. " 'I by a Double Right Thy Bounties Claim': Aphra Behn and Sexual Space." *Curtain Calls: British and American Women and the Theater, 1660–1820.* Ed. Mary Anne Schofield and Cecilia Macheski. Athens: Ohio UP, 1990. 193–210.

Shakespeare, William. *The Riverside Shakespeare.* Ed. G. Blakemore Evans. Boston: Houghton Mifflin, 1974.

Sharp, Jane. *The Midwives Book.* London, 1671.

Stone, Lawrence. *The Road to Divorce: England, 1530–1987.* New York: Oxford UP, 1990.

Trumbach, Randolph. "London's Sodomites: Homosexual Behavior and Western Culture in the Eighteenth Century." *Journal of Social History* 11 (1977): 1–33.

————. "Sodomitical Subcultures, Sodomitical Roles, and the Gender Revolution of the Eighteenth Century: The Recent Historiography." *Eighteenth-Century Life* 9 (1985): 109–21.

Underwood, Dale. *Etherege and the Seventeenth-Century Comedy of Manners.* New Haven, Conn.: Yale UP, 1957.

Weinreb, Ben, and Christopher Hibbert, eds. *The London Encyclopedia.* London: Macmillan, 1983.

Wilmot, John, second Earl of Rochester. *The Poems of John Wilmot, Earl of Rochester.* Ed. Keith Walker. London: Blackwell, 1984.

Wycherley, William. *The Country Wife. Restoration and Eighteenth-Century Comedy.* Ed. Scott McMillin. New York: Norton, 1973. 3–78.

Zimbardo, Rose. "Aphra Behn: A Dramatist in Search of the Novel." *Curtain Calls: British and American Women and the Theater, 1660–1820.* Ed. Mary Anne Schofield and Cecilia Macheski. Athens: Ohio UP, 1990. 371–82.

PART 2

Chased Desire:
Women and Feminism
in Plays by Men

Tupping Your Rival's Women: Cit-Cuckolding as Class Warfare in Restoration Comedy

J. Douglas Canfield

An old black ram / Is tupping your white ewe. —Iago in Othello *I.i.89–90*

Therefore let no man be urgent to take the way homeward until after he has lain in bed with the wife of a Trojan to avenge Helen's longing to escape and her lamentations. —Nestor in Homer's Iliad *2.354–56*

Women are raped by Serbian soldiers in an organized and systematic way, as a planned crime to destroy a whole Muslim population, to destroy a society's cultural, traditional and religious integrity. —Drakulic, "The Rape of Bosnia-Herzegovina"

He tops upon her still, and she Receives it. —Contentious Surly, watching his wife courted before his face, in Leanerd's Rambling Justice *I.8*

*I*n war—from the mythical past of the Trojan War to today's all-too-real postcolonial conflicts—conquerors and conquered alike have attempted to demonstrate dominance over their rivals not just by fancied but by actual tupping of their opponents' women. I choose the verb *tupping* not only because of its Renaissance and Restoration reverberations, especially germane to my topic, but also because of its connotations of animal behavior and of the brutal sexual dominance implied by *topping,* or climbing on top. Slavenka Drakulic's poignant description of systematic rape in Bosnia-Herzegovina gets to the heart of the psychology: an attempt to destroy the cultural integrity of the enemy by contaminating the vessels of his patriarchal genealogy, by impregnating those vessels with his enemy's seed, the final cruel joke of hatred and revenge. Iago's taunting of Brabantio adds the dimension of fear of racial contamination, fear of the potency of the Other. Contentious Surly's agony is made especially torturous by his fear of class domination: he is a typical Restoration cit, who is portrayed as gracelessly impotent in the face of his wife's seduction by the Cavalier rake.

I am interested in pursuing this unpleasant topic because of the way it has been politely glossed over in histories of Restoration drama. Most notably, John Harrington Smith set the stage for the last half century's worth of criticism by delineating a subcategory of Restoration comedy "cynical comedy." He wanted to contrast plays in this group with those comedies that featured his chosen—and admired—trope of the gay couple. Smith points out that cuckolding is central to these comedies about "the gallant in the ascendant" (see Smith, chap. 4). He means gallants that are not paired with socially equal, equally witty women to form the gay couple, but his phrase glancingly though unintentionally alludes to the class warfare embedded in Restoration comedy—and ignored in its criticism. This warfare is imaged especially in the trope not just of cuckolding in general but of cit-cuckolding in particular, wherein representatives of the dominant class tup with impunity the women of the emergent middle class.

I do not use the metaphor of warfare loosely. I am thinking of Michel Foucault's inversion of the notion that war is just politics extended into the notion that politics is extended war (90–91). In words that seem to me applicable to the period after the restoration of the Stuarts and their continuing struggle for power, Foucault writes: "If it is true that political power puts an end to war, that it installs, or tries to install, the reign of peace in civil society, this by no means implies that it suspends the effects of war or neutralises the disequilibrium revealed in the final battle. The role of political power, on this hypothesis, is perpetually to re-inscribe this relation through a form of unspoken warfare; to re-inscribe it in social institutions, in economic inequalities, in language, in the bodies themselves of each and every one of us" (90). Restoration drama is one of the social institutions that continues the class warfare of midcentury England. Conflict in Restoration drama, as elsewhere in Restoration society, can be seen—at least in part—as an extension of the civil war between the old feudal class and the emergent bourgeoisie, or better, between the Court and the Town and their allies against the City of London and, occasionally, its allies among the country gentry.

I have previously examined ways in which the ideology of a restored Stuart hegemony was reinscribed in the Restoration rhymed heroic play, tragicomedy, and political tragedy of the decade 1679–89 (see Canfield, "Significance," "Ideology," and "Royalism's Last Dramatic Stand"). I should like now to argue that the conflict of those Restoration comedies featuring cit-cuckolding is related to the same class warfare, reinscribes the same ideology, and does so, in Foucault's terms, not only through *language* but through the *body-language* of stage performance and, indeed, through *bodies* themselves, where the perfect, potent bodies of Cavalier rakes dominate the imperfect, impotent bodies of cits, and where the bodies of women become the contested ground for class dominance and, ultimately, symbols of the contested land of England itself. However much wit these women are given, however much sexual energy of their own they display, in these wars between men they are merely counters.

Present in comedies from the early 1670s, this displaced warfare breaks out with an unprecedented aggressiveness in the rampant cit-cuckolding of Restoration comedy of the Exclusion Crisis. On the eve of England's last great dynastic struggle, the revolution called glorious by the winners, as the Exclusion Crisis came to a climax at Oxford, English comic playwrights turned cit-cuckolding into a particularly virulent example of the erotics of power. Edward Ravenscroft's *The London Cuckolds* was produced in November 1681, Aphra Behn's *The Roundheads; or, The Good Old Cause* in December, Thomas D'Urfey's *The Royalist* in January 1682, and John Crowne's *City Politiques,* scheduled for production in June 1682, was delayed by censorship until January 1683.[1] All four of these plays portray cits as silly, cowardly, impotent Whigs who meddle in politics; Cavaliers as handsome, witty, libertine, potent Tories who are worthy to dominate; and women as generally witty, attractive, sexually active, and naturally attracted to the dominant males. The Cavaliers tup their rivals' women, often in their faces, and force them to accept it. And this is all performed before an audience, as is now commonly recognized, that included cits, as if to rub in class dominance.

Ravenscroft's *London Cuckolds* is the least overtly political of these plays. But there is no mistaking the class warfare.[2] Three cits—Wise-acre, Doodle, and Dashwell—are cuckolded with impunity by three Cavaliers—Townly, Ramble, and Loveday. They are abetted by two witty, rebellious wives—Eugenia and Arabella—and by one ignorant country wife, Peggy. Arabella is prescient about Peggy's fate, for her husband will not succeed in keeping her ignorant: "[T]his is not an age for the multiplication of fools, in the female sex" (I.i; 451). Indeed, Ramble ends up instructing her in "the duty of a wife" (V.ii)—that is, satisfying a real (read Cavalier) man sexually and cuckolding her cit husband. When Arabella's cit husband leaves her for his business at the Exchange with no more than a kiss (a typical portrayal of cits as negligent of their women in favor of trade), she reveals that her unsatisfied sexual appetite has a class bias: "I have a month's mind to greater dainties, to feast in his absence upon lustier fare than a dull City husband" (I.i; 451), who is "without a sting" (III.i; 480). She prefers to cuckold him with Townly, but if chance throws Ramble in her lap, she will take him. They court in explicit, blasphemous bawdry:

> *RAMBLE.* I have both faith, hope and charity; faith to believe
> you dissemble, hope that you love me, and charity enough to
> supply your wants in your husband's absence. . . .
> *ARABELLA.* Take notice then, thou desperate resolute man, that
> I now go to my chamber, where I'll undress me, go into my bed,
> and if you dare to follow me, kiss or come to bed to me; if all the
> strength and passion a provoked woman has, can do't, I'll lay
> thee breathless and panting, and so maul thee, thou shalt ever
> be afraid to look a woman in the face.
> *RAMBLE.* Stay and hear me now: thou shalt no sooner be there
> but I'll be there; kiss you, hug you, tumble you, tumble your
> bed, tumble into your bed, down with you, and as often as I
> down with you be sure to give you the rising blow. [III.i; 481–82]

Arabella takes great delight in belittling her husband, by making him jump over a stool, for example (IV.iii; 517), and even greater delight in outwitting his injunction that she must answer every question put to her by a man with no. She manipulates the questioning in such a way as finally to get Townly into bed with her (V.i).

Eugenia proves equally witty—and equally voracious—as she takes Townly by mistake for Ramble, then tricks Dashwell not only into sitting in the garden, disguised as her and waiting for Loveday, while she and Loveday frolic in his bedroom, but even into taking a humiliating beating from Loveday when he is finished. That Dashwell deserves such treatment is manifest in this exchange between Ramble and Townly:

> *TOWNLY.* What is her husband?
> *RAMBLE.* A blockheaded City attorney; a trudging, drudging,
> cormudging, petitioning citizen, that with a little law and much
> knavery has got a great estate.
> *TOWNLY.* A petitioner! Cuckold the rogue for that very reason.
> [I.i; 454–55]

Here not just class but topical politics is evident: a petitioner is one who supported the Exclusion Bill. And Dashwell identifies himself further when he protests, "Cuckold the foreman of an *Ignoramus* Jury" (V.iii; 528)—that is, foreman of Shaftesbury's hung jury. So when Dashwell is dressed as a woman in the garden and called a "Cotquean" (V.v; 543)—that is, a man who does women's domestic chores—and when Loveday administers to him a flailing, he has himself been symbolically tupped by the dominant males. And it is no accident that twice in the play Ravenscroft refers to the king, once as Arabella playfully makes her husband jump over the stool—first "for the king" and then "for the queen" (IV.iii; 517)—and once, more explicitly, as Peggy, like Wycherley's country wife, naively protests to her husband that the "gentleman" (Ramble) who just courted her and kissed her hand in public "might be the king, they say he is a fine man" (II.iii; 474). This seemingly throwaway line, which alludes to Charles II's own sexual prowess, clearly associates the Cavaliers of the play with the Court party and gives a royal sanction, as it were, to their tupping their rivals' women. After all, Charles obviously flaunted his sexuality as a sign of potency, and potency was a sign of inherent class superiority, as well as—central to the Exclusion debate—inherent monarchical authority. Ravenscroft's epilogue might serve for all these cit-cuckolding plays, but especially those of the Exclusion Crisis: Ramble says,

> every cuckold is a cit.
> But what provoked the poet to this fury,
> Perhaps he's picqued at by the ignoramus jury,
> And therefore thus arraigns the noble City.
> No, there are many honest, loyal witty,
> And be it spoke to their eternal glories,
> There's not one cuckold amongst all the Tories.

We can cuckold you with impunity, but you cannot cuckold us, for we are the superior class—and therefore deserve to rule.

Two recent articles on Behn's *Roundheads*—one by Robert Markley and the other by Elizabeth Bennett Kubek—have thoroughly analyzed the sexual politics of that play.[3] Let me just say here that Behn's Cavaliers—tellingly referred to throughout as "Heroicks"—who have lost their estates to the likes of Ravenscroft's Dashwell, consider cuckolding Cromwell's generals, whose sexual as well as political ineptitude proves their lack of worth to dominate. The Cavaliers view the potential cuckolding as "an Act of honest Loyalty, so to revenge our Cause" (IV.i; 1:389), especially if Loveless can "cuckold the Ghost of old *Oliver*" by sleeping with Lady Lambert, Cromwell's former mistress (I.i; 1:349). General George Monck's taking of the City of London is appropriately described by cits as a rape, for he uprooted her gates and "lay her Legs open to the wide World, for every Knave to view her Nakedness" (V.iv; 1:420).[4] In other words, disloyal cits deserve to be cuckolded, and the City of London herself, for her infidelity, deserves to be raped into submission by the real men of

England, the Royalists. Here the body of woman is clearly a metonymy for the contested land, and rape is clearly both a literal and a metaphoric weapon in wars between men. The witty women themselves, as Kubek demonstrates, despite the fact that this play was written by a woman, are put back in their place—supine before real men.

Like Behn, D'Urfey sets *The Royalist* during the Interregnum and intends it—especially the first act, that ends in the title character's being stripped of his estate—as he says in the preface, as a "*Memento* of *past* or as a *Caveat* of *future* Mischiefs and Diabolical Practices" (sig. A2r; italics reversed). The danger posed by Roundhead republicans in the past—as by exclusionist Whigs in the present crisis—seems perhaps best epitomized in this stanza from a witty song sung by the loyal lieutenant Broom. Note how the political and the sexual are compounded:

> The Name of *Lord* shall be Abhorr'd,
>   For every Man's a Brother;
> What Reason then in Church or State
>   One Man should Rule another?
> When we have Pill'd and Plunder'd all,
>   And Levell'd each Degree,
> Wee'l make their plump young Daughters fall,
>   *And Hey then up go We.*
>   [IV.ii; 50. Italics reversed]

Not only will distinction be destroyed, but our women will be tupped and our genealogical eggs scrambled. The theme of leveling gets played out especially in the low-plot, low-class scenes, where Slouch and Copyhold, two tenants of the Cavalier Sir Charles Kinglove, come to London to exercise their heady sense of elevation, only to be jostled about by lords' pimps and pretentious footmen. Copyhold says, "If these doings last, woe be to all merry Meetings ifaith; why one knows not now who's the Landlord, nor who's the Tenant; which is the King, and which the Cobler" (III.ii; 26). They go on to argue that there is no refuge in the law, for the strongest control it. Might now makes right, for "the Head and Fountain of the Law"—that is, Charles I—"lyes a bleeding" (III.ii; 27). Ironically, class rape can be used to symbolize both Puritan leveling and "natural" aristocratic dominance. There is no real difference between class rape that goes low-high and class rape that goes high-low: both are acts of dominance, cloaked in whatever language of legitimacy, even religious.

D'Urfey focuses the high plot of the play on sexual warfare, on cit-cuckolding, ostensibly as revenge but really as naked power. The libertine Royalist Heartall—the two terms are virtually synonymous, for the surplus sexual energy of the Cavaliers is the sign of their potency and right to reign—first seduces the niece of the chairman of the Committee of Sequestrations, Sir Oliver Oldcut, then palms her off on the corrupt justice Sir Paul Eitherside. On their wedding night she makes Eitherside promise abstinence under pretense of keeping their marriage a secret from her uncle for the nonce, but at the same time she gives him the key to her chamber. Unable to restrain himself, the old lecher discovers his bride in bed asleep with her lover—onstage. Seizing Heartall's breeches, he plans to get her portion by law and turn her out of doors, but when he demands her portion from Oldcut, the latter reveals that she has no money. Meanwhile, Eitherside has publicly humiliated himself as a cuckold.

Because Oldcut sequesters his estate, Sir Charles Kinglove, the Royalist of the title, decides to take revenge by cuckolding him with his wife, Camilla, who like all the women in these plays is spontaneously attracted to the manly Cavalier. Camilla repeatedly portrays her husband as impotent and knows she "was design'd for nobler Fortune" (II.i; 11). She insists to Sir Charles that "though I am fetter'd to this tainted Limb, this Canker of the festring Common-wealth, yet I have Loyal blood within my veins" (III.iii; 35). They speak delightfully thus, breaking into a form of duet:

> *SIR CHARLES*. Thou must [have loyal blood], I know it.
> Thou soft lovely Creature. Those that have Wit like thee, must
> needs be Loyal.
> This Marry'd Lump, this, Husband, is thy shame:
> *CAMILLA*. My shame indeed, and Husband but in Name.
> And tho in Name I must his Wife appear.
> *SIR CHARLES*. And tho in Name thou must his Wife appear,
> Thou art the Mistress of a Cavalier.
>
> [ibid.]

As in *The Roundheads,* the latent loyalty within witty women in *The Royalist* is ostensibly a sign of the *naturalness* of Royalist supremacy. These women's wit is linked to their sexuality and shows their fitness for Cavalier "tupping." Since Marx's *German Ideology* we have known how to critique dominant systems that portray their foundations as natural and universal. But the real foundation here has to do more with what Nietzsche calls *virtù* in *The Genealogy of Morals*—the sheer male power of dominance. The loyalty of the submissive woman here is like the loyalty of the submissive land before power that succeeds in portraying itself as legitimate and natural.

Sir Charles and Camilla contrive to trick Oldcut out of two of his teeth, which are delivered to Sir Charles, and into patiently bearing fillips on his nose—both acts of symbolic castration. Most outrageously, they make him witness their embraces while he sits in a supposedly enchanted pear tree and comments thus on their "Carnal Copulation": "Now, who's that? 'dsheart the Colonel, and Kissing her, and she Clasping him. . . . what still cling'd? still lockt together? why Colonel, Goat, Stallion, how eagerly the strong-backt Dog gripes her?" (V.i; 56). The animal references underscore the aggression of such tupping—and undercut any rhetoric of legitimacy.

Typically, this play ends with the cits announcing their cuckoldry to the world—that is, to the audience. Addressing and taunting that audience in a way that implicates them in his rebellion, Captain Jonas, described in the dramatis personae as "A Seditious Rascal that disturbs the People with News and Lyes, to promote his own Interest," as he is led off to prison for consorting with a whore, says with heavy irony, "Therefore good people, what ever you think of me, I believe you to be good people; very good people; as good Subjects; as true to th'King and Kingly prerogative; as unwilling to Rebell and Mutiny; and as heartily Conscientious in your dealings as my self. And so farewell t'ye" (59). In the prologue D'Urfey has insulted the Whigs in his audience by saying only they would refuse an adulterous intrigue—implicitly because they lack Tory potency. At the end he forces them to watch their party humiliated sexually through the trope of synecdoche, cuckolded cits standing for the whole of that party and identified with regicide rebels.

On the other side of the political symbolism, aside from the central character, there are two important symbols for loyalty. At the opening of the play in the center of the stage is a royal oak fenced around that Sir Charles Kinglove apostrophizes as a symbol of legitimate Stuart hegemony. The oak was by this time a well-recognized symbol for the same, as it harbored Charles II after the battle of Worcester and allowed him to escape the regicide Roundheads. The other symbol is in a way related: Philipa, a rich heiress in love with Sir Charles but abandoned by him because her father became a traitor, is a character, like Wycherley's Fidelia, out of romance. She follows Sir Charles dressed as a man and surreptitiously defends her absent self as being not incompatible with Sir Charles's loyalty: "A Roundhead's Daughter might have got a Cavalier, that might have liv'd to take his Grandfather by the Beard" (I.i; 6). When Charles II in exile needs twenty thousand pounds posthaste, Philipa does not hesitate a minute to send it, and Sir Charles's union with her at the end represents the triumph of loyalty and the reunion of "Great *England's* Monarchy" (V.i; 63) with the body of its loyal land. Although Philipa is a romanticized heroine, she shows the same willingness—read loyalty—as do the city wives; loyalty is essentialized through this construction of female subjectivity, becoming the necessary subordinate partner for royalty.[5]

In Crowne's *City Politiques* class warfare rises closer to the surface than in any of these plays—so close to the surface that the play's production was delayed from spring 1682 to winter 1683. Though the locale is displaced to Naples, there is no doubt that we are in London, where city rebels defy the legitimate government, arm themselves, and speak sedition. Critics have attempted to identify several of the characters as representatives of specific individuals during the Exclusion Crisis, and there are some important resemblances, as between Doctor Sanchy and Titus Oates, the infamous perpetrator of the Popish Plot, and the Catholic Bricklayer and the "Protestant Joiner," Stephen College, one of the perjurers in the plot who was executed for treason. Several characters have traits of Shaftesbury; the Podesta has traits of Slingsby Bethel, one of the defiant Whig sheriffs of London during the crisis; the Viceroy in some sense could be seen to represent the duke of York; and both Cavaliers at points represent Buckingham and/or Rochester.

But it is important to see that these characters embody types as well, that Bartoline, for example, does not represent necessarily any particular Whig lawyer but the class of corrupt lawyers who would sell their opinions to the highest bidder, who are really Antinomians. And it is important to recognize such a portrayal as a salvo of political propaganda from Royalists who claim that theirs is the party of de jure power. When the Governor tells the Podesta that the Viceroy will not knight him until he proves himself, the Podesta threatens (behind his back, of course),

> Since he is so huffy and stormy I'll be a storm. . . . A whirlwind
> that shall rumble and roar over his head, tear open doors by day
> and by night, toss his friends out of their coaches and beds into
> jails; nor shall all the preachings and pulpit-charms of their priests
>
> Dispossess me or fright me in the least;
> A Whig's a devil that can cast out a priest.
> [I.ii.133–41]

Despite all of their own sanctimonious rhetoric, these Whigs are portrayed as religious hypocrites, defiant of the divine sanction that supposedly underwrites de jure rule and poised to wreak havoc on their country. Dr. Sanchy says of praying that "it is but a thing of form to please the people" (II.i.289), and the Bricklayer obtusely opines, "I care not a farthing for reason, law, nor Scripture if they side with the Tories. I prefer Whig nonsense before Tory reason" (IV.i.79–81). Indeed, the Whig claim to government is portrayed as de facto power. Concerning the question whether their cause is right, the Bricklayer and the Podesta have this telling exchange:

> *BRICKLAYER.* We have a hundred thousand men, and they are al-
> ways in the right. Set me in the head of such a general council,

and I'll be pope, the only infallible judge.
PODESTA. Ay, and have what forms of worship you will. When
a cannon's the preacher [pun intended], who dare shut up the con-
venticle? And nothing opens and divides a text like gunpowder.
[IV.i.396–401]

This battle over the right or power to govern is figured especially
in the play as a battle over estates, over land, because, although England
was in transition from a land-based to a trade-based political economy,
land remained the ultimate status symbol for both the threatened aristocracy and the emergent bourgeoisie. When Florio, the Cavalier disguised as
a reformed Puritan in order to have access to the Podesta's wife,
hypocritically pretends to be concerned for the misguided Tories and
prays, "Heaven turn these wicked men; I love their souls," the Bricklayer
responds with the rhetoric of power instead of religion, "Heaven turn 'em
out of the kingdom, for I love their lands" (IV.i.402–3). The Podesta allows
the reformed Florio, who is apparently dying of syphilis, to live in his
house and be nursed by his wife, Rosaura, out of greed for his "estate,"
which he hopes Florio will bequeath to her (II.i.434) and which the equally
greedy Bartoline hopes Florio will bequeath to his child-bride, Lucinda.
The Cavalier Artall remonstrates with his erstwhile witty companion Florio,
accusing him, as now one of the Whigs, of trying to "babble and scribble
us out of our estates" (I.i.127). Artall employs the metaphor of swallowing
estates whole (I.i.137), a metaphor elaborated on by Craffy, the Podesta's
son, whose rebellion against his father culminates in giving evidence
against him and his faction: "They are moderate drinkers o' wine, but will
carouse water abundantly; for they'll drink your rivers, fish and all, and put
your land into it for a toast, if you'll let 'em. And yet sometimes they have
very narrow swallows; they cannot down with a little church ceremony [as
in taking communion in the Anglican Church, according to the Test Act],
but they'll swallow church lands, hedges, and ditches" (V.iii.206–11).
The battle over landed estates itself gets figured as a battle over
women, over the wives of these seditious cits. Artall disguises himself as
Florio in order to seduce the wife of the lawyer who corrupts the whole
process of the transfer of property and who would cheat his fellow Whig
out of Florio's estate. The closing words of act IV are the Podesta's frantic
ravings about losing his "estate" because of his rebellious knavery
(IV.iii.168–69), and act V immediately opens with Artall's rhapsody over his
affair with Lucinda: "I am strangely taken with this sweet young creature;
'tis so pleasant to drink at such a fresh spring, which never brute defiled or
muddied" (V.i.1–3). On the surface, this is a hit at Bartoline's impotence, an
impotence that he acknowledges throughout the play and that he forces
the Podesta to acknowledge (see esp. II.i.384–87, where he calls wearing

breeches at their age an imposture, for they "prechend cho what yey ha' not"). But it also identifies women with the springs that run through the land. It is no accident that Bartoline, when he catches Artall and Lucinda in each other's arms, threatens to take away Artall's estate. When Artall protests he has too good a title, Bartoline boasts that he and his fellow Whig lawyers have infinite tricks to poke holes in titles and that the only title Artall will end up with is to "the jail," which will become his family seat (V.i.53–69). Artall responds by taking Lucinda under his wing and threatening Bartoline with the power that has always been symbolic of feudal hegemony, as well as of potent virility—the power of swords. He threatens to let into the country French swords (just what the Whigs always feared—and justly), and the threat is a clever ruse to draw Whig wrath onto Florio, for whom Bartoline still takes him. But it is also a revelation of the force that always lies behind supposed de jure power, despite his Royalist rhetoric: "I'll let in the enemy, and cut the throats of such rogues as you, who abuse your trade, and like so many padders make all people deliver their purse that ride in the road of justice. Better be ruled by the swords of gallant men than the mercenary tongues of such rascals as you are" (V.i.101–5).

Florio, a libertine whose scam is as outrageous as Horner's, delights in the prospect of being called the "———" of the Podesta's wife (I.i.10). The text is left blank for the actor or reader to fill in, but if the word were as mild as *seducer,* surely Crowne would have filled it in himself. Surely he invites us to supply a more aggressive word. In a speech by Florio, Crowne also makes the analogy between Rosaura's body and an estate explicit:

> I do not know
> But my fair love, like an o'er fertile field,
> May breed rank weeds if she be idly tilled [that is, by cits or their
> sons];
> Lest love for fools should in her bosom live,
> She shall have all the tillage I can give.
>
> [I.i.337–41]

When he finally seduces Rosaura, he proclaims triumphantly, "Then we may securely hoist sail for the haven of love. All the mud that barred it up we have conveyed away, and I will come ashore on these white cliffs, and plant my heart there forever" (V.ii.199–202). The "white cliffs" are not only her breasts and/or her mons veneris, but they are also the very White Cliffs of Dover. For the power struggle comically portrayed in these plays is ultimately over the control of Albion herself.

One of the subtler jokes in this play is the way in which these Cavaliers' pretended rhetoric of reformation echoes (as in Lee's *Princess of*

Cleve) Rochester's deathbed conversion. It is as if Crowne the Royalist wrenches Rochester's dead body back from the Whig moralizers who had temporarily triumphed over it. Rochester's libertinism, a function of aristocratic class superiority at the moment when its hegemony was being most seriously threatened, is hurled back in the teeth of the emergent bourgeoisie and its middle-class morality as a sign of the Stuarts' right to rule with impunity, not because of law or morality but because of sheer amoral power. Caught in flagrante delicto, Florio and Rosaura brazen it out at the end, turning Whig principles against the Podesta:

> *FLORIO.* Our [Whig] principles are: he is not to be regarded who has a right to govern, but he who can best serve the ends of government. I can better serve the ends of your lady than you can, so I lay claim to your lady.
> *ROSAURA.* And you have my consent.
> *FLORIO.* So, I have the voice of the subject too; then you are my wife and I'll keep you.
>
> [V.iii.179–85]

Of course, no real theory of contractual government is here being affirmed. Florio gets and keeps Rosaura by the felt power of class supremacy.

In the end the Whigs defeat themselves, appropriately, by their own hypocrisy, lack of loyalty among themselves, and their own false witnesses gone amok. But they are also defeated by Craffy's Oedipal rebellion against his father, a rebellion figured throughout the play as his incestuous desire for his father's wife. His story can be read as the anarchy that inevitably follows from Whig disrespect for the law. But it can also be read as an allegory of Monmouth's own Oedipal rebellion against his father. Of course, no father's wife was literally involved in that rebellion. But on the symbolic level, once again the body of woman can be seen as a figure for the land itself. If the king's bride is his loyal country (as figured throughout the period), then the confusion Craffy makes throughout this play between his father's wife and his father's estate enhances the possibility of an allegorical reading. Perhaps that possibility more than anything else resulted in the play's being banned temporarily.

The rhetoric at the end of Crowne's play is not that of the typical providential justice underwriting legitimate rule. It is the rhetoric of class. The Governor warns the rebels, whose power has now been quashed, "And so, gentlemen, henceforward be wise, leave off the new trade you have taken up of managing state affairs, and betake yourselves to the callings you were bred to and understand. Be honest; meddle not with other men's matters, especially with government; 'tis none of your right"

(V.iii.390–95).[6] Rights are thus functions of class, and the class superiority of England's aristocracy has been vigorously reasserted in these plays about cit-cuckolding.

Cit-cuckolding is finally a trope not just for class dominance, however. It is obviously a trope for gender dominance as well. The seduced women in these plays are figures for the contested land itself. They along with the estates are symbols for the power of the dominant class. But the women are also figures for real women, who unfortunately throughout human history have been tokens in power relations between men. When those relations break out into real, open warfare, women really get raped. Even in the displaced warfare of these plays, there is no real liberation for women. They may escape oppressive relationships with cits, but they still remain objects of exchange between men as men vie for control. Tupping your rivals' women, especially in their very faces, is a sign of class dominance, but it is always the men who are on top—of both the rivals and the women.

Notes

1. Dates are from *The London Stage,* checked against Hume. I omit consideration of Behn's *The False Count; or, A New Way to Play an Old Game,* apparently also produced in the fall of 1681, because it indeed is a "compromise-formation" (the term is from Rothstein and Kavenik) involving the legitimation of the middle class. Behn appears to have offered her audience an ending that embodies not class warfare but a truce. On the other hand, we do not know when she wrote either play, but if *The Roundheads* was written and performed subsequently, Behn may perhaps have despaired of truce in the light of what she and the Royalists would have considered Whig intransigence over the problem of succession and its attendant constitutional crisis. I also omit discussion of Behn's *City Heiress* (April 1682), partly because its politics is so well treated by Markley and partly because the play does not really feature cit-cuckolding as I am treating it here.

2. *Pace* Hume, who maintains that the play "is rollicking good fun with no ulterior point whatever" and denies that the play is political because it was performed annually on the Lord Mayor's Day for years (355). Hume's protégé, John Harwood, follows suit (87–88), despite flirting with a sociopolitical reading of the play along class lines, a reading he dismisses by baldly asserting that "no political or theological metaphors seem very probable constructs by which the play can be understood beyond its literal dimension" (97). By "literal dimension" he means that the play is simply a farce that delights in sex for sex's sake. With regard to audience response, the fact that the play was performed for the next century, especially on the Lord Mayor's Day for half of it, rather than denying the play's power relations seems to me to underscore the aggressive nature of performing such plays in the teeth of middle-class audiences, who during the Exclusion Crisis

apparently sat there and took it and even laughed and enjoyed it and perhaps even internalized it, like the cuckolded cits portrayed by Nokes and
Leigh. After 1688 Whigs could afford to indulge themselves; besides, an
audience always considers itself superior to objects of satire, even those of
their own class or group. Like Swift's tennis players, they deftly stroke the
ball into someone else's court.

In this and the other plays I treat, farce physically fills the stage
during most of them. In the light of all the slapstick action and especially
of the bodies of Nokes and Leigh, as they run around impotently protest-
ing cuckolding and class dominance, one is tempted to apply the theories
of Bakhtin, the concepts of the carnivalesque and the grotesque body, especially expounded in *Rabelais and His World*. But as a Marxist, Bakhtin
exalts and romanticizes the folk; he portrays folk humor as subversive of
official discourse. Here, it seems to me, the folk elements of farce and particularly the grotesque body serve to underwrite official discourse, to reaffirm hegemonic ideology. Bakhtin's essential (and essentializing) optimism
about the lower classes needs to be tempered by Foucault's insights into
the myriad ways state power can co-opt elements that might be potentially
radical but that can be brought into the service of the state. Moreover, that
which at first glance strikes a modern audience as subversive in these plays—
the cuckolding itself, subversive of patriarchal genealogical control—turns
out upon closer inspection to be actually reactionary, an aggressive reaffirmation of aristocratic hegemony at the very moment it is about to be
overthrown.

Finally, with regard to tropes of power beyond the literal, it is
hoped that this essay's analysis will convince the Humes and Harwoods,
Rothsteins and Kaveniks that Restoration comedy has profound political
meaning—not topical but structural, deeply ideological—even when it is
superficially meaningless (for Rothstein and Kavenik's treatment of *The London Cuckolds*, see 248–50).

3. The articles complement each other's political readings, but Kubek goes on
   to argue that women are put back in their places in the aristocratic order
   and disallowed any real feminist political liberation (cf. Harwood 97).

4. Cf. Behn's source in Tatham's *The Rump:* "Was ever such a Rape committed
   upon a poor She City before: Lay her legs open to the wide world, for every
   Rogue to peep in her Breech" (V.i; 58). The apprentice who speaks this
   line reveals both sympathy for the City and embarrassment at the country's
   shame. Behn's character, the essentially unsympathetic Joyner, reveals less
   of both. Despite the fact that Tatham's apprentice goes on to blame the Rump
   and not finally General Philagathus (read Monck) for the violation, the
   mood of Tatham's play is less aggressive than that of Behn's, perhaps because he could afford, in the spirit of the Restoration compromise, to be
   more benevolent. But the differences between these two plays—especially
   Behn's addition of the gay-couple motif into the relations between Cavalier heroes and Commonwealth women—underscore my main point
   about the particular aggressiveness of the sexuality in these Exclusion
   Crisis comedies.

5. Backscheider suggests that Sir Charles's union with Philipa also represents an appeal for healing the Cavalier-cit rift (256 n. 98). Perhaps, but the play is so stridently anti-cit that the union would seem to symbolize more probably dominance and submission.
6. Cf. Crowne's *Regulus* and my article on it.

Works Cited

Backscheider, Paula. *Spectacular Politics: Theatrical Power and Mass Culture in Early Modern England*. Baltimore: Johns Hopkins UP, 1993.

Bakhtin, Mikhail. *Rabelais and His World*. Trans. Hélène Iswolsky. 1968. Bloomington: Indiana UP, 1984.

Behn, Aphra. *The Works of Aphra Behn*. 6 vols. Ed. Montague Summers. London, 1915; New York: Benjamin Blom, 1967.

Canfield, J. Douglas. "The Ideology of Restoration Tragicomedy." *ELH* 51 (1984): 447–64.

———. "*Regulus* and *Cleomenes* and 1688: From Royalism to Self-Reliance." *English Culture at the End of the Seventeenth Century*. Ed. Robert P. Maccubbin and David F. Morrill. Special issue of *Eighteenth-Century Life*, n.s., 12.3 (Nov. 1988): 67–75.

———. "Royalism's Last Dramatic Stand: English Political Tragedy, 1679–89." *Studies in Philology* 82 (1985): 234–63.

———. "The Significance of the Restoration Rhymed Heroic Play." *Eighteenth-Century Studies* 13 (1979): 49–62.

Crowne, John. *City Politiques*. Ed. John Harold Wilson. Lincoln: U of Nebraska P, 1967.

Drakulic, Slavenka. "The Rape of Bosnia-Herzegovina." *Arizona Daily Star.* 16 Dec. 1992. A17.

D'Urfey, Thomas. *The Royalist*. London, 1682.

Foucault, Michel. *Power/Knowledge: Selected Interviews and Other Writings, 1972–1977*. Ed. Colin Gordon. Trans. Colin Gordon, Leo Marshall, John Mepham, and Kate Soper. New York: Pantheon, 1980.

Harwood, John T. *Critics, Values, and Restoration Comedy*. Carbondale: Southern Illinois UP, 1982.

Homer. *The Iliad*. Trans. Richmond Lattimore. 1951. Chicago: U of Chicago P, 1962.

Hume, Robert D. *The Development of English Drama in the Late Seventeenth Century*. Oxford: Clarendon, 1976.

Kubek, Elizabeth Bennett. " 'Night Mares of the Commonwealth': Royalist Passion and Female Ambition in Aphra Behn's *The Roundheads*." *Restoration* 17.2 (Fall 1993): 88–103.

[Leanerd, John.] *The Rambling Justice; or, The Jealous Husbands. With the Humours of Sir John Twiford*. London, 1678.

Markley, Robert. " 'Be Impudent, Be Saucy, Forward, Bold, Touzing, and Leud': The Politics of Masculine Sexuality and Feminine Desire in Behn's Tory Comedies." *Cultural Readings of Restoration and Eighteenth-Century Theater*. Ed. J. Douglas Canfield and Deborah C. Payne. Athens: U of Georgia P, 1995. 114–40.

Ravenscroft, Edward. *The London Cuckolds*. 1682. *Restoration Comedy*. Ed. A. Norman Jeffares. 4 vols. London: Folio, 1974. 2:435–551.

Rothstein, Eric, and Frances M. Kavenik. *The Designs of Carolean Comedy*. Carbondale: Southern Illinois UP, 1988.

Shakespeare, William. *The Riverside Shakespeare*. Ed. G. Blakemore Evans. Boston: Houghton Mifflin, 1974.

Smith, John Harrington. *The Gay Couple in Restoration Comedy*. Cambridge, Mass.: Harvard UP, 1948.

Tatham, J[ohn]. *The Rump; or, The Mirrour of the Late Times, a New Comedy*. The Second Impression, Newly corrected, with Additions. London, 1661.

Van Lennep, William, ed. *The London Stage, 1660–1800. Part 1: 1660–1700*. Carbondale: Southern Illinois UP, 1965.

Almahide Still Lives: Feminine Will and Identity in Dryden's *Conquest of Granada*

Katherine M. Quinsey

*J*ohn Dryden's play *The Conquest of Granada* does not immediately strike the mind as a feminist critique of male domination. Its main female characters embody the extremes of traditional myths of the good and evil of woman, and its hero's name was a byword for bombast on the Restoration stage well before the play's first appearance in print.[1] The play attempts an essentialist redefinition of patriarchy and kingship, opposing them to a shifting pattern of revolution and counterrevolution wherein the position of king and husband and father is shown to be untenable as exercised by word of law, and wherein the rhetoric of that authority is exposed as false, exploitable, and arbitrary. It thus creates a double-edged critique and affirmation of patriarchal power, exposing the falsity of certain social and political constructs while affirming a "natural" patriarchy. Within this debate, however, *The Conquest of Granada* focuses with remarkable precision on questions of feminine identity, contrasting the identity assigned through patriarchal constructions of woman to the identity achieved through the expression of female subjectivity and will.[2]

This feminine focus appears in the play's two-part structure, in which a deeply flawed and fractured patriarchy is replaced by a somewhat feminized paternalism. In the process female figures play dominant roles in restoring social and familial bonds, gender roles are explored and redefined, and concepts of identity and relationship are reestablished on a new basis. Indeed, the play is notable for the centrality given its female characters: leadership roles—though clearly qualified and limited—are given to almost all its women.[3] This phenomenon may reflect in part the appeal of heroic plays to a female audience, as well as the female-centered nature of the romance-chivalric tradition behind them (Righter

Frontispiece to *The Rehearsal* (1714 edition), in *The Dramatick Works of his Grace George Villiers, late Duke of Buckingham* (1715), vol. 2, 32. By permission of the Department of Special Collections, Stanford University Libraries.

138–40). Nevertheless, both within itself and in its relation to its sources and to contemporary discourse, theatrical and otherwise, *The Conquest of Granada* explores with unusual specificity the issue of female subjectivity and the imposition of male constructions and power upon it. Dryden's play exploits and adapts the romance conventions of his sources, George de Scudéry's *Almahide* and Perez de Hita's *Los guerras civiles de Granada,* in various ways, in order to tighten the play's focus on the oppositions and ironies inherent in the female position. For example, to the (traditional) story of the sultana's trial for adultery Dryden adds the story of Almanzor's attempted seduction and Zulema's attempted rape, drawing the different forms of patriarchal domination into a culminating point. He also develops the character of Almahide far more fully (cf. Roper 414), making her inner and outer conflicts a locus for these issues.[4] Moreover, he strips the conventions of romance throughout, blurring metaphorical power with literal power, both political and psychological.

In engaging the issue of feminine identity and subjectivity within patriarchal structures, this play also diverges from the representation of the romance heroine on the contemporary heroic stage. The idealized heroines of Thomas Killigrew and William Davenant, even if they transcend gender boundaries in some respects—fighting or leading men in battles, for example—are firmly located in the ideal of woman as the embodiment of virtue.[5] Their minds and wills are constructed in accordance with patriarchal conventions: in Davenant's *Siege of Rhodes,* for example, Ianthe's sole passion is her wifely virtue, and she carries this even to the extent of blaming herself for resenting her husband's jealousy (25). Moreover, *The Conquest of Granada* represents a significant departure in the representation of women in Dryden's own opus, particularly in the heroic plays. It has recently been argued that the virtuous heroines of Dryden's heroic dramas are self-asserting reiterations of a deeply conservative patriarchal ideology (Evans 16–17); in this essay I will contend that *Tyrannick Love* strains that ideal to its limits and that *The Conquest of Granada* diverges significantly from that pattern in representing female subjectivity much more fully in resistance to such an ideology.[6]

The female characters whose careers illustrate most dynamically these questions of feminine independence, will, and identity are Lyndaraxa and Almahide.[7] These two appear to embody the two extremes of the traditional masculinist myth of woman: Lyndaraxa as the feminine expression of Machiavellian political will and overweening individualism, and Almahide as the pattern of sacrificial female virtue.[8] Nonetheless, although both characters affirm patriarchal values and speak its language, they turn patriarchy against itself, challenging it from within. Furthermore, it is not the domineering Lyndaraxa who affirms feminine subjectivity more positively but rather the good wife Almahide. The energy of Almahide's characterization is sustained through most of the play by the conflict between her assertions of her own will and identity and the various impositions placed upon her by patriarchal society. Her own attempts to construct herself according to marital convention expose the inadequacy of those conventions, ending in her near destruction; by force of that realization, she separates herself from her patriarchally assigned role and from all male expectations, to declare her own identity. At the end, however, when a new, feminized patriarchal order is established and conflicts appear to be resolved, Almahide is neutralized; both her desire for Almanzor and her resolute assertion of her autonomy retreat into the negating convention of an authority that disposes of her as an object without a will of her own. Her dramatic career thus raises certain unanswered questions about feminine will and identity and their relation to social order.

Lyndaraxa appears to personify the independent female will, conventionally presented as villainous. She is imbued with the traditionally negative characteristics attributed to female dominance and the female will: she is ruthless, devouring, incapable of love, moved only by the lust for power. Parallels between Lyndaraxa and Almanzor have been noted (Hughes 91–101; King 73–75; Alssid 217), and Lyndaraxa appears to illustrate the misogynist commonplace that certain heroic virtues in the male become distorted into villainy and moral inversion in the female. The antifeminist slant of this characterization is unsettled, however, by her overt exploitation of the prescribed image and role of woman. In a patriarchal society, the height of feminine ambition is to be the consort of a king, her identity defined by his; Lyndaraxa turns that on its head by defining herself as a king's consort independent of an actual marriage. She will be a queen, let Fortune but name the man. She defines the role of queen as a position of complete self-sufficiency: a queen is one who lives "without controul" and whose happiness is hers alone (pt. 1, II.i.146–50). Ultimately, when marital conventions fail her, she takes her own action, to become a queen without a consort, a status achieved on the basis of her own political and military leadership, however traitorous. Although at this culmination of her power the play erases her almost immediately, as a kind of horrific monstrosity, her exaltation occurs in a general context of praise of women's leadership in battle (2.V.iii.164–71, 230–35), and she is murdered not as a faithless mistress but as a traitor to her country.

More subtly, throughout the play Lyndaraxa's rhetoric and self-description consistently parody and utilize traditional images of women, exposing them as emblems of falsity. In an early scene she and Almahide are contrasted in their response to the noise of Abdalla's rebellion. Almahide is struck within herself, affirming a unity of body and spirit—

"The noise, my Soul does through my Sences wound" (1.III.i.251)—
whereas Lyndaraxa appropriates conventional feminine images, picturing
herself as both an iconographic abstraction and a prize of war:

> like his better Fortune I'le appear:
> With open Arms, loose Vayle, and flowing Hair,
> Just flying forward from my rowling Sphere.
> My Smiles shall make *Abdalla* more than Man;
> Let him look up and perish, if he can.
>
> [1.III.i.265–69]

Later, when pressed for moral consistency—a promise to Abdalla—
Lyndaraxa retreats into the antifeminist commonplace that women are
incapable of consequential reasoning and thus lack a rational and
conscious center:

> I know not what my future thoughts, will be:
> Poor women's thoughts are all *Extempore.*
> Wise men, indeed,
> Before had a long chain of thoughts produce;
> But ours are only for our present use.
>
> [1.IV.ii.179–83]

The falsity of this claim is ironically underlined by Abdalla's awareness
that, on the contrary, she has a very clear agenda: "Those thoughts you
will not know, too well declare / You mean to waite the final doom of
Warr" (1.IV.ii.184–85). Thus, although Lyndaraxa is a thoroughly conventionalized figure of the "heartless Fair" who destroys men in her will
to dominate, her embodiment of these traditionally assigned evils of female ambition is subverted by the insistence that conventional images of
women are false and arbitrary.

In a related pattern, Lyndaraxa explodes and exploits romance
convention throughout, by blurring or eliminating the distinction between
metaphor and literal sense; the absolute rule of the mistress is, for
Lyndaraxa, identifiable with the political and military rule of a queen. She
consistently utilizes the language of dalliance to dupe lovers who are
themselves thoroughly aware of the deception; yet the convention becomes exposed by being made literal—it is both contrasted to and has a
powerful effect on real human feelings. The cruelty lamented by Abdelmelech is not the conventional cruelty of the chaste mistress but literal mental
cruelty, evinced by his literal tears.[9] Lyndaraxa's power is real, not illusory;
the romance conventions of *bienséance,* of the power of the mistress and
the humble service of her knights, become transplanted to what Derek

Hughes terms a "Hobbesian jungle" (109), where power is the fundamental principle. One of the more notable examples of this combined exploitation and deconstruction of conventional amatory language is Lyndaraxa's victory over Abdelmelech when he comes to claim the fort she has been defending. Lyndaraxa takes a literal war engagement—her defense of the fort and Abdelmelech's capture of it—and casts it into the metaphor of love-play, blurring the distinction between her military action and her plays on lovers' hearts:

> She who is lov'd must little Letts create;
> But you bold Lovers are to force your Fate.
> This force you us'd my Maiden blush will save;
> You seem'd to take what secretly I gave.
>
> [2.II.ii.49–52]

The conventions of the romance novel—here, the salon-type debate on the nature of love, beauty, and friendship (Schweitzer, *Scudéry's "Almahide"* 112–15)—masks a power game in which Lyndaraxa easily manipulates her lover. And the game is played with men's lives:

> *LYNDARAXA.* Reverse your orders, and our
> Sentence give; My soldiers shall not from my Beauty live.
> *ABDELMELECH.* Then, from our Friendship they their lives shall gain.
>
> [2.II.ii.69–71]

This entire scene is conducted in joint awareness not only of Lyndaraxa's falsity but also of the falsity of the metaphors; it is entirely self-reflexive and self-parodying. Ultimately the metaphors divide: Lyndaraxa both forces Abdelmelech to admit his love for her and succeeds in playing for time so that Abdalla's troops can rescue the fort; Abdelmelech ends the scene by stripping the metaphor, dividing love-play from war absolutely, while turning it into literal assault. "Though not thy fort, thy person shall be mine" (2.II.ii.135).

In spite of what seems to be her aggressive individualism, however, Lyndaraxa's drive does not affirm feminine subjectivity or independence of identity and will. Although she plays on the elusiveness of female identity, she never affirms its independence or existence, and most of her assertions are patently false, mere techniques of manipulation. Her ambition seems rather to be predicated on external social forms that deny any inner identity: any man will do as long as he is a king. Thus both men and women under Lyndaraxa's external imposition of patriarchy become mere social forms whose substance is meaningless. Her climactic encounter with Almanzor in act III, scene iii, of Part 2 juxtaposes two opposing definitions of love and of humanity: in Almanzor's definition, "My Love's my Soul," inseparable from identity; in Lyndaraxa's, identity and desire do not exist—" 'tis Inclination all"—and Almahide is not a person but a name that Almanzor can apply to any female who will accommodate his sexual urges. Indeed, Lyndaraxa herself appears to lack any kind of subjective center. She speaks in the sort of cliché allotted to the stock overreaching villain: "O, how unequally in me were joynd / A creeping fortune, with a soaring mind!" (2.III.ii.27–28). Her passions and desires are mere reflections of outward events:

> For I my self scarce my own thoughts can ghess,
> So much I find 'em varied by success.
> As in some wether-glass my Love I hold. . .
> [1.IV.ii.3–5]

She embodies a satire of feminine inconstancy carried to the furthest extreme of the assumption: there is nothing inside. In the particular nature of her villainy, then, Lyndaraxa embodies in herself a critique of patriarchal constructions of woman, raising the question of the relation of such social constructs to inner identity.

The relation of feminine will and identity to patriarchal conventions is most searchingly explored, however, in the career of Almahide. Almahide consistently affirms her own will, her own identity, and her own subjectivity in response to her lover, her father, and her husband. This self-assertion is equally evident in her response to Almanzor's passion and in her thoroughgoing attempt to fulfill of the role of the virtuous wife and dutiful daughter. Hughes argues that Almahide is a flawed and deluded character, one whose platonic-romantic and marital ideals are shown to be insubstantial and inadequate for dealing with human passions, even her own (103–14). These assertions of virtue, however, are also part of her attempt to determine and define her own identity, paradoxically, by asserting her independence from the impositions of male constructions and male desires. In this she departs notably from the pattern of virtuous wives elsewhere in Dryden's heroic drama, as outlined by David Evans, who argues that Dryden's heroically virtuous women are the moral exemplars of a deeply conservative patriarchal ideology; they assert the interdependence of familial and social order, as Dryden defines their public virtue through the "private greatness" of wifely submission (Evans 16–17). Evans does not deal extensively with Almahide and the *Conquest*—indeed, he refers to Almahide, erroneously, as "the most normative of Dryden's heroines" (17), without mentioning her eventual rejection of her role as Boabdelin's wife—and thus he ignores the significant changes in the representation of this type of heroine over the corpus of Dryden's plays.

In *Tyrannick Love* Berenice strains the representation of wifely virtue to its limits, applying the abstract concept so strictly as to push it to logical extremes, putting her lover in danger of death in order to uphold the authority of a preposterous tyrant who seriously problematizes the monarchic as well as the marital ideal. Berenice completely submerges her identity in wifehood—she is no longer "Berenice" but "the Wife of *Maximin*" (II.i.16–18; cf. Evans 14)—exposing a badly fractured and questionable subjectivity that expresses itself in parodic pseudo-platonic fantasies (e.g. III.i.312–28) that were easy meat for the creators of *The Rehearsal*. Almahide is obviously a far more fully realized character, who is given complex and witty speeches and a central role in the play's argument. More important, she also embodies a far more dynamic and questioning representation of the concept of wifely virtue, one that focuses specifically on the relation of female subjectivity to an externally determined patriarchal role and identity. The play's action is structured by a process whereby Almahide attempts to live by the patriarchal code, even to the extent of constructing her own mind and heart in accordance with its demands, only to find this choice both a logical and a moral impossibility. For Almahide, the observance of paternally prescribed conventions becomes in itself an assertion of her own will and identity; and whereas Berenice succeeds only in pushing those conventions to ludicrous and destructive extremes, Almahide ultimately separates herself from them, to declare an independent identity by her own name, in words that almost exactly invert those of Berenice. Like Almanzor, then, she embodies an essentialist critique of external laws of patriarchy, but as a woman she presents a challenge not easily answered, and at the end of the play her reabsorption into a redefined paternalism proves difficult.[10]

In her absolute observance of the laws of daughterhood and wifehood, Almahide exposes the inadequacy, inconsistency, and falsity of the patriarchal model, replacing the traditional idea of female "virtue"— usually negatively defined as chastity—with an older sense of Stoic *virtus,* or inherent moral power and integrity. When her father urges that she must be "taught, by force," to know happiness in marriage, she speaks from within the claim of patrilineal succession to affirm her own identity and will:

> To force me, Sir, is much unworthy you;
> And, when you would, impossible to do.
> If force could bend me, you might think with shame,
> That I debas'd the blood from whence I came.
>
> [1.V.i.328–31]

Note that she insists here on her own paternally prescribed identity as a seed of patrilineal stock, not as a mere vessel of transmission. Her subsequent submergence of her identity and desires in those of her father and her husband paradoxically affirms her own moral independence and integrity, in response both to the imperious possessiveness of passionate love and to the legalized subjugation hallowed by marriage and kingship: "[K]now, that when my person I resign'd, / I was too noble not to give my mind" (2.I.ii.148–49). More tellingly and most obviously, her complete fulfillment of the laws of wifely submission overtly dramatizes the no-win situation implicit in the laws of marital authority. She embodies perfectly both the ideal and intent of the patriarchal wife and, in doing so, shows up that ideal as inadequate and false:

> But, your Command I prize above my life:
> 'Tis sacred to a Subject and a Wife.
>
> . . . .
>
> Grant that I did th'unjust injunction lay,
> You should have lov'd me more then to obey.
> [2.I.ii.172–73, 182–83]

In the scene in which she denies to Almanzor that Boabdelin has been unkind to her, describing his kindness in extravagant metaphors, Boabdelin's ironic comment, "O goodness counterfeited to the life! / O the well acted vertue of a wife" (2.III.i.78–79), touches on a central truth. The virtue is indeed acted. It cannot be otherwise, and it finds its vindication only in Almahide's own independent will, as she stated it earlier: "Yes; for my Love I will, by Vertue, square; / My Heart's not mine; but all my Actions are" (2.I.ii.219–20).

This pattern reaches its inescapable conclusion in Almahide's near rape, arraignment for adultery, and subsequent trial by combat. Here is the quintessence of the patriarchal subjugation of woman, in which the woman herself is silenced, on trial as an impure vessel for the royal seed, to be "proved" innocent or guilty by arbitrary male action. In this case, however, it appears as the logical culmination of the no-win pattern, highlighting its fundamental injustice and artificiality. The contrived improbability of the situation provides its own critique. This critique is reinforced structurally by the assault scene immediately preceding the trial (2.IV.iii). This scene raises questions through the obvious parallels between Almanzor's intentions and Zulema's, which frame the seduction argument between Almanzor and Almahide with the stark exposé of the Hobbesian power base under social and sexual convention, and with the stripping of the romantic language of courtship into a chilling reminder of the social reality of female silence and male violence: "Perhaps my

Courtship will not be in vain: / At least few women will of force complain"
(2.IV.iii.25–26). Almahide's climactic refusal of Almanzor, presented as a
Stoic feminist victory over both her own passions and an importunate man,
is framed, even encased, by the forces of manipulation and male desire
imposed upon it. Her honor, so powerfully asserted in this dialogue, is
erased immediately afterward in the sudden assault. In becoming the
ravished or near-ravished woman of contemporary tragedies and tragicomedies—"*Enter* Almahide; *schrieking: her hair loose*"—Almahide is
turned from a self-asserting subject into an object, both of villainous male
desire and of the audience's prurient interests. Her honor is also negated in
the trumpeted claims of both Boabdelin and Almanzor, who are fighting
not for her honor but for their own:

> *BOABDELIN.* O proud, ingrateful, faithless, womankind!
> How chang'd, and what a Monster am I made!
> My Love, my Honour, ruin'd and betray'd!
> *ALMANZOR.* Your Love and Honour! mine are ruin'd worse:
> Furies and Hell what right have you to curse?
> Dull Husband as you are,—
> What can your Love, or what your Honour be?
> I am her Lover, and she's false to me.
>
> [2.IV.iii.362–69]

Their voices echo one another, just as Almanzor's libertine language and
intent in the attempted seduction echo and anticipate Zulema's. Thus
Almanzor is linked here with both figures of abusive male power, the
rapist and the jealous husband.[11]

Almahide is not permitted to speak again until she is cleared in the
same arbitrary way practiced here by Boabdelin and Almanzor—male
vaunting and military prowess—and by Zulema's confession—a man's
word. It is only at this point that she can invoke the common laws of
human justice and decency:

> Could you, denying what our Laws afford
> The meanest subject, on a Traytors word,
> Unheard, condemn, and suffer me to goe
> To death . . . ?
>
> [2.V.ii.139–42]

Here Almahide anticipates the feminist argument that male domination
denies women the laws of ordinary human justice. It is notable that here
too Almahide breaks the traditional injunction of wifely silence and insists
on her right to speak and be heard: "[F]or I must speak" (2.V.ii.134). In-

deed, she sees that right of speech and self-presentation as fundamental to the laws of justice for women. (In her speech she tells the story of her marriage to Boabdelin, rewriting the events of the play from the wife's perspective. It is the speech she might have given in her defense had she been permitted to speak earlier.) Here, specifically, the laws of marriage decree the woman guilty until proven innocent; it is clear that such a practice belongs in a disordered world where "Heav'n is not Heav'n; nor are there Deities" (Abdelmelech, 2.V.i.15). What is curious is that although the scene thus allows an alternate humane justice—indeed, it implicitly equates humane with feminist—it still contains Almahide within the arbitrary male construct implied by the trial. She is vindicated not by her own honor or by recognized justice but by arbitrary action, even that of a villain; Zulema's word, evidently, carries more weight with both Almanzor and Boabdelin than the word of Almahide herself. Since her honor has presumably been vindicated already for the audience by her own speech and action, the effect of containment here is marked. Dramatic irony makes the feminist point—or at least engages the audience to consider it.

The trial also culminates the ongoing question and assertion of Almahide's inner identity, which is explored and developed through the play, mainly in contrast to the constructs men attempt to impose upon it. Even her initial encounter with Almanzor, and the shock of realizing her own passion for him, elicit an assertion of the continuity and independence of her selfhood as distinct from his.

> Your passion, like a fright suspends my pain:
> It meets, 'ore-powr's, and bears mine back again.
> But, as when tydes against the Current flow,
> The Native stream runs its own course below:
> So, though your griefs possess the upper part,
> My own have deeper Channels in my heart.
> [1.III.i.411–16]

In response to Almanzor's attempts to know her full mind concerning him, Almahide holds herself aloof and sovereign, seeing his desire as invasive: "Why do you thus my secret thoughts pursue, / Which known, hurt me, and cannot profit you?" (1.IV.ii.436–39). It is notable that this entire debate centers on the question of her freedom; Almanzor's love is compared with the possessiveness of a pirate—he uses metaphors of plunder and purchase, reiterating patriarchal concepts of Almahide as a commodity—and this in response to her direct question, which gets straight to the point: "Once more, *Almanzor*, tell me, am I free?" (1.IV.ii.399). Her defiance of her father locates the independence of her identity within its elusiveness and softness, actually exploiting masculinist stereotyping to assert her own independence from male power:

> My soul is soft; which you may gently lay
> In your loose palm; but when tis prest to stay,
> Like water it deludes your grasp, and slips away.
>   [1.V.i.332–34]

Boabdelin's torment stems mainly from his inability to know and thus possess Almahide's inner nature: "O Heav'n, were she but mine, or mine alone! / Ah, why are not the Hearts of Women known?" (2.III.i.37–38). All he can possess is the social form of an utterly chaste and obedient wife. He wants her love, that is, to control and possess her desire; he gets it, couched in phrases of perfect duty, a form he finds unacceptable.

Almanzor is equally guilty of imposing an external construct of expectation on Almahide's self. Immediately before the debate on Almahide's freedom, in an argument between Almanzor and Zulema over the status of Almahide as a prize of war, Zulema describes her implicit objectification in its most brutally reductive terms:

> If you will free your part of her you may;
> But, sir, I love not your Romantique way;
> Dream on; enjoy her Soul; and set that free;
> I'me pleas'd her person should be left for me.
>   [1.III.i.487–90]

This proposal completely obliterates any female subjectivity and exposes male objectification of the female as an assault on identity in one of its most traditional formulations, that is, as the union of body and soul. It fragments, even kills, the female self. Yet Almanzor is drawn into this way of thinking; Zulema's challenge to him here will be taken up in his subsequent debates with Almahide, most notably in his attempted seduction, when he tries to persuade her to separate her body from her rational soul, "dull Reason" and the "Maximes of the Day" (2.IV.iii.215, 196). In that scene Almanzor's customary heroic hyperbole is disturbingly replaced by conventional libertine jargon straight from the comic stage, a jargon that both erases and constructs female sexual desire and that exposes his complete failure to understand the independent selfhood on which she insists. He twists her admission of love for him into the commonplace of "half-yielding" generally used to excuse rape and seduction, and he gives her beauty the standard misogynist epithet "killing fair," also frequently used to excuse acts of aggression by implying that the female's beauty has given her the upper hand in a power struggle, for which she deserves whatever blows she gets.[12]

Almanzor's inability to possess or understand Almahide's inner self culminates immediately after this scene, in which his shocking and seemingly incredible naïveté in immediately believing her guilt exposes his complete inability to grasp who she is. It also seriously damages the credibility of his earlier mythologizing. Indeed, it can be argued that his attempted seduction leads naturally into his belief in her falsehood, for he has already constructed her as a transferable sexual object.

The debates between Almanzor and Almahide bear a superficial resemblance to those between Maximin and Catherine in *Tyrannick Love,* as she allies thought and reason with heroic honor governed by Stoic rational principles and a will committed to them. Unlike Catherine, however, Almahide is emphatically represented as having sexual desire and the ability to love passionately; this is no simple opposition between male appetite and female virtue. Furthermore, Almahide's sexuality and desires are central to her identity; her admission of her passion for Almanzor coexists with her assertion of her own feeling and identity as distinct from his. Throughout the play Almahide's sexual nature is portrayed in relation to the various ways in which patriarchal structures and discourse contain, constrain, and construct female sexuality. Marital conventions attempt to negate it as obedience or contain it as love given only as bidden by the husband—a distinction clearly outlined by Almahide when she first looks within and admits her love for Almanzor: "How blest was I before this fatal day! / When all I knew of love, was to obey!" (1.V.i.367–68).

Conversely, libertinism, although it supposedly celebrates a freer expression of sexuality, is merely another expression of the same male-centered authoritarian structure, based on the Hobbesian power principles of Zulema, which contains and constructs female sexuality even more completely than does marital convention. Libertinism is associated with Almahide from the beginning, not only in her casting as the distinctly unvirtuous Nell Gwyn but also from her first contribution to the drama, in the Zambra song performed to encourage peace and to celebrate her impending nuptials (1.III.i.198–232). The song is a scorned lover's account of how a dream of his loved one causes him to have a nocturnal emission and thus gives him what she will not. Not only does this song reduce love to the most basic satisfaction of (male) physical needs, but it also constructs and then eradicates female subjectivity. As usual, no does not mean no—"She bid me not believe her, with a smile"—and the central act itself seems to be more than half a rape:

> Then dye, said I. She still deny'd:
> And, is it thus, thus, thus she cry'd
> You use a harmless Maid? And so she dy'd!

The song ends by eradicating the female will altogether: "You must ease my pain" whether you will or no, through the power of my fantasy. This song establishes the theme of the imposition of male passion on female subjectivity, to be associated with Almahide throughout. In its themes of erotic fantasy, the imposition of male desire, and female death, it also anticipates directly Almanzor's attempted seduction, Zulema's attempted rape, and the linking of both acts with Almahide's death—her threatened suicide and execution.

Although the virtuous and desiring heroine is frequently a construct, or fantasy, of that same patriarchal ideology, Almahide's passionate love resists these constructions. It is associated with her integrity and her identity; the fact that she expresses (and examines) it verbally gives her a subjectivity not usually allotted to chaste heroines who are the prizes of noble action. Her victories over Almanzor's desire are equally victories over her own; her female desire is essential to her feminine "virtue"—a substantial and active virtue not to be confused with passive obedience and negation of desire. It confers a sense of self and independence, rather than conformity to male expectations. Indeed, it defeats male expectations. Certainly Almahide herself attempts to construct her own subjectivity and passion in accordance with patriarchal convention: "But know, that when my person I resign'd, / I was too noble not to give my mind" (2.I.ii.148–49). She does this, however, in order to assert her own sense of self. Here, echoing and inverting the language of Zulema, she declares the unity of her mind and body in an effort to resist the same fragmentation he exposes so ruthlessly. Almost immediately after this declaration, however, Almahide shows her awareness of the impossibility of achieving such a self-unity within patriarchal convention, as she explores her own subjectivity and realizes to herself its elusiveness:

> Yet, for *Almanzor* I in secret mourn!
> Can Vertue, then admit of his return?
> Yes; for my Love I will, by Vertue, square;
> My Heart's not mine; but all my Actions are.
> · · · · · · · · · · · · · ·
> What will he think is in my Message meant?
> I scarcely understand my own intent:
> But Silk-worm-like, so long within have wrought,
> That I am lost in my own Webb of thought.
> [2.I.ii.217–20, 223–26]

The speech moves through a pattern of resolve and question, ending in irresolution; it epitomizes the conflict between public identity and private self, showing with unusual vividness the confusion found in seeking identity within.[13] Although throughout the play Almahide attempts to contain and construct her own desire as that of the virtuous wife, the patriarchal system refuses to recognize her efforts—a failure dramatically underlined by her near rape, arraignment, and near execution for the very crime she would avoid, as all the most oppressive aspects of paternalism converge following her climactic renunciation of Almanzor. It is only when she realizes how completely this system has let her down—"[My chastity] has betray'd me to this publick shame: / And vertue, which I serv'd, is but a name" (2.V.ii.7–8)—that she is able to separate her own desire and self from the role it dictates.

Almahide's declaration of independence, once she is vindicated by combat and confession, appears to be entirely conventional: she retreats to one of the usual fates of chaste women whose virtue has been somehow tarnished—the self-silencing and self-negation of the cloister. Yet this act in itself is political and affirmative. In fact, it is her culminating assertion of her own identity as distinct from the roles imposed upon it by men. She speaks as herself, not as submissive wife or virtuous virgin, clearly distinguishing her own self from the role defined by a male society: "Though *Almahide* still lives, your wife is dead" (2.V.ii.150). The love for Boabdelin that dies with her role as wife is "a love [as] pure and true" as an abstract ideal (151). In killing it she finally separates her own feeling and identity from an externally defined role. Her renunciation of both Boabdelin and Almanzor is not so much self-negation as an attempt to free herself from the expectations of possessive male desire in the only way open to her.[14] Conversely, her farewell to Almanzor asserts her own desire with remarkable frankness, both revealing the infinite possibilities available through it and reiterating the restrictions placed upon it. Her heart is "boundless," not subject to limitations any more than Almanzor's is, except those set by herself; but the boundless heart cannot function within the rules of the love and marriage game and so must give over play.

> Then, since you needs will all my weakness know,
> I love you; and so well, that you must goe:
> I am much oblig'd; and have withal,
> A Heart so boundless and so prodigal,
> I dare not trust my self or you, to stay,
> But, like frank gamesters, must forswear the play.
>   [2.V.iii.45–50]

After this climactic affirmation of feminine desire and selfhood, there is a sense of disjunction, as Almahide is reabsorbed into a renewed patriarchal order, retreating into a highly conventional rhetoric of widowed modesty—her last speech in the play, accepting Almanzor from Isabella, consists of nothing but obedience—and losing the name by which she had affirmed her identity. Possibly, having explored dramatically the ideal of virtuous womanhood, having found it to be self-possessing and predicated on a sense of moral independence, and having found that it deeply challenges paternalistic assumptions and structures, Dryden finds the discovery unsettling. He thus attempts to integrate the feminine ideal into a milder and somewhat feminized patriarchal order. The possibilities raised by Almahide might explain some of the divergence in audience response to *The Conquest of Granada*. Although mocked for its bombast by the male playwrights of *The Rehearsal*—and thereafter by those men who have shaped the literary curriculum—most of whom focus on the figure of Almanzor, the play was admired by a female spectator for its representation of ideal virtues in both sexes. She wrote that "love is made so pure, and valor so nice, that one would imagine it designed for an Vtopia rather than our Stage. I do not quarrell with the Poet, but admire one borne in the decline of morality should be able to feign such exact virtue" (Mrs. Percy Evelyn to Dr. Bohun, in Evelyn 742–43). In its uneasy balance of heroic affirmation and parodic deflation, the play evidently reaches through to conflicting assumptions about human nature and the basis of society. The figure of Almahide presents questions and potentialities that challenge even more fundamental assumptions, and these are left unanswered.

Notes

1. See Roper 412. Roper's headnote to *The Conquest of Granada* in Dryden's *Works* provides a valuable critical and historical discussion.
2. For discussion of the interaction of differing views of patriarchy in *The Conquest of Granada,* see Barbeau; Kropf, "Political Theory" and "Patriarchal Theory"; and Fisher 422–23. Feminist issues in this play, on the other hand, are usually notable for their absence in critical discussion. Alssid, for example, analyzes the centrality of Almahide's education of Almanzor (201–7) without even mentioning Almahide's own love for Almanzor—a major source of dramatic conflict. More recently, however, Berry notes how the female characters of *The Conquest of Granada* think of themselves as individuals (106–7), and Canfield comments on the misogyny evident in the final acts (38).
3. Part 2 highlights particularly the authority of Queen Isabella. Ferdinand of Aragon and Isabella of Castile were of course joint monarchs in historical fact. Carrasco-Urgoiti points out that Isabella, "who tried to be always near the battlefront," was a key figure in unifying the nobility, partly through her promotion of the cult of chivalry and courtly love (27).
4. As contemporary editions of Dryden's sources were not available to me, my description of the plots comes from the full accounts given by

Schweitzer (*Scudéry's "Almahide"*) and Carrasco-Urgoiti. Edward Phillips's translation of *Almahide,* which makes much of the attempted seduction and rape, was published in 1677 and clearly shows the influence of Dryden's play (Schweitzer, "Dryden's Use"). The story of the falsely accused queen comes from local ballads of Granada (Carrasco-Urgoiti 90); de Hita adds the element of a chivalric trial by combat. Almahide's personality bears no resemblance to that of her namesake in Scudéry and is not defined at all in de Hita.

5. Killigrew's female warrior Clorinda (*Love in Arms,* 1663 [Van Lennep 1:54]) has of course a long history in romance, but the role is used to assert gender differences, and Clorinda is idealized as a shrine of virtue and honor in both body and mind. Her body is a "Temple where Honour, Love, and Beauty, with a perfect vertue, [are] enshrin'd in those chaste Veins" (Killigrew 231). In *The Siege of Rhodes* (first performed in 1661, and frequently thereafter [Van Lennep 1:29–30, 42, 46, 51, 60, 108–9, 255]) Ianthe is represented as leading men in battle on at least two occasions and is described androgynously ("Fairer than Woman, and than man more fierce" [Davenant 21]), but it is her distinctively feminine virtue and beauty that do the leading. She has an iconographic and visual function on the battlefield.

6. The term *subjectivity* here refers simply to woman as a perceiving, thinking, and feeling subject, as opposed to woman as an object of male desire or action, or woman as a construct that reflects male desire. The play highlights this definition—and this contrast—to the extent of making it dramatically pivotal. As my argument will show, the *Conquest'*s focus on female subjectivity contrasts significantly with Dryden's treatment of female heroism and marriage in earlier heroic dramas. *The Conquest of Granada* also bears an interesting relation to the emerging ideology of the essentialized feminine evident in the conduct literature of the early eighteenth century, in which female subjectivity was acknowledged and then appropriated, and the female mind, will, and feeling were constructed to meet the needs of a paternalistic society (cf. Shevelow; LeGates). Dryden's play, rather than constructing female subjectivity to fit the masculinist agenda, seems consciously to explore the divergence of female subjectivity from male construction and imposition and to associate expressions of female will and feeling with issues of identity and separateness.

   The focus on feminine subjectivity and the problematizing of gender types occurs in various forms elsewhere in Dryden's work but has not been discussed extensively. Winn discusses Dryden's tendency to a fluidity of gendered representation and his generally supportive and rational relationships with women, particularly women writers (*Beauty,* chap. 7). Winn does mention how in spite of these progressive views Dryden is still caught by convention in his discourse with and about women (e.g., 432–33). This is the ambivalence we see informing and unsettling the treatment of patriarchy and women in *The Conquest of Granada.* More might be inferred from various readings of Dryden's opus. In his *Ilias,* for example, the influence of the romance tradition informs the portrayal of Briseis so as to emphasize her subjectivity, as opposed to the Homeric original, where she is merely a prize of war (Roper 418). In *The Conquest of Granada* Dryden invokes these oppositions, specifically in the debates of act I concerning Almahide's freedom. More complex problems of female subjectivity and desire are represented in the *Sigismonda* translation (see Reverand).

While any ideas about Dryden's position on women's rights at the time of writing *The Conquest of Granada* must necessarily be extremely speculative, some observations can help contextualize the play's engagement of women's issues. The play seems to exist in a general context of debate surrounding marriage and gender roles. (Winn suggests that Dryden may have been experiencing marital difficulties, pointing to the prologue to Part 1 and to Dryden's supposed affair with Anne Reeves, who played the Christian slave Esperanza and who may have sung the Zambra song [Winn, *Dryden* 212–13; idem, *Beauty* 391–92, 396]). *The Conquest of Granada* is written while Dryden is preparing for publication *Tyrannick Love,* a play that strains and fractures conventional ideals of marital virtue. It is followed almost immediately by *Marriage A-la-Mode,* one of the most famous examples of the dynamic disjunction created when the libertine cynical view of marriage is juxtaposed with heroic love—a duality that also informs *The Conquest of Granada.* Thereafter, in *The State of Innocence* (1673), Dryden has Eve voice a politically charged critique of the assumptions underlying

female subjection in terms anticipating those of later feminist essayists such as Astell: "Th'unhappiest of creation is a wife, / Made lowest, in the highest rank of life: / Her fellow's slave; to know and not to chuse: / Curst with that reason she must never use" (act V; cited in Winn, *Beauty* 400).

7. The "exact[ly]" virtuous Benzayda is in some ways more purely a figure of romance than either Lyndaraxa or Almahide, and her characterization does not focus so directly on questions of female subjectivity and identity. Nonetheless, she is remarkable in her assertion of female nature as inherently active and heroic; she plays the dominant role in an action that exposes traditional patriarchal expectations as false and inadequate in the light of individual human "virtue"—specifically, the traditionally feminine virtues of love and self-sacrifice. The subplot redefines patriarchy in sentimental terms, anticipating the domestic scenes of later eighteenth-century drama and novels, and the virtue of Benzayda is instrumental in bringing this about. Although it can thus be seen as anticipating the later eighteenth-century essentializing of woman as the shrine of moral virtue, this subplot differs from that construct in that Benzayda's virtue is emphatically active, as opposed to the (feminized) Ozmyn's passive resignation. It is notable that, in the scene where Benzayda's love, courage, and self-sacrifice triumph over Abenamar's obtuse patriarchalism, she is cross-dressed. The cross-dressing here departs from contemporary stage practice in that it is not a means of intrigue or disguise. Her breeches do not hide who she is; rather, they function as a visible sign onstage of her active redefinition of female virtue.

8. Hughes explores parallels between Almahide and Lyndaraxa, even in phraseology (104–12) suggesting that these ironic similarities show the insubstantial and delusive nature of Almahide's "cult of appearances." These parallels,

however, are also exploited for contrast. Lyndaraxa's focus on female subjectivity leads only to emptiness—she is pure type—whereas Almahide's is part of a process by which the formulae of "exact virtue" are shown to be inadequate and by which she ultimately separates herself from them.

9. Powell notes that Michael Mohun, the actor cast as Abdelmelech, appears to have had the ability to cry at will (118).

10. The gap between patriarchal idealism and feminine subjectivity is nicely epitomized in Dryden's casting. The role of Almahide was played by the distinctly unvirtuous Nell Gwyn, in between the births of two of her royal children. Nell had already been used to break up the boundaries between theatrical fiction and the audience's and players' reality, in the notorious epilogue to *Tyrannick Love* ("I am the ghost of poor departed *Nelly*"). Her appearance in the prologue of Part 1 of *The Conquest of Granada*, wearing an absurdly large hat and making salacious references to the war of the theaters, seems almost to pick up where *Tyrannick Love* leaves off. In both these roles, but most particularly in that of Almahide, the body of the actress, and the audience's extratheatrical knowledge of her life, become the site of the charged and unsettled questions of the relation between inner self and outer role, as Almahide's sexual idealism is inhabited by Nell's sexual realism. This disjunction exemplifies in itself the disjunction between individual subjectivity and constructed public role, suggesting the implied similarity between theatrical and social roles.

11. Canfield notes the link between Almanzor's seduction attempt and Zulema's rape attempt, "as if to underscore the nature of Almanzor's assault as a form of rape" (38). He also notices the misogyny evident in the parallel between Boabdelin and Almanzor, both of whom immediately conclude that all women are false (38). It should also be noted that the trial of the innocent sultana for adultery was folk material used by de Hita (Carrasco-Urgoiti 90). What is new in Dryden is Almanzor's role and the linking of Almanzor's attempted seduction to Zulema's assault, as well as the linking of Almanzor and Boabdelin.

The link between Zulema and Almanzor has been noted independently by Hughes, who sees this scene as Almanzor's moral nadir, the point at which he is most fully of the villains' world (99). What Hughes does not mention is that that villainy is defined most notably by its misogyny.

12. Winn suggests that in combining the heroic dialogue of the play with the libertine discourse of the prologues, epilogues, and songs, Dryden is appealing to two different segments of his audience: "A female sensibility nurtured by the reading of French romances" and "what he imagined to be a male sensibility honed on libertine lampoons" (*Beauty* 395–96). The two kinds of discourse are, however, deeply intertwined in the play, as this scene demonstrates: the two frameworks of value comment on each other, a conjunction that heightens the misogynistic elements in libertinism.

13. Dryden's source for the image of the silkworm is in Jonson's *Timber,* where the silkworm emphasizes the difficulty in knowing truth through the senses and the subjective activity of the soul: "*Knowledge* is the action of the *Soule;* and is perfect without the *senses* . . . but not without the service of the

senses: by those Organs, the *Soule workes;* She is a perpetuall Agent, prompt and subtile; but often flexible, and erring; intangling her selfe like a Silke-worm: But her *Reason* is a weapon with two edges, and cuts through" (8:588).

14. Cf. Berry: "Not even the virtuous Almahide . . . thinks of herself as merely a wife. Her cowardly king-husband she rejects in favor of convent life, where she may keep intact her individual soul" (106–7).

Works Cited

Alssid, Michael M. *Dryden's Rhymed Heroic Tragedies: A Critical Study of the Plays and of Their Place in Dryden's Poetry.* Vol. 1. Salzburg: Institut für Englische Sprache und Literatur, Universität Salzburg, 1974.

Barbeau, Anne T. *The Intellectual Design of John Dryden's Heroic Plays.* New Haven, Conn.: Yale UP, 1970.

Berry, Margaret. "Almanzor and Coxinga: Drama East and West." *Comparative Literature Studies* 22.1 (Spring 1985): 97–109.

Canfield, J. Douglas. *Word as Bond in English Literature from the Middle Ages to the Restoration.* Philadelphia: U of Pennsylvania P, 1989.

Carrasco-Urgoiti, Maria Soledad. *The Moorish Novel: "El Abencerraje" and Perez de Hita.* Boston: Twayne, 1976.

Davenant, Sir William. *The Siege of Rhodes: The First and Second Part. . . .* 1672. *The Works of Sir William Davenant.* London, 1673; New York: Benjamin Blom, 1968. 1–66.

Dryden, John. *The Conquest of Granada by the Spaniards.* 1672. *The Works of John Dryden.* Vol. 11. Ed. John Loftis and David Stuart Rodes et al. Berkeley: U of California P, 1978. 1–218.

———. *Tyrannick Love; or, The Royal Martyr.* 1670. *The Works of John Dryden.* Vol. 10. Ed. Maximillian E. Novak and George R. Guffey. Berkeley: U of California P, 1970. 105–93.

Evans, David R. " 'Private Greatness': The Feminine Ideal in Dryden's Early Heroic Drama." *Restoration* 16.1 (Spring 1992): 2–19.

Evelyn, John. *Memoirs of John Evelyn, Esq., F.R.S. Comprising His Diary, from 1641 to 1705–6, and a Selection of His Familiar Letters.* Ed. William Bray. London: Frederick Warne, n.d.

Fisher, Alan S. "Daring to Be Absurd: The Paradoxes of *The Conquest of Granada.*" *Studies in Philology* 73 (1976): 414–39.

Hughes, Derek. *Dryden's Heroic Plays.* Lincoln: U of Nebraska P, 1981.

Jonson, Ben. *Ben Jonson.* Vol. 8. Ed. C.H. Herford, Percy Simpson, and Evelyn Simpson. Oxford: Clarendon, 1947.

Killigrew, Thomas. *The First Part of Cicilia & Clorinda; or, Love in Arms.* 1663. *Comedies and Tragedies by Thomas Killigrew.* London, 1664; New York: Benjamin Blom, 1967. 215–64.

King, Bruce. *Dryden's Major Plays.* New York: Barnes and Noble, 1966.

Kropf, Carl R. "Patriarchal Theory in Dryden's Early Drama." *Essays in Theatre* 6.1 (Nov. 1987): 41–48.

————. "Political Theory and Dryden's Heroic Tragedies." *Essays in Theatre* 3.2 (May 1985): 125–38.

LeGates, Marlene. "The Cult of Womanhood in Eighteenth-Century Thought." *Eighteenth-Century Studies* 10.1 (Fall 1976): 21–39.

Powell, Jocelyn. *Restoration Theatre Production.* London: Routledge, 1984.

Reverand, Cedric D., II. "Dryden's Nobly Ignoble Heroine: Sigismonda from *Fables.*" *Studies in Eighteenth-Century Culture* 19 (1989): 23–37.

Righter, Anne. "Heroic Tragedy." Restoration Theatre. Stratford-Upon-Avon Studies 6. Ed. John Russell Brown and Bernard Harris. London: Edward Arnold, 1965.

Roper, Alan. Headnote to *The Conquest of Granada by the Spaniards.* By John Dryden. *The Works of John Dryden.* Vol. 11. Ed. John Loftis and David Stuart Rodes et al. Berkeley: U of California P, 1978. 411–35.

Schweitzer, Jerome W. "Dryden's Use of Scudéry's *Almahide.*" *Modern Language Notes* 54 (March 1939): 190–92.

————. *Georges de Scudéry's "Almahide": Authorship, Analysis, Sources, and Structure.* Baltimore: Johns Hopkins UP, 1939.

Shevelow, Kathryn. *Women and Print Culture: The Construction of Femininity in the Early Periodical.* New York: Routledge, 1989.

Van Lennep, William, ed. *The London Stage, 1660–1800. Part 1: 1660–1700.* Carbondale: Southern Illinois UP, 1965.

Winn, James Anderson. *John Dryden and His World.* New Haven, Conn.: Yale UP, 1987.

————. *"When Beauty Fires the Blood": Love and the Arts in the Age of Dryden.* Ann Arbor: U of Michigan P, 1992.

Resisting a Private Tyranny in Two Humane Comedies

James E. Evans

*L*et the business be carried as Prudently as it can be on the Woman's side, a reasonable Man can't deny that she has by much the harder bargain. Because she puts her self entirely into her Husband's Power, and if the Matrimonial Yoke be grievous, neither Law nor Custom afford her that redress which a Man obtains. . . . For whatever may be said against Passive-Obedience in another Case, I suppose there's no Man but likes it very well in this; how much soever Arbitrary Power may be dislik'd on a Throne, not *Milton* himself wou'd cry up Liberty to poor *Female Slaves,* or plead for the Lawfulness of Resisting a Private Tyranny.

> —Mary Astell, *Some Reflections upon Marriage*

Mary Astell's *Some Reflections upon Marriage* provides an Enlightenment feminist perspective on marital issues that are dramatized in William Congreve's *The Way of the World* and George Farquhar's *The Beaux' Stratagem*. Astell's essay was first published in 1700, the same year as Congreve's play; the third edition of *Reflections,* with an angry preface, appeared in 1706, the year before Farquhar's comedy. Astell's work describes uncompromisingly the hard bargain that marriage presented to a woman, loss of liberty to a tyrant in law and custom; the two plays each confront the grievous matrimonial yoke experienced by one female character, even as their comic endings celebrate a match that seems likely to result in more benign private tyranny for another. Congreve's and Farquhar's comedies also include a perspective on marriage that implicitly questions, as Astell's essay does more directly, assumptions about individual liberty associated with the Glorious Revolution of 1688. Their female characters encounter a paradox resulting from the recent change in England's government, that its rhetoric of liberty brought no increase in the liberty of women and, indeed, probably made them more vulnerable because of its emphasis on the contractual basis of society. As Astell observes, men who vigilantly resisted a monarch's arbitrary power were content to preserve their own in private life. This paradox became more acute for Astell and for Farquhar's female characters when a queen became ruler of the nation in 1702.

Astell, a moralistic author who distrusted wit and the theater (Perry, *Astell* 160–61), may seem an unlikely interpretative guide to comedies by Congreve and Farquhar. As Shirley Strum Kenny points out, however, many plays by Colley Cibber, George Farquhar, and Richard Steele, and some by John Vanbrugh, William Congreve, and Susannah Centlivre, constitute "a distinct and significant kind of comedy" that presents a "humane vision of life, complex modes of characterization, realistic dialogue to emphasize character" ("Humane Comedy" 30, 43). The "humane comedy" of the 1690s and 1700s is also characterized by its representation of marital issues, which, according to Kenny, these authors faced "with genuine interest, some perception, and even originality." As comic plots focused more often on serious problems in courtship and married life, such subjects "helped turn the theater from satiric comedy to a more compassionate, less ironic view of life" (Kenny, "Elopements" 85). What Kenny does not account for is the fact that some humane comedies, written in the decades following the Glorious Revolution, explore ways that questions about liberty in married life relate to answers provided to those questions in the public sphere.

The Way of the World and *The Beaux' Stratagem* contain voices of resistance akin to "the feminist critique of possessive individualism" that Ruth Perry finds in Astell's *Reflections*. Perry views Astell's essay broadly as a response to the Glorious Revolution (and especially to John Locke's rationalization of it in *Two Treatises of Government*), a revolution marked by "a paradigm shift from a political world populated by men and women involved in a web of familial and sexual interconnections to an all-male world based solely on contractual obligation" (Perry, "Astell" 449–50). While the Revolution authorized greater liberty for men to resist tyranny, "it tightened the reins on women and reaffirmed men's power over them . . . in separating the rights of citizens from the obligations of families." Astell was convinced that in these "new ideological scripts" only men were "theorized as individuals," who had "the right—and the propensity—to strive for the unlimited accumulation of property" (Perry, "Astell" 449, 450, 451). C.B. Macpherson, in discussing the emergence of possessive individualism characteristic of these decades, remarks that such contradictions in Locke's theory express "the ambivalence of an emerging bourgeois society which demanded formal equality but required substantive inequality of rights" (247). W.A. Speck adds, "Although 'Liberty and Property' was the motto for the revolutionaries, the emphasis soon came to settle on the second word" (247–48). Astell was alert to the gap between political rhetoric and social practice as it concerned women.

Her *Reflections* undertakes, in part, a reply to Locke's *Two Treatises*. To justify changing the monarchy in England, Locke dissociates patriarchal from political authority, a linkage traditionally used to rationalize absolute monarchy. More concerned to establish the individual's right to property, he pays little attention to government of families. He does allow that "the *Power of the Husband*" is "far from that of an absolute Monarch" and grants to a wife "full and free possession of what by Contract is her peculiar Right" (339). While finding in Adam's superiority over Eve no justification for monarchy, though, Locke nevertheless locates in the biblical story a "Foundation" for the "Subjection" that "every Wife owes her Husband" (192). Lois G. Schwoerer argues that Locke's *Two Treatises* "had the effect of weakening in theory the notion of the subordinate role of women in the family" (217). But as Gordon J. Schochet more convincingly points out, "Locke does not seem to have questioned this aspect of the traditional patriarchal family" (250).

Astell challenges Locke's preference for "the Arbitrary Power of 100000 single Men" to that of a king (Locke 378). Preferring Stuart monarchy to the political society that followed 1688, she questions Locke's position: "Is it not then partial in Men to the last degree, to contend for, and practise that Arbitrary Dominion in their Families, which they abhor and exclaim against in the State? For if Arbitrary Power is evil in itself, and an improper Method of Governing Rational and Free Agents, it ought not to be Practis'd any where; Nor is it less, but rather more mischievous in Families than in Kingdoms, by how much 100000 Tyrants are worse than one" (76). Astell's bitter words, first added to *Reflections* in the 1706 preface, four years after Anne became England's queen, make it impossible to ignore private tyranny as an impediment to female liberty. In her minority report on this early Whig interpretation of history, Astell identifies wives bluntly as "poor *Female Slaves*" and insists that her reader recognize that the allegedly postpatriarchal story told by Locke and others is not the whole story. As a woman, she turns upside down the rhetoric of liberty; Locke's "100000 single Men," from her vantage point, produce an equal number of private tyrants. Astell thus identifies the ambivalence described by Carole Pateman in her recent analysis of contract theorists: "The social contract is a story of freedom; the sexual contract is a story of subjection. . . . Contract is far from being opposed to patriarchy; contract is the means through which modern patriarchy is constituted" (2). Sensitive to this problem for those theoretically "Free Agents" who were female, Astell exposes the contradictions in Locke's viewpoint.

A similar, if less angry, awareness of the discrepancy between the social contract and the sexual contract emerges within the comic conventions of *The Way of the World* and *The Beaux' Stratagem*. Female characters in these comedies find themselves facing circumstances that apologists for the Revolution judged unacceptable for men, a form of slavery, chosen in choosing to marry. In Astell's view, "She who Elects a Monarch for Life, who gives him an Authority she cannot recall . . . had need be very sure that she does not make a Fool her Head, nor a Vicious Man her Guide and Pattern" (103). Confronted with male characters holding various forms of contractual authority, Millamant, Mrs. Fainall, Dorinda, and Mrs. Sullen share something of Astell's political understanding, if not her political edge. For example, in Farquhar's *The Beaux' Stratagem* Dorinda tells Mrs. Sullen, who is married to a brutal tyrant, that "your Example gives me such an Impression of Matrimony, that I shall be apt to condemn my Person to a long Vacation all its Life" (II.i.10–12). Late in Congreve's *Way of the World* Millamant laments to Mrs. Fainall, half of that play's most cynical marriage, "Well, If *Mirabell* shou'd not make a good Husband, I am a lost thing;—for I find I love him violently" (IV.i.315–16). While Dorinda's inclination to "condemn my Person" to a single life and Millamant's fear that she could become "a lost thing" in marriage echo the fashionable jargon of their society, their words also reveal their personal fears, which the plays situate amid questions about liberty as theorized following the Revolution.

In *The Way of the World* Millamant discovers a strategy to reduce, though not eliminate, her anxiety about marriage. In the famous proviso scene she and Mirabell agree upon a private contract, witnessed, after the fact, by Mrs. Fainall. Millamant negotiates for "My dear Liberty" with the recognition that she will, in subscribing to the agreement, "by degrees dwindle into a Wife" (IV.i.185, 226–27). Her immediate focus on liberty, wittily echoed in other language—"liberty to pay and receive visits," "what I please," "when I please," "to be sole Empress" (212–22)—draws attention to the scene's central political issue for a woman soon to be subject to the power of her husband. Susan Carlson believes that Millamant is "conscious of but does not fully articulate the losses she will suffer in marriage" (84). Fortunately Mirabell does not wish to "be beyond Measure enlarg'd into a Husband," and he grants her "Dominion" so long as she "exceed not in [her] province" (*WW* IV.i.230–31, 263–64). That Mirabell intends to be "a tractable and complying Husband" (277) is welcome news, given the probable alternative; in a comedy Millamant can take part in shaping a more favorable private contract and can expect greater happiness. Indeed, this witty dialogue seems to displace her unarticulated misgivings through attention to apparently trivial matters (sleeping and waking, endearments, visits, masks, beverages, toasts). Several of their metaphors—"Empress," "Dominion," "province"—politicize the dialogue and suggest some discrepancy between the theoretical liberty of individuals in society and the loss of liberty experienced by Englishwomen in marriage.

Much has been said about the contractual structure of the proviso scene. For instance, Richard W.F. Kroll discovers a Lockean agreement in it (749), and Richard Braverman argues that this is "a true settlement," which "symbolizes the polity as a civil union that originates in consent" (234). The proviso scene contains aspects of a social contract based upon consent, the foundation in Locke for authority in marriage as well as in society. In his *Two Treatises* Locke stipulates "a voluntary Compact between Man and Woman" as the basis of "*Conjugal Society*"; he also observes that in marriage "the last Determination, *i.e.* the Rule, should be placed somewhere" and that this "naturally falls to the Man's share, as the abler and the stronger" (337, 339). In Locke's theory women are thus "naturally subordinate to men and the order of nature is reflected in the structure of conjugal relations" (Pateman 52). Like Astell, Congreve also discloses the less hopeful story of the sexual contract. Millamant is aware of her subordination when she negotiates. Her provisos, as Robert Markley observes, "exchange one set of restrictions for another"; she knows she "will be confined within the patriarchal order under the designations of 'wife' and eventually 'mother' " (245–46). Mirabell's provisos follow Millamant's and incorporate hers into *his* vision of primogeniture and her reproductive role. He has, even in this comic scene, the customary "last Determination." Millamant's virtual silence at the play's end reinforces this impression. In marrying Mirabell she will be complicit in, if not passively obedient to, patriarchy. As Carlson notes, "In spite of Millamant's strong campaign for self-preservation, her power and individuality are in the end subsumed" (84).

Act V translates the private contract of Millamant and Mirabell into public acceptance amid the play's exposure of the kind of authority represented by Fainall, a satiric version of Astell's tyrant. His motive is acquisition of wealth; his method, the contract that will subject characters otherwise joined by family and sexual desires to the interest of his acquisitiveness. Taking advantage of female powerlessness, he demands control of Lady Wishfort's estate, the remainder of his wife's fortune, and half of Millamant's fortune. His wife's maintenance will "depend entirely on my Discretion," and Lady Wishfort's matrimonial hopes, on his reserved "Power" (*WW* V.i.270, 266). Lady Wishfort, with uncharacteristic astuteness, associates Fainall's plans with foreign tyranny—"the Barbarity of a *Muscovite* Husband"—and Fainall seems to agree, attributing them to contact with the monarchists in "his *Czarish* Majestie's Retinue" (V.i.271–73). Fainall even mocks his opponents in the language of consent and rights when he tells them, "I suppose *Madam,* your Consent is not requisite in this Case; nor Mr. *Mirabell,* your resignation; nor Sir *Wilfull,* your right" (V.i.437–39).

Enforcing Fainall's demands is the threat of divorce, with the accompanying public infamy vividly depicted for Lady Wishfort. His strategy, forcing the consent of others through power, suggests that Fainall represents values more characteristic of English society before 1688, whether described as "debased Hobbesianism" or "the arbitrary patriarchal will" (Markley 239; Braverman 228). While the Revolution reformed monarchy in political society, however, it did not, as Astell points out, reduce patriarchy in the family but only recast its basis in a new paradigm. Fainall evidences this aspect of the post-1688 patriarchal world—the possessive individualism manifested in his desire to accumulate property, to control it through contract, to tighten the reins on women. His focus on money rather than land also makes him a potential player in the financial revolution that began with the new institutions of the 1690s.

Appropriately, the drawing up of Fainall's contract is the central issue in the fifth act, and his defeat, the crucial moment of the denouement. This action occurs without his consent and depends upon another contract, a deed of trust voluntarily signed by Mrs. Fainall when, as a widow, "she was at her own disposal" and when, demonstrating her rationality in a fashion Astell could approve, she suspected Fainall's "Tyranny of temper" (*WW* V.i.536, 542). The patriarch's tyranny gives way, temporarily, in a comic resolution, to more favorable economic status for a single adult woman. Her status is complemented by Lady Wishfort's role, when she agrees to "consent to any thing to come" in reward for Mirabell's help (V.i.455). Kroll observes that readers often "believe that Mirabell is the direct and effective agent in securing Millamant and her fortune intact. . . . But the fact is that Millamant's dowry remains undivided at the end solely because Lady Wishfort is grateful to Mirabell" (734). Mirabell renegotiates his relationship with Millamant's aunt and her family, for whom Fainall's defeat is a triumph. According to Susan McCloskey, Mirabell "moves to re-vitalize the decaying family, first by guaranteeing its future, then by direct-ing its present," and so "forges the divided kin into a community" (72).

Upsetting Fainall's contractual scheme, the ending restores a web of familial and sexual interconnections as the basis of its settlement, but the restoration remains uneasy. Mirabell's final speech, after all, proposes reuniting Mrs. Fainall, his former mistress, with her husband. He says, "For my part I will Contribute all that in me lies to a Reunion. . . . in the mean time, *Madam,* let me before these Witnesses, restore to you this deed of trust. It may be a means well manag'd to make you live Easily together" (*WW* V.i.615–19). Congreve wrote no reply for Mrs. Fainall, who earlier declares, "This is the last day of our living together, that's my Comfort" (V.i.82–83). While she is protected socially from the infamy of divorce and economically from the tyranny of Fainall, her victory is bittersweet. Witness to the contract of Mirabell and Millamant, she silently laments her status. Astell's work renders Mrs. Fainall's silence eloquent, for she has indeed managed her recent business "as Prudently as it can be on the Woman's side." Even Mirabell, responding to a suggestion early in the play that "No Man in Town lives well with a Wife but *Fainall,*" indicates, "You had better step and ask his Wife; if you wou'd be credibly inform'd" (I.i.264–67). From Astell's point of view a single life would certainly be happier than the reunion that Mirabell projects for Mrs. Fainall. Instead, she becomes the final instance of "Passive-Obedience" in a stratagem that renews the customary sexual contract.

Kenny finds that the focus on marriage in humane comedies often results in "less believable denouements in plots too flimsy to sustain the weight of the marital questions" ("Elopements" 85). Her assertion less convincingly describes *The Way of the World,* which, as Markley points out, attempts to "accommodate morality and ideology" in its resolution and thus to avoid either the open-ended or the fantastic conclusions typical of many earlier wit comedies (249–50). Endings are especially significant, Rachel Blau DuPlessis argues, as the moment of "ideological negotiation" for a work's "fundamental contradictions," at the point "where ideology meets narrative" (3, 19). She elaborates: "Any resolution can have traces of the conflicting materials that have been processed within it. It is where subtexts and repressed discourses can throw up one last flare of meaning; it is where the author may side-step and displace attention from the materials that a work has made available" (3). In *The Way of the World* Congreve steps back from the full implications of a position like Astell's when Millamant and Mrs. Fainall acquiesce in Mirabell's stratagem.

Since Farquhar is less willing than Congreve to comply with an available social script, *The Beaux' Stratagem* does not present the same kind of closure. Judith Milhous and Robert Hume, for example, believe that act V of this play is "deliberately overdone," that Farquhar is "either mocking the conventions of comedy or taking refuge in farce and Cloud Cuckooland" (315). Mrs. Sullen expresses her discontent with private tyranny so much more openly than Mrs. Fainall that there is little dramatic possibility of reunion with her husband. Moreover, because of English laws, "making a marriage was far easier than breaking one." "Legal escapes from miserable marriages" included separations based on mutual consent or by decree of ecclesiastical courts, annulments of child or adult marriages under certain limited conditions, and parliamentary divorce on grounds of adultery or cruelty, a painfully public process, as envisioned in Congreve's play (Kenny, "Elopements" 93). In portraying the Sullens' marriage, Farquhar creates a desire for liberty from the sexual contract that is clearly not so easily satisfied.

Resolving the fundamental contradictions of *The Beaux' Stratagem* requires a deus ex machina in the form of a gentleman from London, Mrs. Sullen's brother Sir Charles Freeman. He makes his first appearance in act V to justify her divorce and to compel Sullen to give up his wife and her fortune. Sullen, Sir Charles's antagonist, is a private tyrant like Fainall and, even more, the brute that Astell thought most husbands to be. Indifferent rather than adulterous, Sullen married "To get an Heir to my Estate" (V.iv.219). His admission vocalizes Astell's assumption that a man merely wants "One who may breed his Children, taking all the care and trouble of their Education, to preserve his Name and Family" (105). Perhaps this explains Sullen's drunken insistence on sharing his wife's bed, even though he clearly has no regard for her. He is, as he admits to Sir Charles, no rake.

Like Fainall, Sullen is defeated by others' holding crucial documents, in this instance when "all the Articles of Marriage with your Lady, Bills, Bonds, Leases, Receipts to an infinite Value" are taken by Archer and given to Sir Charles (*BS* V.iv.276–78). Farquhar places Sullen's striving for property in the context of the play's savage criticism of prudential marriages. While Sullen's mother, Lady Bountiful, spends half of her annual income on charity for the benefit of her neighbors, this member of the younger generation shows again how possessive individualism affects patriarchy. Arranged hastily by Mrs. Sullen's father, this marriage is Sullen's primary means to the end of increasing wealth. He may hate his wife, but he has "no Quarrel at her Fortune" (V.i.81–82). Like the financial adventurers who arrive in Lichfield searching for an heiress, Sullen's character supports John McVeagh's assertion that Farquhar portrays "a society quite thoroughly given over to money pursuits and to commercial habits of thought in spite of its adherence to an apparently other mode of existence" (80). Ronald Berman similarly finds money the "final cause of the play" and suggests that "the dominant mode of language and conception is transactional" (161, 164). By equating the fortunes of Mrs. Sullen and Dorinda at ten thousand pounds, Farquhar emphasizes the parallel between husband and beaux in this postrevolutionary society.

Farquhar resorts to a social contract in order to overcome Mrs. Sullen's unhappiness with the sexual contract. The play presents a scene of voluntary compact, akin to that joining Mirabell and Millamant, prior to Sullen's relinquishing of his wife and her fortune. It begins with Mrs. Sullen's remarking that "all things here must move by consent, Compulsion wou'd Spoil us" (*BS* V.iv.194–95). But this compact differs from the proviso scene in *The Way of the World* in being more public—several witnesses are asked to judge—and, initially, in failing. When Sir Charles asks, "What are the Bars to your mutual Contentment?" the couple's bitter replies end this way:

> *SULLEN.* Is there on Earth a thing we cou'd agree in?
> *SULLEN.* Yes—To part.
> *MRS. SULLEN.* With all my Heart.

SULLEN. Your Hand.
MRS. SULLEN. Here.
SULLEN. These Hands join'd us, these shall part us—away.
[*BS* V.iv.230, 244–49]

Amid its ironies, the scene may convey the Lockean notion that "the *Wife,* has, in many cases, a Liberty to *separate* . . . where natural Right, or their Contract allows" (Locke 339). But the justification for divorce concluded in *The Beaux' Stratagem*—while it contrasts "consent" and "Compulsion"—Farquhar probably derived from Milton's divorce tracts (see Larson).

As Eric Rothstein remarks, "Farquhar uses Milton's ideas as his enabling clause to ratify the final actions of Sir Charles and his sister" (149). Milton's arguments and images appear primarily in two other scenes— Mrs. Sullen's final speeches to Dorinda in act III, scene 3, and Sir Charles's words to Sullen early in act V, scene 1. In both of these Farquhar paraphrases passages from *The Doctrine and Discipline of Divorce* and other Miltonic prose to authorize the divorce. According to Milton, if husband and wife are not "enabl'd to maintain a cherfull conversation, to the solace and love of each other, according as God intended . . . then is there no power above their own consent to hinder them from unjoyning" (328). Such an appeal to higher authority provides an appropriate escape for a woman like Mrs. Sullen, subject to private tyranny in law and custom.

Mrs. Sullen's speeches also resonate with language reminiscent of Astell's critique of patriarchy, echoing especially the 1706 preface, and with a similar emphasis on postrevolutionary rhetoric. Complaining to Dorinda about her husband in act II, Mrs. Sullen declares, "[S]ince a Woman must wear Chains, I wou'd have the Pleasure of hearing 'em rattle a little" (*BS* II.i.61–62). She remarks of her status that " 'tis a standing Maxim in conjugal Discipline, that when a Man wou'd enslave his Wife, he hurries her into the Country." In London, she believes, "A Man dare not play the Tyrant . . . because there are so many Examples to encourage the Subject to rebel" (II.i.117–19, 121–22). Mrs. Sullen expresses more optimism than Astell, for whom private tyranny knows no geographic boundaries. In Mrs. Sullen's later flirtation with Count Bellair, this dialogue occurs:

MRS. SULLEN. Alass, Sir, why shou'd you complain
to me of your Captivity, who am in Chains my self?

· ·
COUNT BELLAIR. . . . dis is your Case; you're a
Slave, Madam, Slave to the worst of *Turks,* a Husband.
[III.iii.322–23, 329–30]

Astell, who agrees with such descriptions of marriage, wonders why English society permits a husband to do what is "grievous to a generous Mind, render Life miserable." She asks satirically whether a woman's "being subjected to the *inconstant, uncertain, unknown, arbitrary Will* of Men" is not "the *perfect Condition of Slavery*" (Astell 76). Astell, however, sees no hope for the private slave, for "to struggle with her Yoke will only make it gall the more"; she recommends the Christian virtues "Patience and Submission" (116, 102). Similarly, though Farquhar's Mrs. Sullen imagines rebellion when "the Cruelty of the Governour forces the Garrison to Mutiny" (*BS* III.iii.333–34), she is too conventional to act.

Mrs. Sullen also expresses a paradox not available to Congreve's characters in 1700—the presence of a queen on the throne. During the preceding monarchy of William III "much was made of Mary's obedience as a wife and of her signing over to William her legal right to rule England" (Perry, "Astell" 449). Similarly, the female characters in *The Way of the World* finally capitulate to the patriarchal plans of Mirabell. Queen Anne, on the other hand, provides another kind of example for Mrs. Sullen, so that she asks, "But in *England,* a Country whose Women are it's Glory, must Women be abus'd, where Women rule, must Women be enslav'd? nay, cheated into Slavery, mock'd by a Promise of comfortable Society into a Wilderness of Solitude?" (*BS* IV.i.2–6). Her language resembles that of Astell's preface to *Reflections,* published four years after Anne became queen. Astell's anger increased during the monarchy of a queen "who disposes of Crowns, gives Laws and Liberty to *Europe,*" who is the "Glory of her own Sex and Envy of the other" (87). Astell ridicules advocates of male superiority for even implying that women on thrones are "wicked Violations of the Law of Nature" (71). As angry as Astell about continued submission to the sexual contract, Mrs. Sullen expresses similar grounds for her emotions.

Mrs. Sullen's strong voice of resistance does not permit Farquhar a resolution like Congreve's for Mrs. Fainall, even though Mrs. Sullen once considers a similar script: "I cou'd be contented, with a great many other Wives, to . . . give the World an Appearance of living well with my Husband, cou'd I bring him but to dissemble a little Kindness" (*BS* II.i.145–48). Her condition never met, this character earns the sympathy of reader or spectator. Laura Brown remarks that Farquhar seems "drawn to the beleaguered and injured wife . . . whose response is in some degree imbued with a new and explicitly moral consciousness of personal virtue" (139). Mrs. Sullen's response is also imbued with a consciousness of liberty, which she articulates much more fully than does Millamant. Her brother's appearance recalls that, before marriage, Mrs. Sullen was a Freeman, a free man in theory if not in fact. Locke postulates "Man being born . . . with a Title to perfect Freedom" (341); presumably this theory could include women. But Astell questions sarcastically, "*If all Men are born free,* how is it that all Women are born slaves?" (76).

Mrs. Sullen shares Astell's bitter knowledge about individual liberty for women, and while Farquhar does reveal the limitations of freedom after marriage, he does not let her remain in this slavery. When Sullen agrees to give up his wife's fortune, he says, "If you have a mind, Sir *Charles,* to be merry, and celebrate my Sister's Wedding and my Divorce, you may command my House" (*BS* V.iv.282–84). While separation by mutual consent was legally possible, divorce was not. Nor has Sullen provided grounds for a parliamentary divorce. As Dorinda reminds her sister-in-law, "Your Divisions don't come within the Reach of the Law" (III.iii.423–24). Nonetheless, whether divorced or separated, Mrs. Sullen may return to her brother's guardianship and to a single life that Astell could approve. On the other hand, she may begin a relationship with Archer. In an early textual variant he declares that "if the lady pleases, she shall go home with me" (quoted in Milhous and Hume 293). The opportunity for Archer and Mrs. Sullen to exit together occurs in all versions of the text; he takes her hand to lead off the dance. The possibility exists, however, that if she follows Archer, she may be subjecting herself again to patriarchy, after an interlude of freedom. It is notable that Archer shares Sullen's mercenary motives.

Farquhar's divorce fantasy, though remote from the unvarnished possibilities of Astell's essay, resolves the play's contradiction between liberty and patriarchy.[1] The divorce fantasy also transcends the conventional comic ending by celebrating the dissolution of one marriage simultaneously with the making of another, between Dorinda and Aimwell. Archer observes, " 'Twould be hard to guess which of these Parties is the better pleas'd, the Couple Join'd, or the Couple Part'd?" (*BS* V.iv.289–90). For Carlson the ending of comedy usually signifies the loss of female power temporarily gained: "When a dialogue between the sexes is the subject of comedy (as it almost always is when strong women characters appear), the ending works against women" (22). Her observation applies to Millamant, but not necessarily to Mrs. Sullen. Farquhar restores Mrs. Sullen's liberty in restoring her to her brother's protection.

The Beaux' Stratagem also includes a courtship plot based on love at first sight, culminating in a marriage based on free affection rather than money. When Aimwell follows his heart, his honesty offers him the prospect of happy marriage not granted to Archer, his more mercenary companion. In a sudden confession of their financial scheme, Aimwell prefers "the Interest of my Mistress to my own" (V.iv.30–31) and, through this virtuous action, renders more likely the possibility that Dorinda, like Millamant in *The Way of the World,* will find some happiness within the private tyranny she accepts by marrying. A principle of Farquhar's resolution seems to be, in Dorinda's phrase, that "one generous Action deserves another" (*BS* V.iv.91). Aimwell, therefore, soon discovers that he is the viscount he pretended to be. Though lacking the political overtones of Congreve's proviso scene, then, Farquhar's play suggests, at least, a marriage chosen by individuals acting with some self-determination.

Both *The Way of the World* and *The Beaux' Stratagem* conclude with a festive dance and some final couplets that reiterate the authors' attitudes toward marital discord. Mirabell warns the audience about "mutual falsehood" and adds that "marriage frauds too oft are paid in kind" (*WW* V.i.621, 623). Archer delivers Farquhar's final and some-what more optimistic lines on "*Those parted by consent, and those conjoin'd*" (*BS* V.iv.294). Just as they use male characters to rescue distressed wives, both authors give male characters "the last Determina-tion," to recall Locke's phrase. Although the plays allow women more self-expression and apparently more self-determination, their temporary liberty finally becomes part of the script of patriarchal expectations. In addition, these plays perpetuate the assumption that marriage is still, in most instances, the desirable outcome for younger single women, who are presumed to be better off within a patriarchal marriage than in rebellion against it. Nor do these comedies grant much power to older single women: Lady Wishfort is a foolish victim, while the herbalist Lady Bountiful disappears from the action.

For all these signs of patriarchal society and its discontents, however, *The Way of the World* and *The Beaux' Stratagem* include a perspective on female characters' resistance to marital slavery much like Astell's critique, and both dramatize the need for personal consent in domestic practice as well as in political theory. Both plays present the story of subjection found in the sexual contract that is depicted more polemically in *Some Reflections upon Marriage;* within their comic struc-tures both authors create female characters who "plead for the Lawful-ness of Resisting a private Tyranny" in postrevolutionary England. Milla-mant and Dorinda marry benevolent patriarchs, Mrs. Fainall retains financial independence within an unhappy marriage, and Mrs. Sullen divorces her husband and returns to her brother. On these characters' resistance to private tyranny Congreve and Farquhar base the comic faith of their endings. If comedy is, in Christopher Fry's phrase, "an escape, not from truth but from despair: a narrow escape into faith" (17), then these two humane comedies provide a counterpoint to Astell's pessimistic essay.

Notes

1. According to Robert Hume, contemporary audiences "did not demand conformity to either law or reality" in accepting the "*un*realistic presentation" of divorce (53). The characters' discourse about marriage suffices to justify the Sullens' divorce.

Works Cited

Astell, Mary. *The First English Feminist: Reflections upon Marriage and Other Writings*. Ed. Bridget Hill. New York: St. Martin's, 1986.

Berman, Ronald. "The Comedy of Reason." *Texas Studies in Literature and Language* 7 (1965): 161–68.

Braverman, Richard. *Plots and Counterplots: Sexual Politics and the Body Politic in English Literature, 1660–1730*. Cambridge: Cambridge UP, 1993.

Brown, Laura. *English Dramatic Form, 1660–1760: An Essay in Generic History*. New Haven, Conn.: Yale UP, 1981.

Carlson, Susan. *Women and Comedy: Rewriting the British Theatrical Tradition*. Ann Arbor: U of Michigan P, 1991.

Congreve, William. *The Way of the World*. *The Complete Plays of William Congreve*. Ed. Herbert Davis. Chicago: U of Chicago P, 1967. 386–479.

DuPlessis, Rachel Blau. *Writing beyond the Ending: Narrative Strategies of Twentieth-Century Women Writers*. Bloomington: Indiana UP, 1985.

Farquhar, George. *The Beaux' Stratagem*. Vol. 2 of *The Works of George Farquhar*. Ed. Shirley Strum Kenny. Oxford: Clarendon, 1988.

Fry, Christopher. "Comedy." *Vogue*. Jan. 1951. Rpt. in *Comedy: Meaning and Form*. Ed. Robert W. Corrigan. 2d ed. New York: Harper and Row, 1981. 17–19.

Hume, Robert D. *The Rakish Stage: Studies in English Drama, 1660–1800*. Carbondale: Southern Illinois UP, 1983.

Kenny, Shirley Strum. " 'Elopements, Divorce, and the Devil Knows What': Love and Marriage in English Comedy, 1690–1720." *South Atlantic Quarterly* 78 (1979): 84–106.

———. "Humane Comedy." *Modern Philology* 75 (1977): 29–43.

Kroll, Richard. "Discourse and Power in *The Way of the World*." *ELH* 53 (1986): 727–58.

Larson, Martin A. "The Influence of Milton's Divorce Tracts on Farquhar's *Beaux' Stratagem*." *PMLA* 39 (1924): 174–78.

Locke, John. *Two Treatises of Government*. Ed. Peter Laslett. Cambridge: Cambridge UP, 1960.

Macpherson, C.B. *The Political Theory of Possessive Individualism: Hobbes to Locke*. Oxford: Clarendon, 1962.

Markley, Robert. *Two-Edg'd Weapons: Style and Ideology in the Comedies of Etherege, Wycherley, and Congreve*. Oxford: Clarendon, 1988.

McCloskey, Susan. "Knowing One's Relations in Congreve's *The Way of the World*." *Theatre Journal* 33 (1981): 69–79.

McVeagh, John. "George Farquhar and Commercial England." *Studies on Voltaire and the Eighteenth Century* 217 (1983): 65–81.

Milhous, Judith, and Robert D. Hume. *Producible Interpretation: Eight English Plays, 1675–1707*. Carbondale: Southern Illinois UP, 1985.

Milton, John. *The Doctrine and Discipline of Divorce*. Vol. 2 of *Complete Prose Works*. Ed. Ernest Sirluck. New Haven, Conn.: Yale UP, 1959.

Pateman, Carol. *The Sexual Contract*. Stanford, Calif.: Stanford UP, 1988.

Perry, Ruth. *The Celebrated Mary Astell: An Early English Feminist*. Chicago: U of Chicago P, 1986.

———. "Mary Astell and the Feminist Critique of Possessive Individualism." *Eighteenth-Century Studies* 23 (1990): 444–57.

Rothstein, Eric. *George Farquhar*. New York: Twayne, 1967.

Schochet, Gordon J. *Patriarchalism in Political Thought: The Authoritarian Family and Political Speculation and Attitudes Especially in Seventeenth-Century England*. Oxford: Blackwell, 1975.

Schwoerer, Lois G. "Women and the Glorious Revolution." *Albion* 18 (1986): 195–218.

Speck, W.A. *Reluctant Revolutionaries: Englishmen and the Revolution of 1688*. Oxford: Oxford UP, 1988.

The Way of the Word:
Telling Differences in
Congreve's *Way of the World*

Pat Gill

Villiam Congreve's *The Double Dealer* (1693) met with critical acclaim but not popular success. Anthony G. Henderson, the editor of the 1982 Cambridge edition of Congreve's plays, suggests that Congreve's added dedication, in which he "hectored his critics, and defended in particular his use of soliloquy, the character of his hero, and his satire on women," further antagonized an already unreceptive audience (93). In this dedication Congreve disingenuously confesses:

> But there is one thing at which I am more concerned than all the false Criticisms that are made upon me; and that is, some of the Ladies are offended. I am heartily sorry for it, for I declare I would rather disoblige all the Criticks in the World, than one of the Fair Sex. . . . They who are Virtuous or Discreet, I'm sure cannot be offended, for such Characters as these [in the plays] distinguish them, and make their Beauties more shining and observ'd: And they who are of the other kind, may nevertheless pass for such, by seeming not to be displeased, or touched with the Satire of this *Comedy*. Thus they have also wrongfully accused me of doing them a prejudice, when I have in reality done them a Service. [Henderson 99]

Congreve rather conspicuously continues his satire on women in his apology for it. He warns the offended ladies, guilty or innocent, that their public complaints will reflect badly on them and not on the play. The safest response to comedy, Congreve counsels, is discreet silence: "I have heard some whispering, as if [the women] intended to accuse this Play of Smuttiness and Bawdy: But I declare I took a particular care to avoid it, and if they find any in it, it is of their own making, for I did not design it to be so understood. But to avoid my saying anything upon a Subject which has been so admirably handled before, and for their better instruction, I earnestly recommend to their perusal the Epistle Dedicatory before the *Plain-Dealer*" (ibid., 99–100).

Since William Wycherley, the author of the recommended epistle dedicatory, dedicates it to a famous London bawd, Congreve's endorsement is somewhat tongue-in-cheek. But it is not wholly facetious. Wycherley and Congreve share similar views on the representation of women in comedy and the reception of comedy by women. Wycherley, too, rebukes in harsh terms those women who find his play salacious. Writing to the sympathetic madam of his dedication—and of a well-known house of pleasure—he says: "In short, madam, you would not be one of those who ravish a poet's innocent words and make 'em guilty of their own naughtiness (as 'tis termed) in spite of his teeth; nay, nothing is secure from the power of [ladies'] imaginations, no not their husbands, whom they cuckold with themselves by thinking of other men and so make the lawful matrimonial embraces adultery; wrong husbands and poets in thoughts and word, to keep their own reputations" (Holland, *Wycherley* 347-48). Wycherley finds females' interpretation akin to cuckolding, and just as heinous a crime. Loose women have loose imaginations, and all women who interpret are suspect:

> But why, I say, should any at all of the truly virtuous be con-
> cerned, if those who are not so are distinguished from 'em? For
> by that mask of modesty which women wear promiscuously in
> public, they are all alike, and you can no more know a kept
> wench from a woman of honour by her looks than by her dress.
> . . . But those who act as they look ought not to be scandalised
> at the reprehension of others' faults, lest they tax themselves
> with 'em and by too delicate and quick an apprehension not
> only make that obscene which I meant innocent but that satire
> on all which was intended only on those who deserved it.
>
> [ibid., 349–50]

Both Wycherley and Congreve try to rescue their satire from reproach by allying it with their definition of virtuous women. Virtuous women "ought not to be scandalised at the reprehension of others' faults," and they ought not to possess "too delicate and quick an apprehension." In contrast to their scandalous counterparts, virtuous women, "those who act as they look," simply do not understand sexual innuendo and therefore do not recognize double meanings in the witty phrases they hear. Less honorable women who hope to pass as reputable had best pretend to the same ignorance. Apprehension should never make a lady apprehensive. Like truly virtuous women, then, the dramatists' satire is honest and morally straightforward. The doubleness is all on the outside, all in the duplicitous mind's eye of the beholder, who is convicted of sin the moment she understands.

Wycherley's and Congreve's odd thesis on female interpretation informs the depiction of all heroines in Restoration satiric comedy, and it calls for a kind of double vision in the audience. For Restoration comedy to succeed as both satire and moral commentary, the audience must accede to this "feminine" mode of interpretation. That is, the audience must recognize and then forget the double entendres and ironies in the play—just as it must appreciate and then forget the worldly discourse of the heroine when, after she has established her superior social refinement, she becomes the innocent maid and rake-redeemer. These tasks of willed forgetting are impossible, and neither Wycherley nor Congreve ever convinces his critics that the lewdness in his plays is not implied, but inferred.

In his last play, *The Way of the World* (1700), Congreve creates a heroine who possesses the contrary attributes of being knowledgeable without being in the know. Millamant is lovely, witty, charming, self-confident, cannily playful, and, miraculously, innocent as well. She indulges all her whims and fancies, changes her mind whenever she pleases and without notice, and performs everything in her power to keep herself a mystery, a beguiling uncertainty, to men. This is a consummate portrayal of a typical Restoration comic heroine, and indeed, it is one stereotypical of women in general, at least until recently. Like all Restoration heroines, Millamant excels in crisp dialogue; she is adept in elegant and delightful wordplay. In fact, her conversation entirely lacks that rigorous precept of honest innocence that Congreve and Wycherley pronounce necessary in female members of the audience who hope to be thought virtuous.

Millamant's language has very little indeed to do with straightforward discourse. She depends on Mirabell's—and the audience's—ability to read between the lines to catch her drift, which is the most one can catch, for "Motion, not Method is [her] occupation" (II.i.547–48).[1] Millamant treats words as dangerous entities, discrete material to be withheld, exchanged, disguised, or completely obscured. Alert to every nuance, she makes her way through the minefield of salacious double entendre, attempting to maintain the tenuous balance between an acceptable wit and a too sophisticated understanding. Although Millamant is one of the more refined versions of the type, most heroines of satiric comedy of this era must play out this doubled standard of the (dramatic) feminine ideal. A social position maintained by ever-vigilant linguistic self-awareness may seem uncomfortable, not to mention untenable, but it is the only arena of feminine power available in the play—one might argue, one of the few accessible to women of this class in Restoration life—and Millamant declares her intention to maintain it.

Unlike most Restoration heroines, but again, presumably like most Restoration women, Millamant worries about life after marriage. She quite seriously demands that Mirabell solicit her "to the very last, nay, and afterwards" (IV.i.180–81), explaining that she would think she were "poor and had nothing to bestow" if freed from the "agreeable Fatigues of Solicitation" (183–86). In the wedding proviso scene, Millamant and Mirabell carefully plan the perfect Restoration marriage, a utopic union of elegant discourse, conventional morality, and lively, charming manners.[2] "Let us never visit together, nor go to a Play together," Millamant proposes, "but let us be very strange and well bred; let us be as strange as if we had been married a great while, and as well bred as if we were not married at all" (IV.i.227–31).

Millamant then asserts her right to choose her own garb, companions, and visitors, to write letters and make friends without asking Mirabell's permission, and to refuse to converse with wits and fools even though they happen to be Mirabell's friends and relatives. She stipulates further that she be allowed to "have my Closet Inviolate; to be sole Empress of my Tea-table, which you must never presume to approach without first asking leave. And lastly, wherever I am, you shall always knock at the door before you come in" (IV.i.244–47). Millamant's petition seems fairly modest: she asks for the private space that women of her class generally receive without question, although the common courtesy she demands might not always be so readily forthcoming. Less than a hundred years later, women's attempts to maintain inviolate closets would greatly preoccupy writers such as Samuel Richardson, Fanny Burney, and Ann Radcliffe, but the threat posed by the closet later in the next century—that of women's writing and private meditations—did not obtain as yet. Mirabell's fears concern not Millamant's most private chamber but her more public familial and social activities. Mirabell's qualifications of these latter provisions reveal this worry quite explicitly: "I covenant that your acquaintance be general; that you admit no sworn Confident, or Intimate of your own Sex; no she-friend to screen her affairs under your Countenance and tempt you to make trial of a Mutual Secrecy. No Decoy-Duck to wheedle you a *fop, scrambling* to the Play in a Mask" (IV.i.256–62). After forbidding Millamant vizard masks by day and beauty masks by night, tight corsets when pregnant, and all commerce with street vendors, Mirabell then sets conditions to Millamant's demand for the autonomous rule of her tea table: "Lastly, to the dominion of the *Tea-Table,* I submit—but with a *proviso* that you exceed not in your province, but restrain yourself to native and simple *Tea-Table* drinks, as *Tea, Chocolate,* and *Coffee.* As likewise to genuine and authoriz'd *Tea-Table* talk, such as mending of Fashions, spoiling Reputations, railing at absent Friends, and so forth; but that on no account you encroach upon the men's prerogative, and presume to drink healths or toast fellows" (IV.i.288–97).

While this discussion of domestic restrictions has been viewed as merely an excuse for witty repartee between the two amorous protagonists, it is in fact an integral part of the play's moral satire. With these preconditions, Millamant and Mirabell provide a conservative counterpoint to the ever-changing way of the world.[3] The dialogue suggests that Millamant bargains for an exceptional degree of freedom, yet she asks for nothing unseemly or extravagant. Her connubial stipulations pertain to personal privacy, domestic decorum, and feminine refinement. Millamant fears losing not only her "Will and Pleasure" (IV.i.199) but also the romance of courtship. Her stipulations attempt to sustain the mystery of acquaintance and to prevent casual familiarity, to ward off intimate knowledge and its consequence, satiety. To employ a psycholinguistic analogy, Millamant wants to avoid a marital fall into legibility, wishing rather to become a permanently unreadable sign, forever elusive. Fearing that the attentive devotion of the lover will quickly turn to the "Pedantick Arrogance of a very Husband" (IV.i.196–97), she concocts synthetic divisions to ensure her indecipherability, that strange but familiar otherness that makes her for the moment an ideal love object. Mirroring Mirabell and his desire, available but never entirely approachable, Millamant attempts vigorously to maintain her stasis. What seem like provisions by Millamant for freedom and power are endeavors not to extend her prerogatives but to freeze time, to remain eternally the same.

Mirabell's addenda to Millamant's living arrangement, however, radically alter Millamant's proposed way of life. Millamant's reasonable requests do not challenge the male order, and if there were anything revolutionary in her attempt to remain forever unknown, an attempt already compromised by its uncanny reflection of male desire, it collapses in Mirabell's rearticulation of her stipulations.[4] Tempering her demand to choose her own wardrobe, Mirabell insists that when Millamant is "breeding" she must dress in the manner he directs. Mirabell's healthy notion of maternity attire would be applauded today, but in his era, the free and loose clothing he deems appropriate would put an end to Millamant's social outings. Millamant can neither acknowledge nor discuss this aspect of married life; her proper restraint assures her consent. *Breeding,* of course, implies not only pregnancy but a way of life, one that differs substantially from that which Millamant now enjoys. "Ah! name it not" (IV.i.281), she exclaims as she interrupts Mirabell's description of her productive future. Millamant may disrupt Mirabell's narrative, but she cannot halt the natural progression of married life. Mirabell's sartorial directives harbor within them the more fundamental implications of the profound transformation from "fine lady," as she is called in the dramatis personae, to wife and mother. With trenchant concision, they ensure that Millamant will "by degrees, dwindle into a wife" (IV.i.249).

Mirabell regulates Millamant's personal relations as well as her personal apparel, forbidding her to have a close female friend and to discuss anything but petty concerns. She may indulge in "spoiling Reputations [and] railing at absent Friends," however, since these activities presumably do not "encroach upon the men's prerogative." Female gossip serves to reinforce the fear of social and moral transgression while it dispenses the punishment for it: public exposure.[5] By stressing proper feminine interests and encouraging female hostilities, Mirabell's designations of gender-specific discursive behavior reaffirm and maintain what we now would call an explicitly patriarchal social order. Mirabell shares Millamant's aspiration to freeze time, but a time of his own making. To prevent Millamant from becoming the typical lecherous, duplicitous wife of Restoration satiric comedy, he limits her private and verbal associations. That is, he dictates her friends and conversation.[6] Proscribing personal interchanges with women forbids the sharing of interpretations of events and actions. In the world of Restoration drama, as we learned from Wycherley and Congreve, interpretation by women presupposes or prepares for their loose, duplicitous behavior. Virtuous women do not interpret; on the contrary, they make a show of not understanding. In asserting control over Millamant's discourse, Mirabell endeavors to secure her honesty, both a metaphor for and a metonymy of her virtue.

It is at this point that connubial contracts and public intercourse collide and elide.[7] Mirabell's prerequisites revise the personal boundaries set by Millamant; her private conversation migrates unnoticed to the domain of social dictates. Millamant does not challenge this transposition. Rather, she endorses it by her response to Mirabell's allusion to her potential social violations. Not merely delicate and decorous, Millamant becomes positively prudish in the course of the proviso scene. She responds with haughty indignation to Mirabell's suggestion that she would ever enjoy a close female friend, risqué discourse, or alcoholic beverages, three particulars that seem to be of equal significance to her and to inspire equal disdain. Millamant may be the glory of her sex, but she is no friend to it. Like Angelica in Congreve's earlier play *Love for Love,* Millamant represents and defends her gender in the abstract but has no close, sisterly dealings with particular members of it. This distance is necessary because as heroine, Millamant must demonstrate her exemplary status. She is, quite literally, peerless.

In male-authored Restoration drama, when women band together they generally form unholy unions. In general, female intimacy can only be confessional or duplicitous. That is, a woman makes friends among members of her own sex either to enlist allies to aid and cloak her own immoral activities, or to discover her "friends' " secrets for blackmailing purposes. Virtuous heroines may be affable to, but not intimate with, other female protagonists. Intimacy would strongly suggest a shared moral laxity or a need for a precaution against loss of reputation. For heroines, other women are the enemy, and their social demise serves as the basis for the heroines' elevated status. That is, a heroine has no positive value of her own; rather, she accrues identity by comparison with others. Although Millamant appears to be the most independent and willful female character, she is by far the most proper and conventional—and her prenuptial specifications and Mirabell's proscriptions ensure that she shall remain so.

The other female characters in the play are variations on the theme of hypocrisy, which in women is always linked to sexual license. Lady Wishfort, Millamant's aunt, "full of the Vigour of Fifty-five" (I.i.67–68), hungers pathetically for remarriage. She dislikes Mirabell only because she once entertained the mistaken notion, encouraged by Mirabell, that he desired her. Mrs. Marwood is the lover of Fainall but yearns for Mirabell. Consequently, she does all in her power to prevent his marriage to Millamant. Mrs. Fainall, the daughter of Lady Wishfort and former paramour of Mirabell, still loves Mirabell and plots against her mother to help him marry Millamant. To varying degrees these women engage in dishonest, debased activity that leads to their exposure and humiliation. In the final act Lady Wishfort must swallow her pride and restrain her desire; she promises Mirabell anything in order to obtain his help to prevent her disgrace. Mrs. Marwood, the most dangerous and aggressive female, is exposed as Fainall's mistress, her plots discovered and her reputation ruined. She becomes the butt of the play's satiric joke, a joke that in the process of unfolding subordinates women to male authority.

The case of Mrs. Fainall poses an interesting dilemma. In a way, the young widow doubles for Millamant, representing an amicable worldly feminine presence and allowing the heroine to remain free from the taint of schemes and duplicity. While she is a loyal, invaluable friend to Mirabell, Mrs. Fainall is also a loose woman, false both to her husband and to her mother in the service of her former lover.[8] She abets Mirabell's plot, but as all of Congreve's plays demonstrate, plotting women too closely resemble clever interpreters, and Mrs. Fainall's actions, helpful though they may be, cannot be celebrated unequivocally. Unhappily married to the selfish, unfaithful Fainall, she complains to Mirabell:

> You have been the cause that I have lov'd without Bounds, and
> would you set limits to that Aversion of which you have been
> the occasion? Why did you make me marry this Man?
> *MIRABELL*. Why do we daily commit disagreeable and danger-

ous Actions? To save that Idol Reputation. If the familiarities of our Loves had produc'd that Consequence of which you were apprehensive, where could you have fix'd a Father's Name with Credit, but on a Husband? I knew *Fainall* to be a Man lavish of his Morals, an interested and professing Friend, a false and de-signing Lover; yet one whose wit and outward fair Behaviour have gain'd a Reputation with the Town enough to make that Woman stand excus'd who has suffer'd herself to be won by his Addresses. A better Man ought not to have been sacrific'd to the Occasion; a worse had not answer'd to the Purpose.

[II.i.287–303]

A true rake-hero, Mirabell keeps the secret of Mrs. Fainall's indiscretion and helps her to a husband when it appears their affair might produce offspring. Mrs. Fainall was a wealthy young widow when she met Mirabell, but since she yielded to his seductions, it seems she is not a fit candidate to be his bride. Although he is quick to protect her, Mirabell nonetheless believes that she does not merit an honorable man for a spouse.[9] Fainall is neither honest nor likable, but having bestowed the last favor on a man who is not her husband, Mrs. Fainall could not expect that "a better Man" should be "sacrific'd to the Occasion." Robert Hume remarks, "Within the play, we will find no hint that we should disapprove" of Mirabell's treatment of Mrs. Fainall (*Rakish Stage* 152).[10] It is clear that Mirabell abides by moral principles that limit the extent to which he will assist fallen women, even those he helped to make so.[11]

Women may never be able truly to mean no in the world of manners comedy, but those who say yes lose all claim to the respect and regard of the men to whom they succumb. They owe their good reputation no longer to their adherence to moral principles but to their seducers' discretion, and it is only the code of silence of "honorable" rakes that allows seduced women to remain in genteel society. When in reply to Mrs. Fainall's complaint that she "ought to stand in some degree of Credit" with him, Mirabell says, "I have made you privy to my whole Design, and put in your Power to ruin or advance my Fortune" (II.i.305–9), he is genuinely generous to his cast-off mistress. She can either play the bawd for him and remain his friend or spend her time with a husband she despises and friends she neither trusts nor enjoys. Even though she follows Mirabell's directions to the letter and sacrifices her mother-in-law and an additional portion of wealth at his request, she nevertheless must suffer a cad for a husband, Mirabell's cavalier treatment, and Millamant's cruel teasing. Mrs. Fainall serves as a strategic reminder of the pitfalls of knowledgeable discourse in women. While Millamant repeatedly, if artfully, refuses to look beneath the surface of events, Mrs. Fainall, like Mrs. Marwood, energetically participates in interpreting the actions and motives of the other characters. As a consequence, Mrs. Fainall, like Mrs. Marwood, must suffer the vicissitudes attendant on an easy familiarity with deceit.

Mrs. Fainall's continued support of Mirabell brings her little joy, while it seriously jeopardizes her social standing. In the end she must be rescued from obloquy by the cause of it. Mirabell deflects Mrs. Marwood's exposure of Mrs. Fainall's past amour with him by exposing in turn the adulterous intercourse between Mrs. Marwood and Fainall and by nullifying Fainall's claim to his wife's fortune. In this way, he restores to Mrs. Fainall wealth and a tolerable reputation, but not peace of mind. Although once again in control of her fortune, Mrs. Fainall cannot fully enjoy it; she is still married to a man she loathes, and her power is limited by her status as wife. Mirabell assures Lady Wishfort that he will "[c]ontribute all that in [him] lies to a Reunion" between her daughter and Fainall, and he tells Mrs. Fainall that her wealth "may be a means, well-manag'd, to make [her] live easily together" with her husband (V.677–78, 681–82). These lines may indicate Mirabell's intent to continue deceiving Lady Wishfort, or his cynical notion of the way of the world's marriages, or his sincere interest in sustaining the Fainall union, or all three, but regardless of what they may connote concerning Mirabell, they promise no happiness for Mrs. Fainall. No matter what course of action Mrs. Fainall takes, she can never escape the fact that she married a man she detests at the insistence of the man she loves.

Robert Markley contends that Mirabell's promises of mediation prove him to be a "libertine with a conscience. . . . The morally ambiguous act of marrying off his mistress is thus sanctioned by the playwright ideologically" (240).[12] If this is the case, then the ideological sanction is achieved by a refusal to acknowledge Mrs. Fainall's miserable plight. Mrs. Fainall's rather harsh treatment by Mirabell and Congreve derives, I would argue, from her formal position as the mediating figure between Millamant and Mrs. Marwood, a position that complements that of Mirabell between Fainall and the fops but that places Mrs. Fainall among those women who think "of other men and so make the lawful matrimonial embraces adultery; [who] wrong husbands and poets in thoughts and word, to keep their own reputations." Unlike charming, duplicitous men, charming, duplicitous women earn no desirable, honest spouses. A sympathetic but not admirable character in the play, Mrs. Fainall must pay for her conversance in the discourse of sexual duplicity. In the world of Restoration satiric comedy, even a generous-spirited fallen woman must be one of the butts of the satire's joke and must be made to suffer a certain degree of humiliation.

Mrs. Fainall and Mrs. Marwood are put in their place not only by Mirabell but also by Millamant. Both women suffer from the vexing conversation of the self-possessed heroine, although Mrs. Marwood under-goes by far the most biting attack.[13] Adept at social discourse, Millamant exaggerates, complains, exclaims, observes, and argues with precise gen-eralities and eloquent obfuscation. "Fainall, what shall I do?" Millamant asks.

> Shall I have [Mirabell]? I think I must have him.
> *MRS. FAINALL.* Ay, ay, take him, take him; what shou'd you do?
> *MILLAMANT.* Well then—I'll take my death I'm in a horrid fright.
> Fainall, I shall never say it. Well—I think—I shall endure you.
> *MRS. FAINALL.* Fie, fie, have him, have him, and tell him so in
> plain terms; for I am sure you have a mind to him.
> *MILLAMANT.* Are you? I think I have; and the horrid Man looks
> as if he thought so too. Well, you ridiculous thing you, I'll have you.
> [IV.i.312–24]

While there is no certain indication that Millamant knows of the romantic interlude between Mrs. Fainall and Mirabell, her teasing colloquy hints at her awareness. Unlike Mrs. Fainall, Millamant can marry the man she wants. Her deprecatory treatment of Mirabell, her hesitations, recon-siderations, and final acquiescence, are all acts of power that demonstrate both to Mirabell and to Mrs. Fainall the difference between Mrs. Fainall and herself, a difference that derives from Mirabell's desire. Millamant stresses this point once again in a long and nasty dialogue with Mrs. Marwood.

> *MRS. MARWOOD.* . . . . If you wou'd but appear bare-fac'd now,
> and own *Mirabell,* you might as easily put off *Petulant* and *Wit-*
> *woud* as your Hood and Scarf. And indeed 'tis time, for the town
> has found it; the secret is grown too big for the Pretence. . . . .
> *MILLAMANT.* I'll take my death, *Marwood,* you are more Censori-
> ous than a decay'd Beauty or a discarded Toast. . . . "The Town
> has found it." What has it found? That *Mirabell* loves me is no
> more a Secret than it is a Secret that you discover'd it to my
> Aunt, or than the Reason why you discover'd it is a Secret.
>
> •
> Poor *Mirabell!* His Constancy to me has quite destroy'd his Com-
> plaisance for all the World beside. . . . . If I had the Vanity to think
> he would obey me, I wou'd command him to show more Gal-
> lantry. 'Tis hardly well bred to be so particular on one Hand,
> and so insensible on the other. . . . . I grant you 'tis a little barba-
> rous. Ha, ha, ha!
> *MRS. MARWOOD.* . . . . I detest him, hate him, Madam.
> *MILLAMANT.* O Madam, why so do I—And yet the Creature
> loves me, Ha, ha, ha. . . . . [IV.i.341–89]

These excerpts from this very interesting and brutal exchange amply reveal the privileged status Millamant enjoys. As an exceedingly merry and confident Millamant and an increasingly bitter Mrs. Marwood demonstrate, Millamant is different from other women in the play because it is she whom Mirabell desires. She is also the "virtuous" woman who conceals her own desires and thus perfectly mirrors Mirabell's. Presumably Mirabell desires Millamant because she is different from other women in ways that are not merely the consequence of his desire. Yet it is not so much that Millamant is different as that other women have lost their difference; they have become substitutable links in a series, familiar but not uncanny and, as a consequence, no longer of interest to Mirabell. These women have made known their passion for Mirabell, while Millamant sends up smoke screens on which Mirabell can read only his own desire.

Both Mrs. Fainall and Mrs. Marwood point to Millamant's refusal to speak her desire, her refusal to "have [Mirabell], and tell him so in plain terms" (Mrs. Fainall, IV.i.319–20), to "appear bare-fac'd . . . and own *Mirabell*" (Mrs. Marwood, IV.i.341–42). Millamant never does tell Mirabell that she cares for him, although she confesses it to Mrs. Fainall. Millamant's withholding of that particular speech is very much like her withholding of the last favor: she stays honest (virginal) by holding her tongue, by keeping her feelings unspoken. Completely in keeping with the traditional double standard, Millamant's virtue is her lack of experience, a virtue that acquires its value when set off by women who lack that lack. She wins Mirabell's heart not by not giving her own but by showering him with general conversation to forestall particular admissions.[14] In short, she links her discursive behavior to her physical integrity, thereby embodying the Restoration's double meaning of *honesty*.

Although Millamant at times seems perfectly aware of the relative nature of her status as an object of desire—as her attempts by proviso to sustain this status after marriage prove—she at one point argues for the intrinsic nature of her desirability. This thesis seems both perverse and infeasible, but it is important to Millamant, and to the odd moral operations of the play, that she engage it with ardor. Millamant points out that

> when one parts with one's Cruelty, one parts with one's Power; and when one has parted with that, I fancy one's Old and Ugly. *MIRABELL.* Ay, ay suffer your Cruelty to ruin the object of your Power, to destroy your Lover—and then how vain, how lost a Thing you'll be! . . . For Beauty is the Lover's Gift; 'tis he bestows your Charms, your Glass is all a Cheat. The Old and Ugly, whom the Looking-glass mortifies, yet after Commendation can be flatter'd by it, and discover Beauties in it; for that reflects our Praises, rather than your Face.

MILLAMANT. . . . Lord, what is a Lover that it can give? Why, one makes Lovers as fast as one pleases, and they live as long as one pleases, and they die as soon as one pleases; and then, if one pleases, one makes more.

. . . .

One no more owes one's Beauty to a Lover, than one's Wit to an Echo. They can but reflect what we look and say; vain empty Things if we are silent or unseen, and want a being. [II.i.427–55]

Under the guise of polite conversation in St. James's Park, the two protagonists dispute fairly complicated philosophical concepts. Mirabell claims that beauty is in the eye of the beholder, that the observer designates what is and is not beautiful. Millamant declares that beauty is an innate property of the object, that observers' opinions cannot affect what is inherent.

All of Restoration drama militates against Millamant's contention. She herself recognizes that her argument does not apply to her own situation. Indeed, Millamant works very hard to stimulate artificially Mirabell's interest and desire. Her attraction of Mirabell is all a matter of position, completely subject to comparison and alteration. The song, "agreeable to [her] humor," that only an act later she longs to hear testifies to a savvy appreciation of the workings of preference. In what appears to be an ode to triangular desire, the song affirms:

Tis not to wound a wanton boy
Or am'rous youth, that gives the joy;
But 'tis the glory to have pierced a swain,
For whom inferior beauties sighed in vain.

Then I alone the conquest prize,
When I insult a rival's eyes;
If there's Delight in Love, 'tis when I see
That Heart Which others bleed for, bleed for me.
[III.i.415–18, 420–24]

Mirabell describes his attraction to Millamant in slightly different terms, terms that anticipate Jacques Lacan's account of sexual division by several centuries. Despite their markedly gender-specific relation to the play of desire, both protagonists characterize their affection as a process that allows them to see themselves with pleasure by the manipulation of others' responses. Mirabell explains:

I like her with all her Faults; nay, like her for her Faults. Her Follies are so natural, or so artful, that they become her; and those

Affectations which in another Woman wou'd be odious, serve but to make her more agreeable. I'll tell thee, *Fainall,* she once us'd me with that Insolence, that in Revenge I took her to pieces, sifted her, and separated her Failings; I study'd 'em, and got 'em by rote. The Catalogue was so large that I was not without hopes one Day or other to hate her heartily: to which end I so us'd myself to think of 'em that at length, contrary to my Design and Expectation, they gave me every Hour less and less distur-bance; 'till in a few Days it became habitual to me to remember 'em without being displeas'd. They are now grown as familiar to me as my own Frailties; and in all probability, in a little time longer I shall like 'em just as well. [I.i.177–94]

Millamant has become both a part and a mirror of Mirabell: he finds he likes her almost as much as he likes himself. She is his missing rib as well as his desirable Other. It is not that Millamant bewitches him but that Mirabell decides to love her. Millamant must take some credit for this decision, but it has nothing to do with inherent beauty. Rather, Millamant acts as a screen, throwing back the projections of others. While her virginity (honesty) demands that she possess no secrets, that she be innocent and hence transparent, hers is nonetheless a painstakingly studied pose. Millamant argues against her own modus operandi because as heroine she represents traditional values and universal standards. She must seem the antithesis of superficial considerations and relative worth, although, as her conjugal negotiations attest, she founds her future on both. In the debate in St. James's Park, Congreve's inconsistent moral philosophy is caught out. Millamant voices the conservative ideology of ultimate truths, caught in and representative of the play's contradictory attitude toward appearance and reality, word and deed.

Congreve's dedicatory polemic depends on this distinction be-tween virtuous integrity and vicious doubleness to free the play's moral satire from charges of salaciousness. It is the way of the world to attempt to halt promiscuous interpretations—the unrestrained way of the word—by using connubial contracts to define and reflect proper feminine public intercourse. The two different descriptions of feminine response to improper conversation reflect the two opposing characterizations of the heroine—innocent, straightforward, unaware of sexual reference, unac-quainted with double meaning, and urbane, circumspect, savvy, wittily articulate. Wit and morality are uneasily wed in heroines, who reveal one or the other but never both at the same time. Just as the two charac-terizations cannot unite to form a sophisticated but naive heroine, one that can both win the urbane hero and represent traditional values, Congreve's two depictions of innocent female readers cannot merge to form the impossible female auditor, that woman who does not apprehend prurient remarks but yet somehow knows that they refer to other women.

The play ends on a surprisingly pedantic moral note. Unlike Wycherley's *The Country Wife,* which closes with the cynical "Dance of the Cuckolds," *The Way of the World* distributes retribution and moral maxims with only the slightest, if any, trace of irony. Mirabell, the charming deceiver and seducer who uses fraud and duplicity to gain his ends, intones the final lines of the play to the assembled cast:

> From hence let those be warn'd, who mean to wed,
> Lest mutual Falsehood stain the Bridal-Bed;
> For each Deceiver to his Cost may find,
> That Marriage Frauds too oft are paid in kind.
>
> [V.682–85]

While this motto seems rather strange and inappropriate issuing from a rake who, after all, was the reason that falsehood stained the bridal bed of the Fainalls, it is perfectly in keeping with the play's discursive privileging of masculine authority.[15] Mirabell's sententious moralizing at the play's end and the careful parceling out of just deserts strongly suggest that moral "truth" wins out over ambiguous appearance, and that word and deed—in the person of Millamant and in the form of marriage—can (and must) be united. Edward Burns remarks succinctly, "The play ends with reality rediscovered, not transformed" (209).[16] Yet Millamant's coy behavior and future provisos and Mirabell's reasons for loving Millamant argue with equal force against that reading. The difficulty in restoring "reality"— in restoring a status quo that is also an ideal—is reflected in Millamant's contradictory philosophical positions. She argues earnestly for natural essence while everything about her speaks eloquently of artful construction. It is only the satiric joke—the exposure and humiliation of duplicitous women—that deflects attention away from the unresolved double nature of the heroine and provides the fragile moral basis for the play's satire.[17]

The Way of the World is not unique among manners comedies in its depictions of women or in its struggles with (mis)interpretations. Restoration satiric comedy and its heroines purport to reflect and yet fail to sustain a coherent, clearly moral position. Both mirror worlds in which the act of moral assessment becomes a difficult, almost impossible task, and both depend on a knowledge of duplicity that they condemn. I do not claim that these confusing dramatic renderings represent contemporary social conditions, that they realistically reflect the actual circumstances of women during the Restoration and eighteenth century.[18] Rather I argue, much more particularly, that the paradoxical demands made on female characters by playwrights of manners comedy slide into those made on female auditors. The dramatists' arguments in defense of their satiric treatments of female hypocrisy, duplicity, and sexual desire expose the gap in the moral premises of Restoration comic satire, a gender gap that has as much to do with putative female spectators as with female characters. Those arguments, made half in jest and half in defensive justification of the plays, project their troubling gendered interpretive strategy beyond the confines of the plays. The honesty and virtue that authors purport to depict depends on the contrast between the heroine and the rest of the female protagonists in the play, and the approval or mute acceptance of this contrast by female spectators or readers. That is, the moral integrity that the plays link to the possibility of the heroine's discursive honesty must find a referent outside itself in the moral understanding of virtuous women. And yet, at the same time, virtuous women—both within the play and in the context of its reception—are not supposed to understand a word.

Notes

Portions of and elaborations on this article can be found in my book *Interpreting Ladies: Women, Wit, and Morality in the Restoration Comedy of Manners* (Athens: U of Georgia P, 1994).

1. All citations of the play refer to Henderson.
2. In his important study, Norman Holland finds that the proviso and contract scenes reveal the inner feelings of Mirabell and Millamant and emancipate them, especially Millamant, from oppressive familial authority. Holland theorizes that the discussions bring Millamant "from girlhood to maturity" (185) yet claims as well that her provisos endeavor to maintain her prenuptial allure. Novak ("Love, Scandal") and McDonald (155–56) postulate that these stipulations protect both characters from the world of gossip, knaves, and fools. Brown reads the provisos as attempts to find "mutual private happiness within the confines of a rigid and demanding social context" (133).
3. Peter Holland (*Ornament of Action* 240) thinks the provisos constitute an attempt by Mirabell to confine the "whirlwind" Millamant. See Markley 244–47 for a fine exposition of the social and linguistic implications of this scene.
4. This reading is informed by the Lacanian notion of the Other, which, in psycholinguistic terms, is the nonexistent lost object of desire—actually a version of oneself—that one seeks in imaginary relation to others. See Lacan's "The Mirror Stage as Formative of the Function of the I" and "The Freudian Thing," in *Ecrits* 1–7, 114–45. For an excellent explanatory discussion of this and other related aspects of Lacan's theory, see Jacqueline Rose's "Introduction—II" in Lacan, *Feminine Sexuality* 27–57.
5. See Spacks 124–26 for an alternative reading of the power and politics of gossip.
6. Roper discusses the provisos as they relate to Mirabell's pursuit of mastery over Millamant's language. He writes: "Mirabell fears that Millamant's ten-

dency to use words to distract herself from obligations might lead her to engage, carelessly, in social folly or actual iniquity" (67).

7. For critical assessments that primarily address the language of the play, see Kaufman; Roussel 124–59; and Markley 233–50.

8. In an interesting recent article, Elizabeth Kraft makes use of Amazonian literature as well as Spacks's argument in *Gossip* of the transgressive and subversive aspects of female discourse to read Mrs. Fainall as both a threat and reproach to Mirabell and, by extension, men in the seventeenth century, a threat and reproach Congreve recognizes and obscures.

9. Norman Holland comments that there is very little difference between Mirabell and Fainall, and that Mirabell treats Mrs. Fainall "very shoddily indeed" (188; see 175–98). Wain calls Mirabell a "cad," pointing out that both Mirabell and Fainall have behaved abominably to Mrs. Fainall (384). Brown, too, finds Mirabell and Fainall indistinguishable at first (133). For a full elaboration of their troubling similarities, see Hawkins 115–38.

    Some critics think that the play carefully elaborates the differences between Mirabell and Fainall. Peter Holland, in *Ornament of Action*, discusses the play in relation to the conflict between the two male protagonists for moral and social primacy as well as the rivalry between the two leading-man actors who played their parts, Thomas Betterton and J.B. Verbruggen (235). Braverman sees this as the primary concern of the play. McCloskey offers a persuasive account of the play as a series of judiciously conceived occasions demonstrating the moral and familial authority of Mirabell. Markley, although stressing the properties of the language, agrees that Congreve's play teaches the audience to distinguish the moral discourse of Mirabell from the immoral discourses in the play, primarily that of Fainall (233–50), and Weber proposes that the play "establishes the philosophical libertine's distance from the Hobbesian libertine" (123).

10. Weber comments: "An audience may feel, of course, that Mirabell should have sacrificed himself, but that is not the way of this world" (125).

11. For an indication of Congreve's fairly misogynistic view of women, see Hodges 183.

12. Markley also argues that Mirabell is genuinely concerned about Mrs. Fainall and her family and that his schemes "promote both their interests" (240).

13. See Birdsall 235; Novak, *Congreve* 146–49; and McDonald 150–51.

14. Markley provides very good discussion of Millamant's wit (242–43).

15. See Peter Holland, *Ornament of Action* 233–43; McCloskey; and Markley 240–42. They argue that by this time Congreve has cleverly established Mirabell as a proper moral (discursive) authority to rule women and lesser men.

16. Burns argues provocatively that the play "takes great risks . . . to decoy us with plot into confronting relationship" (204). He calls the play a "summation of Restoration comedy" (205). "Congreve invents nothing," Burns concludes; "his plays are virtuosic arrangements of received ideas . . . [that] imply no further comedies" (211).

17. For recent interpretations of the play's satire, see Bruce 80–81; Love 85–107; Brown 128–35; and Hawkins 115–38. Some critics consider the play to lack a satiric approach or to produce a confused or contradictory moral

perspective: see Donaldson 154–58; Parfitt 21–38; and Hume, *Development* 435–37.

18. A few studies that provide descriptions and examinations of the predicament of women in the seventeenth century are Clark; Gagen; Stenton; Reynolds; Latt; Fraser; Schofield and Macheski; and George.

Works Cited

Birdsall, Virginia Ogden. *Wild Civility: The English Comic Spirit on the Restoration Stage*. Bloomington: Indiana UP, 1971.

Braverman, Richard. "Capital Relations and *The Way of the World*." *ELH* 52 (1985): 133–58.

Brown, Laura. *English Dramatic Form, 1660–1760: An Essay in Generic History*. New Haven, Conn.: Yale UP, 1981.

Bruce, Donald. *Topics of Restoration Comedy*. New York: St. Martin's, 1974.

Burns, Edward. *Restoration Comedy: Crises of Desire and Identity*. Basingstoke, Eng.: Macmillan, 1987.

Clark, Alice. *Working Life of Women in the Seventeenth Century*. London: Routledge, 1919.

Donaldson, Ian. *The World Turned Upside-Down: Comedy from Jonson to Fielding*. Oxford: Clarendon, 1970.

Fraser, Antonia. *The Weaker Vessel*. New York: Random House, 1984.

Gagen, Jean. *The New Woman: Her Emergence in English Drama, 1600–1730*. New York: Twayne, 1954.

George, Margaret. *Women in the First Capitalist Society: Experiences in Seventeenth-Century England*. Urbana: U of Illinois P, 1988.

Hawkins, Harriet. *Likenesses of Truth in Elizabethan and Restoration Drama*. Oxford: Clarendon, 1972.

Henderson, Anthony G., ed. *The Comedies of William Congreve*. Cambridge: Cambridge UP, 1982.

Hodges, John C., ed. *William Congreve: Letters and Documents*. New York, 1964.

Holland, Norman N. *The First Modern Comedies: The Significance of Etherege, Wycherley, and Congreve*. Cambridge, Mass.: Harvard UP, 1959.

Holland, Peter. *The Ornament of Action: Text and Performance in Restoration Comedy*. Cambridge: Cambridge UP, 1979.

———, ed. *The Plays of William Wycherley*. Cambridge: Cambridge UP, 1981.

Hume, Robert D. *The Development of English Drama in the Late Seventeenth Century*. Oxford: Clarendon, 1976.

———. *The Rakish Stage: Studies in English Drama, 1660–1800*. Carbondale: Southern Illinois UP, 1983.

Kaufman, Anthony. "Language and Character in Congreve's *Way of the World*." *Texas Studies in Language and Literature* 15 (1973): 411–27.

Kraft, Elizabeth. "Why Didn't Mirabell Marry the Widow Languish?" *Restoration* 13 (Spring 1989): 26–34.

Lacan, Jacques. *Ecrits: A Selection*. Trans. Alan Sheridan. New York: Norton, 1977.

————. *Feminine Sexuality and the Ecole Freudienne.* Ed. Juliet Mitchell. Ed. and trans. Jacqueline Rose. New York: Norton, 1982.

Latt, David J. "Praising Virtuous Ladies: The Literary Image and the Historical Reality of Women in Seventeenth-Century England." *What Manner of Woman: Essays on English and American Life and Literature.* Ed. Marlene Springer. New York: New York UP, 1977.

Love, Harold. *Congreve.* Oxford: Blackwell, 1974.

Markley, Robert. *Two-Edg'd Weapons: Style and Ideology in the Comedies of Etherege, Wycherley, and Congreve.* Oxford: Clarendon, 1988.

McCloskey, Susan. "Knowing One's Relations in Congreve's *The Way of the World.*" *Theatre Journal* 33 (1981): 69–79.

McDonald, M.L. *The Independent Woman in the Restoration Comedy of Manners.* Salzburg: Universität Salzburg, 1976.

Novak, Maximillian E. "Love, Scandal, and the Moral Milieu of Congreve's Comedies." *Congreve Consider'd.* Ed. Maximillian E. Novak and Aubrey Williams. Los Angeles: William Andrews Clark Memorial Library, 1971. 24–50.

————. *William Congreve.* New York: Twayne, 1972.

Parfitt, George. "The Case against Congreve." *William Congreve.* Ed. Brian Morris. London: Ernest Benn, 1972. 21–38.

Reynolds, Myra. *The Learned Lady in England: 1650–1760.* Gloucester, Mass.: Smith, 1964.

Roper, Alan. "Language and Action in *The Way of the World, Love's Last Shift,* and *The Relapse.*" *ELH* 40 (1973): 44–69.

Roussel, Roy. *The Conversation of the Sexes: Seduction and Equality in Selected Seventeenth- and Eighteenth-Century Texts.* Oxford: Clarendon, 1986.

Schofield, Mary Anne, and Cecilia Macheski, eds. *Fetter'd or Free?: English Women Novelists, 1670–1815.* Athens: Ohio UP, 1986.

Spacks, Patricia Meyer. *Gossip.* Chicago: U of Chicago P, 1986.

Stenton, Doris. *The English Woman in History.* London: Allen and Unwin, 1957.

Wain, John. "Restoration Comedy and Its Modern Critics." *Essays in Criticism* 6 (1956): 367–85.

Weber, Harold. *The Restoration Rake-Hero: Transformations in Sexual Understanding in Seventeenth-Century England.* Madison: U of Wisconsin P, 1986.

PART 3

The Gaze Reversed: Theory and History of Performance

Rape, Voyeurism, and the Restoration Stage

Jean I. Marsden

*T*he advent of actresses upon the Restoration stage revolutionized English drama, creating a new climate for sexual display. One extreme form that such display took in the last two decades of the seventeenth century was a new emphasis on the representation of rape. Scenes of rape, carefully staged and lovingly detailed, became a new and erotically potent element of Restoration drama, appearing with particular frequency in the serious drama of the period. Attempted rapes are absent in Shakespeare—the rape of Lavinia in *Titus Andronicus* occurs offstage, so that the spectator sees only the gory aftermath—and relatively rare in Renaissance drama as a whole. When rape occurs, as in *Titus Andronicus* or Fletcher's *Valentinian,* playwrights emphasize the need for revenge but do not represent rape as a titillating sexual exhibition. In contrast, such scenes were routine in the drama of the last decades of the seventeenth century, and their function was decidedly erotic or even pornographic. When Shakespeare was updated for the Restoration stage, playwrights added scenes in which virtuous women were threatened with rape. In Nahum Tate's *King Lear* Edmund attempts to rape Cordelia on the heath, while in Tate's adaptation of *Coriolanus* Aufidius attempts to rape Virgilia. Likewise, in an adaptation of *Cymbeline* Thomas D'Urfey adds a new female character whose sole purpose seems to be to have her virtue attacked by Cloten. By 1697 the spectacle of rape was common enough in drama to be parodied in Vanbrugh's *The Relapse,* where Loveless carries the willing Berinthia offstage as she murmurs—"very softly"—in the manner of serious dramatic heroines: "Help, Help, I'm ravish'd, ruin'd, undone" (IV.iii.79).[1]

Crucially, the proliferation of rape scenes coincides with the appearance of actresses upon the British stage, linking the representation of rape on the stage to visible femininity. Such scenes are fundamentally voyeuristic, depending for their effect on the audience's role as voyeurs and the actress's function as object of their collective gaze. Writing of the visual significance of women in performance, film theorist Laura Mulvey states, "In their traditional exhibitionist role women are simultaneously looked at and displayed, with their appearance coded for strong visual and erotic impact so that they can be said to connote *to-be-looked-at-ness.* Woman displayed as sexual object is the leitmotif of erotic spectacle. . . . she holds the look, plays to and signifies male desire" ("Visual Pleasure" 62). "Displayed" on the Restoration stage, often in sexually revealing costumes, the actress was presented as sexual object and thus the locus of voyeurism. Her "to-be-looked-at-ness" defined her function as object of desire. Although the dynamics of the Restoration stage allowed for a gaze more fragmented and reciprocal, and less narrowly focused, than that of cinema, the actress was still the necessary ingredient that turned tableau into erotic spectacle.

The scenes of rape introduced into Restoration drama demon-strate Mulvey's theory of woman as sexual display in an extreme form. They present an explicitly sexual situation that foregrounds the sexuality of the actress. Dwelling upon the sexual component of rape, these scenes provide a new and effective stage dynamic focused on the body of the actress. As the joint appearance of actresses and scenes of rape indicates, rape becomes possible as theatrical spectacle only when visible signs of the female are present: breasts, bare shoulders, and "ravished" hair. Edward Ravenscroft inserts such visual markers into his adaptation of *Titus Andronicus* (1681), providing new stage directions to describe Lavinia's appearance after her ravishment. She is to appear onstage with "*Loose hair, and garments disorder'd, as ravished*" (26). Both the loose hair and the disordered garments are later read by other characters as indicators of her rape: "And who hath thus torn down thy precious hair / And rifl'd thee?" (27), and later, "By the disorder of thy dress, I fear / Thou wert i'th' Salvage hands of Ravishers" (35). Such coded signs identify the actress as the focus of desire, so that the rape becomes the physical manifestation of the desire perpetrated by the rapist but implicit in the audience's gaze. Thus the audience, like the rapist, "enjoys" the actress, deriving its pleasure from the physical presence of the female body.[2]

Fictions designed as erotic spectacle for an audience that is tacitly assumed to be male, these scenes present rape as both violent and intensely erotic. They bear little resemblance to what we know of actual rapes committed and prosecuted in the early modern period, when convictions were rare and the demands of proof extreme.[3] Likewise, the distinction crucial to most twentieth-century discussions of rape—between rape as a crime of violence and rape as a crime of sexual desire—is absent or irrelevant. Catharine A. MacKinnon uses this distinction to stress the different meanings rape has for men and women, while Susan Brownmiller states baldly that rape is "a conscious process of intimidation by which *all men* keep *all women* in a state of fear" (15), adding later: "All rape is an exercise in power" (256). Displays of masculine power are an inherent part of most stage rapes, often feeding the desire of the rapist. The origin of these rapes, however, is male sexual appetite, a characteristic most visible in Restoration serious drama, where rape is portrayed as a simple matter of evil versus good, and where "bad" sexual desire results in sexual violence. As represented on the stage, the motivation for rape is blatantly, even crudely sexual, and to emphasize the erotic potential of the rape itself, the rapist's desire is explicitly stated. Coupled with the physical display of the actress, these descriptions, often expressed at length and in near-pornographic detail, operate to arouse the audience's desire. The eroticism of the spectacle is intensified by the probity, virtue, and suffering of the victim, which are never in doubt. Stylized and patently unrealistic, the picture of rape presented to Restoration theatergoers represented an erotic fantasy to be vicariously experienced through the act of voyeurism.

The scenes of rape follow the same general pattern. In each, a chaste and virtuous woman is confronted by a powerful, often evil man—usually the play's villain. She is helpless to resist his attack, and the scene ends in one of two ways: either the heroine is rescued by a strong male character, her lover or her father, or she is dragged off to meet a fate worse than death. In addition, the heroine must be established as the eroticized object of desire, so that the attack on her virtue is clearly motivated by lust—the villain's lust and, as suggested above, that of the audience. A subcategory features women who are raped by men impersonating their husbands, as in Thomas Otway's *The Orphan* or John Dryden's *Amphitryon*. In each case, the woman's fate depends upon the outcome of this scene: if she is rescued intact, she can be allowed to survive; otherwise she must die (or kill herself to prevent violation). Only in the comedy *Amphitryon* is the heroine allowed to live, her innocence lost to the amorous Jupiter.[4]

These scenes display in no uncertain terms both the objectification of women and the polarized gender relations that underlie this objectification. As a result, the scenes of attempted rape split gender into extremes of active masculinity and passive femininity. The opposition between male and female that defines these scenes can be expanded into a series of gender-related dichotomies, all of which are reinscribed in the rapes: active/passive, dominant/submissive, sadist/masochist, subject/object— and ultimately desire/object. In their use of sexual violence, the scenes provide perhaps the most graphic possible example of phallocentrism, an effect that is accentuated by verbal descriptions of women as commodities.[5] Such dichotomies were essential parts of the social construction of gender, and in this sense, the scenes of attempted rape present a perverse, but accurate, distillation of Restoration attitudes regarding gender.[6] They are most noticeable in the serious drama—tragedies and tragicomedies or pathetic plays—of the 1680s and 1690s, in which the scenes of rape are most common; these plays derive their emotional impact from the suffering of defenseless women (see Brown). These extremes of gender stand in ironic contrast to the deliberate blurring of gender lines that can be seen, often in the same plays as the attempted rapes, in figures such as cross-dressed women—and men—and the excessively effeminate fop. In the decades following the Restoration, gender lines became more firmly fixed, but the rape scenes remained even as the fops died out and cross-dressed men vanished from the stage.[7]

The scopic appeal of these scenes lies in their volatile blend of sexuality and suffering, a combination recognizable to the late seventeenth-century audience as "pathos." Jean Hagstrum discusses the roots of the term *pathetic,* finding there "ancient associations with passivity in pain and love" (6) and linking the use of pathos near the beginning of the eighteenth century with violence. This violent sense of pathos appears most conspicuously in the scenes of attempted rape, where violence represents an essential part of pathos and where the ravished woman becomes the source of voyeuristic pleasure. The effect of such scenes depends on the objectification of the heroine, on her representation as both object of pity and object of desire. The attempted rapes yoke these seemingly disparate emotions together through violence. Both emotions are made available to the audience through the heroine's desirability and through her suffering. To heighten the effect, victims of rape were usually played by actresses who specialized in pathos, such as Elizabeth Barry or Anne Bracegirdle.[8] The objectification of women appears even in the language of the drama, as the villains express their desire "to enjoy" their victims, grammatically and visually presenting themselves as the active subject and their victims as the passive object.

This amalgam of desire and pity depends on establishing the heroine as both undefiled virgin and erotic object. The lust of the villain sexualizes the chaste heroine, and her status as object of desire for both rapist and audience is emphasized by the scenes' focus on the body of the heroine-actress. Thus in Otway's *The Orphan* Monimia is established as sexual object early in the play, when the page comments:

> Madam, indeed I'd serve you with my Soul;
> But in a morning when you call me to you,
> As by your bed I stand and tell you stories,

I am asham'd to see your swelling Breasts,
It makes me blush, they are so very white.
                    [I.i.221–25]

These lines draw attention to Monimia's sexual attractiveness, establishing her as erotic object. The emphasis is on the act of looking; the page's words invite us to imagine the bed and the white and swelling breasts. The passage also invites the audience to rediscover this erotic spectacle in the person of the actress who enacts Monimia, whose breasts would be clearly visible and emphasized by dress and staging in the intimacy of the Restoration theater.

Despite the heroine's being established as an erotic object for the male gaze of both characters and audience, the particular essence of her chaste desirability paradoxically lies in her unblemished purity. As Susan Staves has observed, the attempts on the heroine's virtue become proof that such virtue exists; the proof of female chastity lies in the very act that could destroy it. As in contemporary legal practice, were the heroine unchaste, there could be no violation, and rape would have no meaning. Virtue is a necessary precondition to both the definition and the representation of rape. Stage rapists are not interested in violating the unchaste. Tate's Edmund finds his desire "kindled" by knowledge of Cordelia's virtue as well as by her appeals to his pity for her father. Even more explicitly, in D'Urfey's *The Injured Princess* the villainous Jachimo explains the erotic stimulation of female pathos. Dragged off into the woods by a band of ruffians, the young maid Clarina pleads with her attackers:

> *CLARINA.* Look on my tears, and let them melt your heart,
> Your rocky hearts, yet harder far than Stone;
> For Stones melt, when relenting Heavens weeps,
> But you grow more obdurate with my tears.
> *JACHIMO.* Tears? Why thou canst not oblige me more than to
> Weep soundly; it makes the flame of Love more
> Vigorous.
>   [38]

Here, pathos stimulates desire rather than dampening it—a fact that undoubtedly explains the popularity of the genre. It titillates both the audience and Jachimo and at the same time arouses the audience's pity, engaging the spectators in a kind of doublethink combining voyeuristic enjoyment with moral essentialism. Clarina is helpless except for her tears in a scene that derives its effectiveness from the opposition of passivity and a highly sexual "vigor."

Scenes of rape represent women as victimized both physically and symbolically: pure women, like Clarina, are inescapably helpless when faced with phallic power. In each scene, the woman is unable to act, her passivity directly contrasted with the active desire of the rapist. Visually, the female characters are represented as kneeling, crying to heaven for help, weeping, and, inevitably, calling for death (thunderbolts from heaven seem to be the favorite method). They are helpless to evade violation; only suicide or the arrival of (male) assistance on the scene can save them. Suicide is the most active response allowed them, but as presented here, it is itself a negation of self. Overall, their behavior echoes that prescribed by contemporary conduct books, which told women that their proper refuge from any threat lay in a passive defense: tears, prayers, and pathos.[9] In the case of Tate's Aufidius, the sight of Virgilia's suffering converts his "Rage" into "Sorrow"—unfortunately not before Virgilia has killed herself—but the other male characters are easily able to resist the "weapons" of their victims, usually by drowning their sobs and cries with music or with thunder, as Edmund explains:

> like the vig'rous *Jove* I will enjoy
> This *Semele* in a Storm, 'twill deaf her Cries
> Like Drums in Battle, lest her Groans shou'd pierce
> My pittying Ear, and make the amorous Fight less fierce.
> [*Lear* III.ii.122–25]

Perversely, while this passive response enables the rape, resisting more actively could make the victim complicit in the rape—at least in literary representation. Discussing the response to rape in literature, Ellen Rooney writes that "phallocentric criticism of texts that pivot on scenes of sexual violence" contrasts seduction and rape (91), an opposition that depends on the helplessness of the victim. Any form of activity—even resistance—is read as complicity, seduction rather than rape. (Rooney cites several readings of *Clarissa,* for example, in which Clarissa is seen as complicit in her own violation and thus not to be pitied.) A seventeenth-century version of this attitude can be found in *The Excellent Woman Described by Her True Characters and Their Opposites* (1692), a conduct book that faults Lucrece for her response to rape: "If she had not been at all Criminal, she might without doubt have found more remedy for her trouble in her Conscience than in Death. They say she resisted more out of humour, or some secret considerations, than out of Vertue" (81). In other words, Lucrece tried too hard and overacted; she would not have had to go to such extremes had she been innocent. In order for the rape to be presented as such and for the victim-heroine to avoid complaints such as those leveled at Clarissa and Lucrece, the dramatic representation must unequivocally establish the dichotomies that underlie the construction of gender: good women must be shown as passive and helpless; otherwise they risk crossing the line between rape and seduction. Thus, instead of resisting their attackers, the victims attack themselves, tearing their hair and ultimately destroying themselves, not their attackers. Such violence only underscores their helplessness and in turn increases the audience's pity.

Nicholas Brady's aptly named tragicomedy, *The Rape; or, The Innocent Imposters* (1692), presents the archetypical representation of rape. It displays, at length, the issues I have delineated as characteristic of rape in the Restoration theater. The play's central incident involves the rape of the virtuous Eurione (played by Anne Bracegirdle) by the evil Genselarick. The play follows the conventional representation of rape but is remarkable for the extent to which it dwells on the vision, real or imagined, of ravished womanhood. This focus begins early in the second act as the villain expatiates upon his desire for Eurione, visualizing the upcoming scene with relish:

> Methinks I see already
> Her dying Looks, her seeming faint Resistance,
> And feel the mighty Transports of hot Love!
> [21]

Like the critics of Clarissa and Lucrece, Genselarick envisions any struggle that Eurione may make as encouragement, so that her "seeming" resistance only arouses his "hot Love" and makes the rape inevitable.

The audience is given ample opportunity to savor the rape themselves; although the rape necessarily occurs offstage, the progress of Genselarick's evil designs is relayed to the audience by the supposed prince Agilmond's description of the shrieks "he" hears. Immediately after the rape, the scene draws to display the erotic spectacle of the ravished woman: "*the Scene draws, and discovers Eurione in an Arbour, gagg'd and bound to a Tree, her hair dishevel'd as newly Ravish'd, a Dagger lying by her*" (25). The elaborately coded tableau carefully presents Eurione to the audience's gaze: Eurione's "Ravish'd" hair becomes the signifier of her violation, the ropes and gag testify to her helpless state, and a dagger, the symbolic representation of her violation, lies by her side. This exhibition of erotic symbols establishes the crisis of ravished womanhood on which the play centers. The voyeuristic import of the tableau is echoed two scenes later when the violated Eurione is again displayed, this time as the object of the collective gaze of the Goth aristocracy, while her mother, Rhadegondra, exclaims, "Behold my Lords, the Ruines of your Princess!" (29).

This vision of the violated woman dominates the last acts of Brady's play. All eyes are upon her, and her response to being the object of such mass voyeurism is one of horror: "I cannot bear their eyes; already see / All turn and gaze, as if they saw a Monster" (53). The repeated exhibitions of Eurione's violated virginity link the sexual with the monstrous, a kind of sexual freak show in which the violated woman becomes the monster, fascinating but unwholesome and ultimately unnatural. Sexually experienced but virtuous, she is not virgin, wife, or whore and thus serves no legitimate function within a patriarchal society. Eurione's repeated descriptions of herself as an abomination, "nothing but a loathsome Leprosie" or contagion that will "blister" all "chaste hands" (5), compound this effect. Her fears are borne out by the behavior of the other characters, who argue that contact with such a creature should disgust the truly noble. One of the king's advisers even designs a trial for the supposed rapist: he will be given the chance to marry Eurione or die. If he is innocent, so the reasoning goes, then contact with such contagion would be too vile to contemplate:

> His Royal Blood will prompt him to endure
> Ten thousand deaths, rather than marry one
> That's Ravish'd by another.
>
> [34]

The emphasis on the accused rapist's "Royal Blood" suggests that the revulsion occasioned by the ravished woman is rooted in her sexual uncleanness. She is no longer the appropriate vessel for the patrilineal seed. Order can be restored only when this manifestation of sexual disorder is annihilated, and in the final act Eurione, inevitably, stabs herself in despair, destroying the "loathsome" threat and allowing the play to end happily.

The fear of the "monstrous" violated woman is taken to its logical extreme in Henry Crisp's mid–eighteenth century play, *Virginia* (1754). The play's story resembles that of Chaucer's Physician's Tale: the title character is threatened with rape when she is claimed as a slave by a lascivious enemy of her father. Her position as slave and as female presents perhaps the most extreme possible image of powerlessness. In this crisis, her father, whose claim to her is disputed, can only counsel patience, the passive response traditionally assigned to women by moralists. In the end, to prevent her violation, Virginia's father stabs her, exchanging one form of penetration for another.

Virginia's predicament hinges on a key question: To whom does she belong? The same question could be asked regarding the other women who, like Virginia, are threatened with rape. The issue is an important component of these scenes and presents another aspect of the objectification of women, namely their repeated representation as commodities. Such representations enact Lévi-Strauss's postulation that women have symbolic value as exchange and as property. The rape scenes clearly express this coding of women in their emphasis on the heroine as commodity and on the rapist as thief. While the motivation may be sexual, the crime itself is one against property. Like Virginia, whose fate is determined by competing claims to "own" her, Dryden's Jupiter in *Amphitryon* and Crowne's Caligula justify their rapes through claims of ownership. Caligula commandeers Julia as part of his empire, while Jupiter claims the right of the father-creator to repossess his work:

> For, when I made her, I decreed her such
> As shou'd please to love. I wrong not him
> Whose Wife she is; for I reserv'd my Right,
> To have her while she pleas'd me; that once past,
> She shall be his again.
> [*Amphitryon* I.i.108–12]

Alcmena here has no claim on her own body or her own sexuality; both are appropriated by the men for whom she is a token of exchange: the father-creator and the husband. In this system of ownership, her husband is wronged by Jupiter's use of his property; the "property" herself is not considered.[10]

Inevitably, when rape occurs it is equated with loss of property, and the metaphor most commonly used to explain the horror of rape is that of the loss of wealth. Nathaniel Lee's Brutus describes the ravished Lucrece looking "as if she had lost her wealth in some black storm" (I.98), in the same way that Julia's husband, Valerius, in Crowne's *Caligula* wishes that Caesar had stolen anything other than his wife's honor, "ravishing" instead "all my lands, / Bottomless treasure, numberless commands" (39). The designation of the female body as male property is most disturbingly expressed by Virgilia in Tate's adaptation of *Coriolanus*. Threatened with rape by Aufidius, she stabs herself, explaining:

> My Noble *Martius,* 'tis a *Roman* Wound,
> Giv'n by *Virgilia*'s Hand, that rather chose
> To sink this Vessel in a Sea of Blood,
> Than suffer its chast Treasure, to Become
> Th' unhallowed *Pyrate*'s Prize.
> [*Ingratitude* 61]

This Virgilia has defined herself as commodity and her own violation as theft, and she describes her suicide as the means to prevent a symbolic theft. She can only save this commodity by destroying it, sinking the vessel rather than allowing it to be boarded and appropriated. Once raped, the virtuous woman becomes symbolically devoid of meaning, because the act of rape leaves the victim a defiled vessel and thus worthless. She represents a cipher that must be destroyed either by her own hand or by an appropriate agent of the patriarchal order, such as her father.

Like the plays of her male colleagues, the works of the Restoration's one prominent woman playwright, Aphra Behn, include scenes of attempted rape (in *The Rover* and *The Luckey Chance*), but her emphasis differs significantly. In these scenes, Behn is more concerned with the male objectification of women than with the display of women as erotic objects, a concern that creates a noticeably different dynamic of rape. *The Rover* contains two attempted rapes, both inflicted upon the virtuous Florinda. In the first (III.v), Florinda is detained in her own garden by the drunken Willmore, but no real danger exists. She calls out, and both Belvile and her brother Don Pedro appear. The second example (IV.v–V.i) presents a more palpable menace, as Blunt threatens to rape Florinda not out of sexual desire—Willmore's motive—but out of his desire to revenge himself upon womankind in general. "Thou shalt lie with me too," he claims, "not that I care for the enjoyment, but to let thee see I have ta'en deliberated malice to thee, and will be revenged on one whore for the sins of another" (IV.v.54–57). Here Behn stresses the violence of the proposed rape, not its potential for sexual titillation. The scene may create tension, but it is in no way an erotic spectacle. Following this, in one of the play's most disturbing scenes, first Frederick, then Belvile, Willmore, and Don Pedro arrive, and all lay claim to Florinda, who has been confined offstage. Each man expresses his desire to enjoy the hidden Florinda, and they finally agree to settle their debate on the basis of a thinly veiled phallic competition: the man with the longest sword will possess the woman. Behn's concern here is less with the sexual dynamics of rape than with the spectacle of male competition for the objectified female—who is notably absent throughout the scene and thus not available to the audience's gaze. Even here, Behn ridicules this male posturing when the foolish Blunt attempts to save face by fabricating a version of events in which Florinda attacks *him*. He says that she "had doubtless committed a rape upon me, had not this sword defended me" (V.73–74).

A different, yet equally disturbing vision of sexual violation appears near the end of another Behn comedy, *The Luckey Chance*. Here Gayman wins a night with his former love Lady Fulbank by playing dice with her husband. Like Polydore in *The Orphan* and Jupiter in *Amphitryon*, he takes the husband's place in Lady Fulbank's bed, in the process "seizing," as he says, his "Right of Love" (V.vii.358). Although not described as a rape, Gayman's copulation with Lady Fulbank is forced upon her without her knowledge or consent, and her response to the act is similar to the response of ravished women throughout Restoration drama. She cries out that her honor has been ruined. Gayman's "right" has been seized at the cost of her identity, making her, as she laments, "a base Prostitute, a foul Adulteress" (V.vii.361). Lady Fulbank's lament is the more remarkable in light of her own earlier seduction of Gayman, in a scene curiously parallel to this one; what has been ravished here is not so much her physical chastity as her own will and subjectivity—herself. In contrast to the patriarchal solution posed in Dryden's *Amphitryon,* where Jupiter "makes up for" the rape by telling Alcmena that she will bear his son, Behn allows her heroine to break from her doddering husband as Lady Fulbank vows "to separate for ever from his Bed" (V.vii.402). Nonetheless, as the play ends, Sir Cautious "bequeaths" his lady and his estate to Gayman, perpetuating the pervasive objectification of women.

In *The Luckey Chance,* as in *The Rover,* Behn presents rape as a social transaction between men, where women are little more than objects. (Similar homosocial economies exist in plays such as Tate's adaptation of *Coriolanus,* where Aufidius uses his lust as a means of challenging Coriolanus, threatening to rape Virgilia in front of her husband.) The woman, once again, becomes the object of this symbolic exchange between the two male subjects. In *The Luckey Chance* Lady Fulbank ultimately has no control over her own sexuality; her desires are irrelevant to the men around her, and her body becomes just another stake in a game of dice, in this case an asset worth three hundred pounds. It is perhaps Behn's starkest representation of the objectification of women in a patriarchal society. Ironically, Lady Fulbank's violation by Gayman immediately follows a scene in which she proudly asserts both her virtue and her freedom, only to find both qualities out of her control. As Behn's play makes clear, such autonomy is nothing more than illusion in a world in which men buy women's sexuality from other men.

Considered as performance, when the body of the actress makes the sexual import of the act of rape apparent, these scenes not only present a disturbing vision of gender relations but also expose the essential problem of voyeurism and the female spectator. Seemingly directed toward an audience assumed to be male, the scenes of rape presented uncomfortable options for the women who made up part of the Restoration audience. Scenes of rape attempt to titillate the audience by portraying rape as sexually satisfying for the male rapist and deadly for the defiled heroine. They objectify women, visually as objects of desire and symbolically as commodities. As a result, these women are victims many times over: of the rapist who immediately threatens them; of the social construction of gender that defines the female as passive and submissive, thus effectively eliminating active resistance; and finally as victims of the audience's desire.

But what of the female spectator and her response to these scenes? Does she also look through the lens of the male gaze? In her article "Visual Pleasure and Narrative Cinema," Mulvey identifies two forms of visual pleasure: voyeurism, which involves objectification of what is seen, and identification with this image. She argues that the members of the audience identify with the active image, the male hero, and, like him, objectify the female character. This model works well for the male spectator but raises problems when applied to the female spectator, an issue that Teresa de Lauretis and Mary Ann Doane, among others, have subsequently addressed.[11] In the theater, these scenes present few favorable options to the female spectator short of removing her gaze entirely. (This is the option Richard Steele advocates for women attending rape trials: until women sit on the juries, "it would be much more expedient that the fair were wholly absent; for to what end can it be that they should be present at such examinations, when they can only be perplexed with a fellow-feeling for the injured, without any power to avenge their sufferings" [*Tatler,* 22 Oct. 1709].) If she identifies with the victimized woman, she erases the distance requisite for voyeurism, a process that is necessarily masochistic. But for her to identify with the male gaze, thus performing what Doane refers to as masquerade, would be equally disturbing and in itself masochistic, as it requires denial of the female spectator's own sex. Even postulating a lesbian gaze is deeply problematic, for such a gaze, like the other responses, is limited by the brutal physicality of rape.

Aphra Behn's plays present our only evidence of a seventeenth-century woman's response to the dramatic representation of rape. In *The Rover* and *The Luckey Chance* she outlines one central problem, the objectification and commodification of women, but while she balances the attempted rapes with suggestions of female sexual autonomy and examples of female power, she provides no solutions. One possible female response to the rapes appears in an anonymous epilogue to Rochester's adaptation of *Valentinian,* where the actress playing the ravished Lucina accepts that the women in the audience will identify with Lucina but advises them to consider the heroine's violation not as rape, but as rape fantasy:

> I know your Tender Natures, did Partake,
> At least in Thought you suffer'd for my sake,
> And in my Rape bearing a friendly part,
> Each had her *Valentinian* in her Heart.
> ["Epilogue" 251][12]

This suggestion that staged rape acts as sexual fantasy conflicts, however, with the brutal nature of the crime. In the adaptation of *Valentinian* the rape is accompanied by offstage shrieks that are graphically described as the rape occurs: Lycinius says, "Bless me, the loud shrieks and horrid outcries / Of the poor lady! . . . She roars as if she were upon the rack" (IV.ii.10–12).[13] In the end, the act of rape reemphasizes an essential male/female division, for, as the ludicrous nature of Blunt's claim underlines, only men can rape. It is the ultimate expression of phallic power. The female spectator, like the heroine she watches, finds gender lines firmly drawn between those who rape and those who are raped, the actor and the acted upon. Stylized, choreographed, and histrionic, rape still generates a cycle of victimization even when its participants are fictional and its scope contained by theater walls.

Notes

1. When Garrick adapted *The Relapse* in *A Trip to Scarborough* (1777), he revised this scene to eliminate the mock rape.
2. For a consideration of rhetorical voyeurism, see Patricia Parker's discussion of rhetoric and "dilation" in *Literary Fat Ladies* and, more recently, in "Othello and Hamlet."
3. Bashar cites the numerous deterrents that made prosecuting rape difficult, such as the difficulties in proving that a rape had taken place; for example, it was believed that if a woman became pregnant, she must have consented to the rape. Of the 38 alleged rapists prosecuted in the five home counties between 1650 and 1700, "32 were found not guilty and 6 guilty of whom 2 were reprieved, a conviction rate of about one in eight. Not only was the total number of rape cases coming to court decreasing markedly, the proportion of men being convicted of rape was decreasing as well" (35).
4. The only other exception to the rape equals death equation occurs in Thomas Shadwell's *The Libertine* (1675), where Don John and his cohorts rape a group of shepherdesses. This exception to the rule suggests that class plays a role in the fate of the violated woman in drama. If rape is envisioned as a loss of property, it would be less serious to women who were worth less—a theory of rape that, of course, completely ignores the experience of the ravished woman.
5. Teresa de Lauretis defines such identification of the female as object and the object as female as a "rhetoric of violence" (*Technologies of Gender* 45), violence that in this case is played out against the body of the female object.
6. Such attitudes can be seen, for example, in conduct books of the late seventeenth century that advocate two distinct realms for the sexes—the active, public world for men and the private, domestic sphere for women. Proper behavior depends on the sphere to which a person belongs. In everyday life such distinctions were undoubtedly less pronounced.
7. One reason for the continuing popularity of breeches roles was that they displayed an actress's legs, thus reinforcing her feminine appearance rather than blurring gender lines. This shift toward more polarized representations of gender can be seen in the revival of Brady's *The Rape* in

1768. The original play had included, along with the rape, both a man dressed from childhood as a woman and a woman dressed from childhood as a man. When the play was revived, the sexually titillating rape and cross-dressed woman were retained, but the cross-dressed man disappeared. Instead of using gender to obscure his identity, the prince in hiding uses class—dressing as a page rather than a woman.

8. Elizabeth Barry inaugurated the roles of Monimia (*The Orphan*), Cordelia (*King Lear*), and Alcmena (*Amphitryon*), while Anne Bracegirdle played Eurione (*The Rape*). Each actress was known for her emotive qualities, Barry so much so that when *The Rape* was first staged in 1692, Shadwell reportedly requested that she take the part of Eurione, with "a mantle to have covered her hips" (cited in Van Lennep, entry for 19 Jan. 1692). Mrs. Betterton and Mrs. Temple also appeared as ravished women, Mrs. Betterton as Lucretia in Lee's *Lucius Junius Brutus* and Mrs. Temple as Julia in Crowne's *Caligula*.

9. See, for example, the Marquis of Halifax's *The Lady's New Years Gift:* "You have more strength in your *Looks,* than we have in our *Laws;* and more power by your *Tears,* than we have by our *Arguments*" (Savile 28). Conduct books did not, of course, provide instructions on how to behave in the case of rape. However, in 1632 Nicholas Brady instructed the raped woman "to go straight way and with Hue and Cry complaine to the good men of the next town, shewing her wrong, her garments torne and any effusion of blood" (cited in Bashar 35). As Bashar observes, such an open display was both difficult for women and largely ineffective.

10. Here it is possible to trace a connection between the representation of rape and historical evidence. Bashar notes that the rape cases that had the highest likelihood of conviction were those in which a virgin was raped: "Only the rapes that had in them some element of property, in the form of virginity, ended in the conviction of the accused" (42).

11. See de Lauretis, *Alice Doesn't,* esp. chap. 5; and Doane. It was precisely this problem that Mulvey addressed sixteen years after writing her influential essay, in "Afterthoughts on 'Visual Pleasure and Narrative Cinema.' " She used King Vidor's *Duel in the Sun* and other Westerns to postulate a female gaze.

12. In contrast, Behn's prologue to *Valentinian* makes no reference to the rape.

13. Neither the shrieks nor the scene that takes place during the rape appear in Fletcher's play.

Works Cited

Bashar, Nazife. "Rape in England between 1550 and 1700." *The Sexual Dynamics of History: Men's Power, Women's Resistance.* Ed. London Feminist History Group. London: Pluto, 1983. 28–42.

Behn, Aphra. *The Luckey Chance; or, An Alderman's Bargain.* 1687. Ed. Jean A. Coakley. New York: Garland, 1987.

———. *The Rover; or, The Banished Cavaliers.* 1677. Ed. Frederick M. Link. Lincoln: U of Nebraska P, 1967.

Brady, Nicholas. *The Rape; or, The Innocent Imposters.* London, 1692.
Brown, Laura. "The Defenseless Woman and the Development of English Trag-edy." *Studies in English Literature, 1500–1900* 22.3 (Summer 1982): 429–43.
Brownmiller, Susan. *Against Our Will: Men, Women, and Rape.* New York: Si-mon and Schuster, 1975.
Crisp, Henry. *Virginia.* London, 1754.
Crowne, John. *Caligula.* London, 1698.
de Lauretis, Teresa. *Alice Doesn't: Feminism, Semiotics, Cinema.* Bloomington: Indiana UP, 1984.
————. *Technologies of Gender: Essays on Theory, Film, and Fiction.* Bloom-ington: Indiana UP, 1987.
Doane, Mary Ann. *The Desire to Desire: The Woman's Film of the 1940's.* Bloom-ington: Indiana UP, 1987.
Dryden, John. *Amphitryon.* 1690. *The Works of John Dryden.* Vol. 15. Ed. Earl Miner and George R. Guffey. Berkeley: U of California P, 1976. 221–318.
D'Urfey, Thomas. *The Injured Princess; or, The Fatal Wager.* London, 1682.
"Epilogue to *Valentinian* by a Person of Quality. Spoken by Mrs. Barrey." *Rare Prologues and Epilogues, 1642–1700.* Ed. Autrey Nell Wiley. London: Allen and Unwin, 1940. 250–51.
The Excellent Woman Described by Her True Characters and Their Opposites. By T.D. London, 1692.
Hagstrum, Jean H. *Sex and Sensibility: Ideal and Erotic Love from Milton to Mozart.* Chicago: U of Chicago P, 1980.
Lee, Nathaniel. *Lucius Junius Brutus.* 1681. Ed. John Loftis. Lincoln: U of Nebraska P, 1967.
Lévi-Strauss, Claude. *The Elementary Structures of Kinship.* Rev. ed. Trans. James Harle Bell, John Richard von Sturmer, and Rodney Needham. Boston: Beacon, 1969.
MacKinnon, Catharine A. "Feminism, Marxism, Method, and the State: Toward Feminist Jurisprudence." *Signs: Journal of Women in Culture and Society* 8.4 (Summer 1983): 635–58.
Mulvey, Laura. "Afterthoughts on 'Visual Pleasure and Narrative Cinema' in-spired by *Duel in the Sun.*" *Framework* 6.15–17 (1981): 12–15. Rpt. in *Femi-nism and Film Theory.* Ed. Constance Penley. New York: Routledge, 1988. 69–79.
————. "Visual Pleasure and Narrative Cinema." *Screen* 16.3 (Autumn 1975): 6–18. Rpt. in *Feminism and Film Theory.* Ed. Constance Penley. New York: Routledge, 1988. 57–68.
Otway, Thomas. *The Orphan; or, The Unhappy Marriage.* 1680. *The Works of Thomas Otway: Plays, Poems and Love-Letters.* Vol. 2. Ed. J.C. Ghosh. Oxford: Clarendon P, 1932. 1-87.
Parker, Patricia. *Literary Fat Ladies: Rhetoric, Gender, Property.* New York: Methuen, 1987.
————. "Othello and Hamlet: Dilation, Spying, and the 'Secret Place' of Woman." *Representations* 44 (Fall 1993): 60–97.
Ravenscroft, Edward. *Titus Andronicus; or, The Rape of Lavinia.* London, 1681.
Rooney, Ellen. " 'A Little More Than Persuading': Tess and the Subject of Sexual

Violence." *Rape and Representation*. Ed. Lynn A. Higgins and Brenda R. Silver. New York: Columbia UP, 1991. 87–114.

Savile, George, Marquis of Halifax. *The Lady's New Years Gift; or, Advice to a Daughter*. London, 1688.

Shadwell, Thomas. *The Libertine*. 1676. Ed. Helen Pellegrin. New York: Garland, 1987.

Staves, Susan. "Fielding and the Comedy of Attempted Rape." *History, Gender, and Eighteenth-Century Literature*. Ed. Beth Fowkes Tobin. Athens: U of Georgia P, 1994. 86–112.

Steele, Richard. *The Tatler,* no. 84. 22 Oct. 1709.

Tate, Nahum. *The History of King Lear*. 1681. *Five Restoration Adaptations of Shakespeare*. Ed. Christopher Spencer. Urbana: U of Illinois P, 1965.

———. *The Ingratitude of a Common-Wealth; or, The Fall of Caius Martius Coriolanus*. London, 1682.

Vanbrugh, John. *The Relapse; or, Virtue in Danger*. 1697. Ed. Curt A. Zimansky. Lincoln: U of Nebraska P, 1970.

Van Lennep, William, ed. *The London Stage, 1660–1800. Part 1: 1660–1700*. Carbondale: Southern Illinois UP, 1965.

Wilmot, John, second Earl of Rochester. *Valentinian*. 1685. *Rochester: Complete Poems and Plays*. Ed. Paddy Lyons. London: J.M. Dent, 1993. 155–246.

Reading Masks: The Actress and the Spectatrix in Restoration Shakespeare

Laura J. Rosenthal

Samuel Pepys left an invaluable diary full of insights about male spectatorship in the early Restoration. Later in the seventeenth century, Jeremy Collier and scores of others debated the pleasures and dangers of stage plays. While no female diarist has left us the minute observation of a Pepys and no female polemicist the diatribes of a Collier, women playwrights, as criticism has begun to illuminate, also struggled with the erotic, ethical, and political issues raised by the specularized female body. Margaret Cavendish, the duchess of Newcastle, for example, became so mesmerized by a woman player that she rented quarters near the mountebank stage just to watch her every day.[1] This Italian performer was

> the Best Female Actor that ever I saw; and for Acting a Man's Part, she did it so Naturally as if she had been of that Sex, and yet she was of a Neat, Slender Shape; but being in her Dublet and Breeches, and a Sword hanging by her side, one would have believed she never had worn a Petticoat, and had been more used to Handle a Sword than a Distaff; and when she Danced in a Masculine Habit, she would Caper Higher, and Oftener than any of the Men, although they were great Masters in the Art of Dancing, and when she Danced after the Fashion of her own Sex, she Danced Justly, Evenly, Smoothly, and Gracefully. [letter 195; 406–7]

While the "breeches" part, commonly believed to indulge male voyeurism (see, e.g., Styan 134), fascinates Cavendish for its liberating and (arguably) erotic possibilities, clearly the performer's femaleness in itself engages her interest as well.[2] Nowhere does Cavendish express such enthusiasm for a

Miniature of Restoration actress Anne Quin with talc overlays
depicting her in her favorite roles. By permission of the Victoria
and Albert Museum.

boy actor. Actresses—their bodies, their dramatic roles, their specularization—fascinated both Pepys and Newcastle. The presence of women onstage changed the experience of playgoing for women as well as for men.

As the novel inclusion of women onstage and the relentless exploration of marriage and sexuality demonstrate, Restoration theater participated actively in the renegotiation of gender relations. The combination of moral concern for the female spectator (Collier) and fascination with the female spectacle (Pepys and Cavendish) suggests the theater's significance as an arena in which the shifting possibilities for women's subjectivity clashed. This instability becomes most apparent in the variety of potential relationships between the positions of actress and spectatrix, from identification to emphatic distinction. In this essay I would like to explore some of the tensions that women in the audience may have experienced with the advent of the woman player and the cultural changes that she both signified and precipitated.

Restoration theater enacts a deeply ambivalent view of female sexuality. On the one hand, sympathetic women characters, played by women, commonly insist on making their own affective, erotic, and marital choices. Even if the seventeenth-century marriage contract, as Carole Pateman has argued, institutionalized the subordination of women, a woman's right to *choose* her husband had enough social meaning to provide a popular source of dramatic conflict. On the other hand, Restoration theater's distinct visual economy provided possibilities for the objectification of women that Renaissance commercial theater did not (see Diamond; King). The particular conflict between subjectivity in the drama and visual objectification in the theater tended to blur the vast social differences between the women onstage and the women in the audience, creating for the elite spectatrix opportunities for identification with the subjectivity of the figure onstage but at the same time vulnerability to forms of aggression from which her status might otherwise insulate her. This dynamic takes place in the context of what Pateman has described as a transition from a classical to a modern form of patriarchy, best articulated by the debate between John Locke and Sir Robert Filmer. Restoration theater negotiates this transition by enacting the decay of some forms of masculine authority, while at the same time intensifying the objectification of the female body (onstage and implicitly in the audience) as a cultural strategy for recapturing eroded masculine authority in a different form. These differences become most apparent in the comparison of plays written for boy actors with their reformulations in the Restoration. Before turning to the plays, however, I would like to qualify and contextualize this argument.

Both the sexual subjectivity and the objectification of women emerge out of active and unsettled tensions. Restoration plays, as Susan

Staves has argued, frequently advocate affective choice in marriage; many plays with prominent women characters—those of Aphra Behn come to mind—specifically advocate this freedom for women. Yet the women in these plays cannot assume this liberty: their insistence on their own sexual subjectivity commonly conflicts with a father's, husband's, or lover's financial or erotic objectification of them. Further, some Restoration plays end up confirming the father's power to choose a spouse for his child (see Wheatley). The conflict between women as subjects and women as sexual and economic objects popularly provides the play's source of tension and theatricalizes the instability of the status of women.

Similarly, the visual objectification of actresses describes only one aspect of a complex and contested economy in which critics located some kinds of power in the spectacle rather than the spectator, and vice versa. René Rapin, for example, insisted on the moral authority of the stage: tragedy can cure "pride and hardness of heart," rectifying "the passions by the passions themselves" (quoted in Rothstein 10). For Dryden as well, the performance of tragedy must have the power to draw tears and emotionally transform the spectator (Rothstein 15–21). Later, and not entirely unlike Dryden and Rapin, Steele and Addison would emphasize the stage's potential for moral instruction through emotional impact (Straub, 421; Carlson, chap. 9). The power of the specularized actress, real or imagined, became a subject of great concern to Jeremy Collier, who worried that gentlemen in the audience would become so enamored with the characters that women portrayed that they would fall in love with and marry the performers (282).[3] Hobbes, on the other hand, located a sadistic power in the spectator, who enjoys the suffering onstage because "it is sweet to see from what evils you are yourself exempt" (cited in Straub, 421). The mechanics of production during the Restoration further argue for the empowerment of the spectator. Managers overran their budgets to create a theater of illusion: complex scenery replaced the bare Elizabethan stage; elaborate costumes and wigs became an important part of any show; women actors achieved fame for their beauty and notoriety for their homeliness.[4] The specularized female body became one of several new visual objects and pleasures of the Restoration.[5] In his prologue to *The Tempest; or, The Enchanted Island* Thomas Shadwell recognizes this:

> Had we not for yr pleasure found new wayes
> You still had rusty Arras had & threadbare playes;
> Nor Scenes nor Woomen had they had their will,
> But some with grizl'd Beards had acted Woomen still.

When the King's Company lost its lavish theater and scenery to a fire in 1672, it attempted to regain its audience by offering all-female performances as visual compensation (Pearson 28). Colley Cibber complained that the "Scarcity of tolerable Women" exceeded any "Deficiency of Men Actors," for the "Life of Youth and Beauty is too short for the bringing an Actress to her Perfection." While Collier represents the actress as exploiting her spectators, Cibber's later *Apology* genders Hobbes's brutal view: unlike women behind the "Iron Grates and high Walls" of a nunnery that the "Architecture of a Theatre will not so properly admit of," beauty onstage "has no Defence but its natural Virtue. . . . But alas! . . . the poor Stage is but the Show-glass to a Toy-shop" (2:222–23).

In order to understand why so many commentaries on the stage express, as Kristina Straub argues, "a pervasive concern for the economy of power between the subjectivity of the spectator and an objectified, and subjected spectacle" (422), we must return to the position of the spectatrix both inside the theater and out. The middle- or upper-class female spectator differed from her Renaissance precursor not only in her experience of watching women portray women characters—which may have encouraged her to relate the conflicts faced by those characters more directly to her own position—but in her place in the social hierarchy as well. The question of how this place changed, however, has been a topic for considerable debate. Lawrence Stone has pointed to the ways in which conditions for middle- and upper-class women improved in this period: the late seventeenth century, he argues, saw a major reconfiguration of domestic organization from the patriarchal household to the affective family. In the absolutist model of patriarchal sovereignty, as Sir Robert Filmer outlines in *Patriarcha* (1680), a father rules his family with the same absolute and natural authority with which the king rules his subjects—and the family responds as the subjects do to the king. The decline of this model rendered archaic some of the grounds by which the culture disempowered women. As Staves further points out, the Civil War and the execution of Charles I themselves irreparably damaged a certain amount of faith in the patriarchal model. "At about the same time subjects asserted their right to elect a sovereign in the Glorious Revolution," Staves succinctly puts it, "women acquired an analogous right to elect husbands" (189). In many of the plays, marriage becomes contested, no longer providing the festive closure of Shakespearean comedies: the absolute dominion of a father or a husband could no longer resolve a plot (Staves, chap. 3). The decline of the patriarchal model removed one of the central justifications for the subordination of women in general and for paternal control of daughters' sexuality in particular: sovereignty and masculine authority would have to defend themselves on different grounds.

On the other hand, Ellen Pollak has argued that the decline of the patriarchal model of authority did not necessarily mean, as Stone would have it, that conditions for women improved. The economic position of middle- and upper-class women, she argues, became in fact quite precarious. With the enclosure of land, these women contributed less and less to the family's economy, while men increasingly found employment outside of the domestic sphere. Traditional occupations for women, such as medicine and education, became the professionalized specializations of men. Women who might have previously held important occupations, then, were edged out of production and relegated to consumption.[6] Exacerbated by an unfavorable marriage market, this social and economic marginalization may further have placed more pressure on women to cultivate their beauty, thus to reinforce their status as objects.

Pateman's *Sexual Contract* offers a productive insight into this apparent simultaneous empowerment and subordination of women. In Filmer's classical patriarchy, families obey the father the way subjects obey the king. In the postrevolutionary modern patriarchy, most cogently articulated by Locke, many men (but not slaves or even necessarily laborers) gain the right to subordinate one woman through the marriage contract. A contract between unequals, Pateman reasons, creates a relationship of subordination. In the seventeenth century women had achieved equality neither in theory nor in practice. The transition from Filmerian patriarchalism to Lockean contract, then, trades one form of patriarchy for another. Yet in much drama at this time, marriage proves ineffective at creating subordination, sexual or otherwise. In plays as different as *The Country Wife* and *The Lucky Chance* some husbands can at best gain the illusion of subordinating their wives. Since the plays themselves so commonly address the vulnerabilities of both classical and modern patriarchy, the visual economy of the theater becomes a significant site of contestation in the shifting politics of gender.

For the women onstage, the tension between subjectivity and objectification commonly emerges in the gap between upper-class characters who often successfully fight against guardians for their own amatory choice and the less privileged performers who perform those roles and become objects of both empowering and appropriative visual attention. For the women in the audience, nothing represents this tension quite so precisely as the mask. When prologues to Restoration plays comment on the "masks" in the audience, sometimes they mean prostitutes, and sometimes they mean the high-born women, like Elizabeth Pepys, who fashionably covered their faces at the theater. Usually, however, they simply mean "women": appearing at the theater in a mask became so widespread a custom that the device that covered the face and the identity became a synecdoche for the whole person. While various garments have become synecdoches for women at various times, "mask" calls attention to women specifically as spectators by naming them after an accessory that covers the area around their eyes but not the eyes themselves. The mask seems to have provided the Restoration spectatrix with a certain amount of freedom to move through the public space of the theater, and perhaps it even did give her, as it was reputed to do, an opportunity to express her sexuality by maintaining her anonymity. In novels and romances, at any rate, men make love to masked ladies without learning their identities until the ladies choose to reveal them. An object that conceals, however, also calls attention to the obscured region as an object of scrutiny. If the mask protected its wearer from too discerning a gaze, it nevertheless, as Mr. Pinchwife well knew when he disguised his wife as a boy rather than letting her appear at the theater in a mask, *attracted* attention by creating an air of mystery. While women of various social positions wore masks, the covered face could be identified with prostitution and sexual availability. The mask's double function of disguise and allure, modesty and immodesty, implies a woman who wishes at once to be seen and not to be seen. The mask, then, signifies two contradicting forms of sexual positionality: it signifies a sexual being in control of her identity and seeking her own pleasure, as well as an infinitely replaceable visual object whose individual identity and desire have no relevance.[7]

Those who used "mask" as a synecdoche for the female spectator, I believe, left an important insight, for this contradictory significance of the mask parallels conflicting constructions of women's sexual subjectivity in Restoration theater. Female desire and women's insistence on sexual self-determination shape the conflicts in many Restoration plays; at the same time, however, the novelty of the female body as a specular and frequently disempowered object contradicted and circumscribed this subjectivity. The dominant, although not the only, subject/object division that emerges constitutes an attempt to secure the social position of women and ensure the domestic authority of men through a sexual objectification of the figure onstage (in her capacity as performer and character) that conflicts with the character's assertions of sexual subjectivity.

The distinct dynamics of the post-1660 theatrical experience with its differently gendered cast become perhaps most apparent in Renaissance plays revised for the new stage. Like many twentieth-century feminist critics, theater managers in the Restoration found Shakespearean drama particularly dependent on antiquated forms of patriarchal authority. Alterations of three Shakespearean plays in particular—*The Tempest* by John Dryden and William Davenant, *The Taming of the Shrew* by John Lacy, and *King Lear* by Nahum Tate—reveal these political differences, but they also reveal the difference in the new stage's specular relationships. Clearly these adapters found the inscribed specular relations between the boy actor and the audience inadequate for the women who now played those parts.[8] One striking change in several instances of this renegotiation of gender, however, is the extent to which the revised female characters endure new forms of violence. While the revisions allow, express, and exploit the sexual subjectivity of women characters, at the same time they tend brutally to repress that subjectivity through everything from rape to dismemberment and (usually self-)murder.[9] This theater's deliberate blurring of the fictional female body of the character with the actual female body of the player implicates the spectatrix in this dynamic. The performance encourages her, as a similar object of visual attention, to identify with both positions.

The Restoration *Tempest* demonstrates a high degree of self-consciousness about the gender of the actors and confronts the erosion of earlier forms of patriarchal authority. In this new version, Prospero can no longer control the sexual curiosity of his daughters (the adapters add a daughter); he lacks the kind of patriarchal authority, as Katharine Eisaman Maus has argued ("Arcadia Lost"), that Shakespeare's duke displays. Dryden and Davenant give the daughters a great deal more sexual curiosity and frankness than Shakespeare gave the innocent Miranda. Yet it is another new character named Hippolito, a young man whose part the prologue specifies as performed by a woman, who calls the greatest attention to the new play's fascination with the dangers of female sexual subjectivity. Hippolito cannot comprehend monogamy, pursues two potential partners instead of Ferdinand's one, and must fall nearly dead in a duel with Ferdinand before he (she) learns to contain his (her) enormous sexual appetite. Socially inappropriate female desire leads to this play's one significant and nearly fatal act of violence: Ferdinand stabs a male character but a woman performer. So while Prospero's daughters comically and seductively discuss their cravings for a husband, Ferdinand battles Hippolito over his (her) uncontained desires.

Ferdinand's near murder of the sexually indefatigable Hippolito attempts to balance the play's anxieties over the new Prospero's inability to exert sexual control over his daughters. The swordfight itself can be read by the audience as a battle between men over women but also as the equally violent defeat of a character whose name recalls the Amazon queen Hippolita. This displaced defeat of female sexuality becomes the play's dramatic climax, but at the same time the weakness of Prospero's paternal authority marks the fundamental difference in the Restoration version. The adapters provide Prospero with two daughters, doubling the challenge to his ineffectual attempts to isolate them from men. Further, the addition of another daughter gives Miranda a friend with whom she can frankly discuss her sexual desires.[10] The difference between the Restoration and the Shakespearean Miranda's sexual subjectivity and defiance of Prospero's control must have been striking to audiences, for this is precisely the change that Thomas Duffet most relentlessly parodies in his *Mock-Tempest*. In the epilogue to this parody, Duffet comments not just on

Dryden and Davenant's play but also on the gendered theatrical dynamic they exploit and reproduce. In the parody, Miranda expands her sexual availability from Quakero (Ferdinand) to the men in the audiences:

> Gentlemen look'ee now, pray, my Father sayes that I and my
> Sister must have ye all i'fads:
> Whereof I can't tell what to do, I'le Swearo;
> If I take you, I lose my dear Quakero:
> His things are precious, and his love is true;
> But there's no trust in ought you say or do:
> Yet for ought that I know,
> My self could serve you all as well as any,
> But my Father says, pray,
> One Dish of meat can never serve so many;
> For though you all agree in one design,
> To feed like Schollers on the tender Loyn;
> In this you differ with them, pray;
> One little Chop, and one plain Dish will do
> You must have Sause, warm Plates, fresh hau-gou's too;
> The large Pottage of glitt'ring show and dress,
> Must cheat you to the little bit of flesh.
> [Duffet, *Three Burlesque Plays* 111]

Parodically caught between obedience to her father and to her lover, Miranda addresses the men in the audience, insisting that her father has told her and her sister to "have" all of them. Duffet's verb *have,* in a not very subtle pun, offers Miranda to spectators as both an actor delivering the epilogue and as a woman offering her body. Miranda explores this predicament. She describes herself as equal to any woman in the task of serving all of them at once but worries that there is simply not enough of her to go around. She teases them for their corrupt tastes in theater: language does not provide sufficient entertainment, and the "glitt'ring show and dress" distracts them from noticing the play's lack of substance. Yet having already referred to the physical presence of a woman standing before men in an audience, this epilogue puns back and forth between the spectatorial pleasure of dress, show, and the woman actor (with the implied possibility of actually gaining sexual access to the body onstage). In fact, Miranda's speech insists that the audience must substitute one for the other: since they all cannot actually enjoy her at once as a lover—"One Dish of meat can never serve so many"—they must satisfy themselves instead by looking at the scenery, the clothes, and of course the performer. For the spectators, whom the epilogue constitutes as male and heterosexual, visual pleasure becomes both the instigator of and the replacement for the desire that the performance generates. Dryden and Davenant's play symbolically stifles female desire and represses female subjectivity through the violent defeat of Hippolito; Duffet's parody achieves the same ends through visual objectification. The epilogue reduces the complex matrix of men and women, spectators and spectacles, subjects and objects, to an empowered masculine spectating subject and a feminine visual object. In this moment, women onstage and in the audience become part of the scenery.

While Duffet's epilogue itself exploits the opportunity to objectify Miranda, it simultaneously attacks Dryden and Davenant's adaptation as a corruption of Shakespeare. And much of this corruption, Duffet's parody implies, originates in the presence of a female body in a Shakespearean role. Miranda's hint that the audience has been cheated implies that they have paid for a dramatic experience but may not have received their money's worth: the audience has paid to see wit on the stage but has ended up with a glittering spectacle instead. In its nonlubricious meaning, the epilogue specifically satirizes Shadwell's highly successful operatic version of *The Tempest,* which indulged the audience in an unprecedented spectacle of flying spirits, raging storms, and dancing sailors, at the expense, Duffet maintains, of "flesh." Yet in the epilogue's extended pun, the cheat also comes to refer to the exchange of money for visual pleasure. The men in the audience whom Miranda addresses may have hoped that their money would buy them more than a look. Thus, Miranda stands before this audience as a recognizably Shakespearean character, though one that the new stage has "prostituted" to late seventeenth-century entertainment demands. With this pun on the "whoring" of a Shakespearean character, Duffet reiterates one of his central parodic accusations against *The Enchanted Island:* Dryden and Davenant's revision of Shakespeare, Duffet's play tries to demonstrate, transforms the innocent Miranda into a woman with active sexual desires—a change in character, the parody hints, precipitated by the presence of the female body itself. And regardless of individual sexual choices, the Restoration actress was commonly signified as a whore.[11]

In both of these versions, the adapters recognize the patriarchal authority of Shakespeare's Prospero as no longer convincing to their own stage. Both, however, find ways to reinscribe the subordination of women. Dryden and Davenant's play displaces the danger of Miranda's and Dorinda's desire onto Hippolito, who falls nearly dead to Ferdinand's (not the father's) sword.[12] In *The Mock-Tempest,* however, women characters become even more pervasively embattled. This play opens with a tumultuous scene of all-out sexual warfare: instead of sailors clinging to a sinking ship, *The Mock-Tempest* shows whores desperately (and scatalogically) defending their house against an angry mob of men who are demanding "free-trade into and out of all your Ports without paying any Custom" (I.i.149–50, in Duffet, *Three Burlesque Plays*). Shakespeare's magical storm becomes a battle of the sexes in which sailors violently insist on their right of sexual access. *The Mock-Tempest*'s first scene only becomes so violent, though, because the prostitutes will not easily be defeated. Prospero, the keeper of Newgate in this play, does not have magical power or even the authority to order them to jail. When offered terms of peace, the prostitutes unanimously declare for war. Thus, the battle brutally continues.[13] In these *Tempests* classical patriarchal authority depends on magic; modern patriarchal authority resorts—not always successfully—to violence. Duffet's Prospero cannot command his daughters, and his sailors cannot command the prostitutes. Nevertheless, Duffet ends the play by giving the men in the audience visual authority over the women onstage, who were themselves encoded as prostitutes. As Duffet's parody so explicitly reveals, while the masculine assertions may no longer wield the power they once did within the fiction of the play, the objectification of the female performing body serves the politically significant compensatory function of reempowering the men in the audience.

While Duffet, and to some extent Dryden and Davenant, enlist objectification of and violence against women as a force to counter female sexual subjectivity, John Lacy's *Sauny the Scot; or, The Taming of the Shrew* places the tension between the domestic and the specular on the stage itself. The play differs from Shakespeare's in both its violent repression of Peg (Kate) and its lack of conviction about the possibility of taming her. When Petruchio and Peg return to her father's house, Peg reveals that she has only pretended to be tamed and refuses to speak to her husband. In revenge, Petruchio pretends to believe she has a toothache and calls a barber to pull out her teeth. Bianca runs offstage to avoid witnessing this, while Sauny, Petruchio's servant, asks the barber if he could pull out her tongue instead. When Peg refuses to respond, Petruchio proclaims her dead and orders a coffin. He ties her down to the coffin, ostensibly so that the body will not fall out, and begins a procession to the family vault. Peg cries out, however, before they can bury her alive.[14] As in Duffet's *Mock-Tempest,* the *Shrew* becomes more violent in the Restoration, because the woman—now played by a woman—fights harder for domestic authority and sexual subjectivity. Just when the audience believes that the husband has succeeded in brutalizing his wife into submission, we learn that Peg has only acted the part of the tamed wife. What assurance, then, do we ever have that Peg truly submits when she finally claims that she does?[15] Peg not only fights her father's choice for her marriage, but she rejects her husband's assumption of his claim to her body.

But while Lacy represents marriage itself as an active conflict rather than a settled, patriarchal institution that the women can only temporarily resist, the visual objectification of the body of the actress competes with Peg's assertions of her subjectivity. She might refuse the pleasures of marriage to her husband, but she cannot, given her position onstage, refuse the audience the pleasures of looking. In a part Lacy wrote for himself, Petruchio's servant Sauny encourages the voyeuristic objectification of Peg's body. When the couple arrives at Petruchio's residence, Petruchio horrifies his new wife by insisting that Sauny, rather than a female servant, undress her. Sauny, however, takes great delight in this assignment and encourages the audience to share his pleasure; he also often appears as an onstage voyeur of the couple's honeymoon battles. As a character marginal to the dominant class and ethnicity, Sauny does not provide a simple point of identification for the English gentlemen in the audience. This marginal position, however, enables Lacy to use him as a particular kind of mediator: the English gentlemen in the audience may share his voyeurism without acknowledging their complicity. Sauny's leering objectification of Peg and encouragement to Petruchio to treat Peg with greater violence enact a stereotype of a marginal masculinity that invites the dominant masculinity to join it for a moment. Further, Sauny's mediating function in performance would be underscored by the audience's recognition of the actor playing Sauny as the author of the alteration. The trope of Scottishness, then, becomes an alibi for "authorizing" a masculine specular objectification of the woman's body. As Peg insists on her own subjectivity, the leering servant insists on her objectification.

Nahum Tate's two revisions of Shakespearean plays complicate onstage specular relations by opposing a good male character, who views the leading lady with sympathy, against an evil male character, who wishes to rape her. Like Lacy's use of an ethnic "Other," Tate's use of a moral "Other" introduces an objectifying gaze through a marginal form of masculinity. In his famous alteration of *King Lear* the play becomes as much Cordelia's story as her father's, for Cordelia refuses to answer Lear's question out of fear that he will force her to marry a man she does not love. She has already chosen Edgar as her future husband. Cordelia's insistence on her own sexual and affective subjectivity, in fact, occupies the center of the tragedy and precipitates the crisis that follows. Tate uses Cordelia to join the two plots: she not only becomes the object of Lear's paternal love and Edgar's romantic love, but she also becomes the object of Edmund's unmerciful lust.

The threat of rape in Tate's version replaces Lear's patriarchal authority in defining Cordelia's limitations. Cordelia can assert her subjectivity in refusing to marry her father's choice, but she cannot escape objectification once she leaves her father's protection. As she follows her father out into the storm, its turbulence becomes a metaphor not just for Lear's inner turmoil but also for Cordelia's vulnerability outside the circle of Lear's protection. Once she defies her father in making her own erotic choice, she becomes vulnerable to Edmund's objectifying gaze and his advances. Edmund desires Cordelia as he watches her unseen and eroticizes her suffering itself: "[H]ow her tears adorn her. . . . I'll gaze no more—and yet my eyes are charmed" (*Lear* III.ii.70, 79). As soon as Cordelia follows her father into the wild, Edmund sends two ruffians out to capture her and her maid Arante, for he plots to rape Cordelia. Edmund represents his own sexuality as godlike:

> like the vig'rous Jove I will enjoy
> This Semele in a storm. 'Twill deaf her cries
> Like drums in battle, lest her groans should pierce
> My pitying ear, and make the amorous fight less fierce.
>
> [III.ii.121–24]

Unlike the cautious and regretful god, though, Edmund actually wants to destroy Cordelia with his lust. His speech articulates a form of sadism that combines the illusion of godlike power with the infliction of pain on the object of his desire. So while Tate's Lear no longer even starts out with the classical patriarchal authority to arrange Cordelia's marriage, a storm fraught with sexual aggression limits how far she can stray. As Pateman argues (chap. 4), while classical patriarchy depends upon the identity of the empowerment of the father and the king, modern patriarchy depends upon the sons' right of sexual access to a woman. In Tate, good sons achieve this through marriage contracts, bad sons through rape.

In his alteration of *Coriolanus,* retitled *The Ingratitude of a Common-Wealth,* Tate adopts a similar strategy. Just as Edmund becomes obsessed with violating the innocent Cordelia, so Aufidius becomes obsessed with violating Virgilia, with whom he falls in love when she arrives with Volumnia to plead for Rome. He desires her but curses his own restraint from rape and murder:

> I am a lazy Trifler, and unworthy
> To be possest o'th' Beauty that I Love,
> Or be reveng'd upon the Man I hate:
> Why forc't I not my passage to his Heart?
> Then pamper'd in the Banquet of his Blood,
> Flown hot, as flame born *Pluto,* to the Rape;
> And quench't the Fevour in *Virgilia's* Arms.
>
> [V.i; 55]

With a sadistic rhetoric equal to Edmund's, Aufidius parallels his desire to force his sword through Coriolanus's heart with his desire to force himself on Virgilia. And while Tate allowed Cordelia to survive and become queen, he ends *The Ingratitude* with a bloodbath. In the midst of their final battle to the death, a wounded Aufidius begs the wounded Coriolanus not to die until

> thou hast seen
> Our Scene of Pleasures; to thy Face I'll Force her [Virgilia];
> Glut my last Minuits with a double Ryot;
> And in Revenges Sweets and Loves, Expire.
>
> [V.ii; 60]

It is the *spectacle* of the raped and objectified Virgilia that Aufidius desires for revenge. The playwright, though, saves him the trouble: when Virgilia comes onstage, she has already been wounded so horribly that even the cruel Aufidius feels pity. She bids her blood to "stream faster." She has mutilated herself, choosing rather

> To sink this Vessel in a Sea of Blood,
> Than suffer its chaste Treasure, to become
> Th' unhallowed *Pyrates* Prize.
>
> [V.ii; 61]

Not only does Tate add a sexualized form of violence against Virgilia to the plot, but the graphic language of the characters demands a spectacle of blood in performance.

What are the implications of these domestic representations and specular relations for the women in the audience? Since the women characters, whether Indian queens or English heiresses, so commonly struggled against fathers and husbands for their sexual subjectivity, perhaps women in the audience identified these conflicts as similar to tensions in their own domestic lives. Many of the plays, then, could have been viewed by them as encouraging their sexual subjectivity. But would these women have identified with the specular position of the actress? Would they experience a similar objectification? Some of the "masks" belonged to the same class as the actresses, but some did not. Still, while Restoration theater remained highly conscious of the class differences in the audience, the specularized position of women in the audience blurred their difference from the women onstage. Duffet's prologue to *The Suppos'd Prince,* for example, suggests that the visual objectification of the actress extended to the spectatrix:

> He that sits next to a pretty female, knows
> His hand trembles, and something comes and goes.
> He gazes, faints and dyes, why all this shows
> The pow'r and pleasure of a sweet suppose.
>
> [*New Poems* 82–83]

In his prologue to *The Armenian Queen* Duffet represents the man in the audience as distracted not just by the women spectators around him but

also by ones he remembers from an earlier adventure. The male spectator sits

> Fixing his Eye upon the very place,
> Where he pick'd up his last obliging Lass,
> He sees her, Courts her, nay while he sits there,
> Carries her to th'Tavern, finds the very Chair;
> Feels her—soft hand, her melting Eye beholds,
> In empty Arms her airy Body folds.
>
> . . . .
> But what dull sport one party makes alone?
> [*New Poems* 84–86]

He remains distracted by his sexual fantasy until "some loud Heroick rant
awakes him."

If many women in the audience felt themselves newly empowered by the plays to choose a husband or reject their father's choice for
them, the prospect of occupying a similar position in the spectatorial
economy to the women onstage—with all the implications for objectification that this entailed—compromised and contradicted their subjectivity.
The erosion of an older patriarchal structure permitted women to represent
women (cf. Maus, " 'Playhouse Flesh and Blood' "). It also rendered
archaic the assumptions about the father's or the husband's authority
found in Shakespearean drama. At the same time, however, the Restoration
stage cultivated—although not without ambivalence and conflict—the
sexual objectification of the female body that the actress and the spectatrix
have had to negotiate ever since.

Notes

I wish to thank Cynthia Lowenthal for her careful reading and helpful comments.

1. Cavendish's own plays were probably never performed in the public theater, but they may have been performed privately.
2. Cavendish's *Convent of Pleasure* also bears examination in this context.
3. I discuss this issue at greater length in " 'Counterfeit Scrubbado.' "
4. See Diamond, whose important essay observes and discusses the significance of the illusionary quality of Restoration theater.
5. For detailed descriptions and analyses of theatrical conditions in the Restoration, see Styan and Holland. Both emphasize the importance of the visual in Restoration theater. The influence of Charles II, who had watched
   women onstage during his exile in France, should not be underestimated
   as a factor in Restoration theater's employment of actresses. At the same
   time, however, this change also indicates a larger reformulation of gender.
   For an interesting suggestion about why this period permitted women on

the commercial stage, see Maus, " 'Playhouse Flesh and Blood.' " Maus argues that gender became a polarity rather than a hierarchy, redefining the feminine as essentially different from the masculine.

6. Laura Brown has argued that this economic reconfiguration generated a new female dramatic protagonist, "passive, defenseless, and impotent," who acts, like the women to whom her character refers, as "an ideological place-holder": "Domestically, psychologically, and sexually she may possess extensive significance, but socially and economically she is an empty vessel" (442). In "Pathos and Passivity," Jean I. Marsden agrees with Pollak and Brown, using the Restoration *Injured Princess* of D'Urfey as a prime example of a newly passive female character.

7. My discussion of the mask is indebted to Gallagher's essay.

8. Colley Cibber considered the addition of women one of the greatest improvements of the Restoration and the lack thereof one of Shakespeare's impediments: "The Characters of Women on former Theatres," he writes, "were perform'd by Boys, or young Men of the most effeminate Aspect. And what Grace or Master-strokes of Action can we conceive such ungain Hoydens to have been capable of? This Defect was so well considered by *Shakespear,* that in few of his Plays he has any greater Dependance upon the Ladies than in the Innocence and Simplicity of a *Desdemona,* an *Ophelia,* or in the short Specimen of a fond and virtuous *Portia.* The additional Objects then of real, beautiful Women could not but draw a Proportion of new Admirers to the Theatre" (1:90–91).

9. Dryden's Cressida, for example, stabs herself in her desperation to convince Troilus of her love. For another discussion of the violence suffered by Shakespearean heroines in the Restoration, see Marsden, "Rewritten Women." Marsden makes a good case for the ways in which Restoration dramatists relegate Shakespearean heroines to the domestic sphere. I hope to show, however, that the revision of these characters might be understood as part of the transition from one form of patriarchy to another, offering new versions of empowerment and new versions of subordination.

10. For an alternative reading of the gender in this play, see Dobson 43–61. Dobson suggestively insists on Dryden and Davenant's interest in the patriarchal family as well as the patriarchal monarchy, the subject of Maus's essay "Arcadia Lost." He places the written and performed texts, with Hippolito's gender marking the difference, in tension with each other as a confirmation and subversion of patriarchal sexual ideology. Wikander also provides an astute and detailed analysis of Hippolito's sexual voraciousness.

11. In " 'Counterfeit Scrubbado' " I argue against the commonplace assumption that Restoration actresses simply *were* whores. The equation of actress with whore, I suggest, performed the cultural work of preventing cross-class marriages between elite men in the audience and the women onstage.

12. Hippolito appears dead after this fight, but Ariel manages to bring him (her) back to life.

13. Jocelyn Powell reports that the whores were played by men and the courtiers by women, but she offers no source for this information (66–67). According to DiLorenzo, no cast list is included in any of the quarto editions

(Duffet, *Three Burlesque Plays* 53). I find the suggestion of cross-dressing in this scene plausible and not inconsistent with my reading, for it dramatizes (and parodies) violent attempts to demand sexual access to women and the visual objectification that depends on the belief in the presence of a female body. Powell does not mention whether or not the entire cast cross-dressed. The casting of the seductive Miranda as a man, though, would extraordinarily heighten the parodic self-consciousness of her offering her body to the audience. If Duffet had a man deliver her lines, he was quite conscious and possibly even critical of the objectification of women onstage.

14. See also James Worsdale's version of 1735. Haring-Smith provides an extensive stage history of this play.

15. As Staves remarks, Lacy's version "on the whole seems to reflect greater tension and even animosity in the sex war" (134).

Works Cited

Brown, Laura. "The Defenseless Woman and the Development of English Tragedy." *Studies in English Literature, 1500–1900* 22.3 (Summer 1982): 429–43.

Carlson, Marvin. *Theories of the Theatre: A Historical and Critical Survey, from the Greeks to the Present.* Ithaca, N.Y.: Cornell UP, 1984.

Cavendish, Margaret, Duchess of Newcastle. *CCXI Sociable Letters; Written by the Thrice Noble, Illustrious, and Excellent Princess, the Lady Marchioness of Newcastle.* London, 1664.

Cibber, Colley. *An Apology for the Life of Mr. Colley Cibber, Written by Himself.* 1739. 2 vols. Ed. Robert W. Lowe. 1889; London: AMS, 1966.

Collier, Jeremy. *A Short View of the Immorality and Profaneness of the English Stage.* 1698. 5th ed. London, 1730.

Diamond, Elin. "*Gestus* and Signature in Aphra Behn's *The Rover.*" *ELH* 56 (Fall 1989): 519–41.

Dobson, Michael. *The Making of the National Poet: Shakespeare, Adaptation and Authorship, 1660–1769.* Oxford: Clarendon, 1992.

Duffet, Thomas. *New Poems, Songs, Prologues and Epilogues.* London, 1676.

———. *Three Burlesque Plays of Thomas Duffet.* Ed. Ronald Eugene DiLorenzo. Iowa City: U of Iowa P, 1972.

Gallagher, Catherine. "Who Was That Masked Woman?: The Prostitute and the Playwright in the Comedies of Aphra Behn." *Women's Studies* 15 (1988): 23–42.

Haring-Smith, Tori. *From Farce to Metadrama: A Stage History of "The Taming of the Shrew," 1594–1983.* Westport, Conn.: Greenwood, 1985.

Holland, Peter. *The Ornament of Action: Text and Performance in Restoration Comedy.* Cambridge: Cambridge UP, 1979.

King, Thomas A. " 'As If (She) Were Made on Purpose to Put the Whole World in Good Humour': Reconstructing the First English Actresses." *TDR* 36.3 (Fall 1992): 78–102.

Marsden, Jean I. "Pathos and Passivity: D'Urfey's *The Injured Princess* and Shakespeare's *Cymbeline.*" *Restoration* 14.2 (Fall 1990): 71–81.

———. "Rewritten Women: Shakespearean Heroines in the Restoration." *The*

Appropriation of Shakespeare: Post-Renaissance Reconstruction of the Works and the Myth. Ed. Jean I. Marsden. New York: St. Martin's, 1991. 43–56.

Maus, Katharine Eisaman. "Arcadia Lost: Politics and Revision in *The Tempest.*" *Renaissance Drama,* n.s., 13 (1982): 189–209.

———. " 'Playhouse Flesh and Blood': Sexual Ideology and the Restoration Actress." *ELH* 46 (Winter 1979): 595–617.

Pateman, Carole. *The Sexual Contract.* Stanford, Calif.: Stanford UP, 1988.

Pearson, Jacqueline. *The Prostituted Muse: Images of Women and Women Dramatists, 1642–1737.* Manchester: Manchester UP, 1988.

Pollak, Ellen. *The Poetics of Sexual Myth: Gender and Ideology in the Verse of Swift and Pope.* Chicago: U of Chicago P, 1985.

Powell, Jocelyn. *Restoration Theatre Production.* London: Routledge, 1984.

Rosenthal, Laura J. " 'Counterfeit Scrubaddo': Restoration Drama and the Woman Actor." *The Eighteenth Century: Theory and Interpretation* 34.1 (1993): 3–22.

Rothstein, Eric. *Restoration Tragedy: Form and the Process of Change.* Madison: U of Wisconsin P, 1967.

Shadwell, Thomas. *The Tempest; or, The Enchanted Island.* London, 1676.

Staves, Susan. *Players' Scepters: Fictions of Authority in the Restoration.* Lincoln: U of Nebraska P, 1979.

Stone, Lawrence. *The Family, Sex, and Marriage in England, 1500–1800.* New York: Harper and Row, 1977.

Straub, Kristina. "Reconstructing the Gaze: Voyeurism in Richardson's *Pamela.*" *Studies in Eighteenth-Century Culture* 18 (1988): 419–31.

Styan, J.L. *Restoration Comedy in Performance.* Cambridge: Cambridge UP, 1986.

Tate, Nahum. *The History of King Lear.* 1681. Ed. James Black. Lincoln: U of Nebraska P, 1975.

———. *The Ingratitude of a Common-Wealth; or, The Fall of Caius Martius Coriolanus.* 1682. London: Cornmarket, 1969.

Wheatley, Christopher J. "Romantic Love and Social Necessities: Reconsidering Justifications for Marriage in Restoration Comedy." *Restoration* 14.2 (Fall 1990): 58–70.

Wikander, Matthew. " 'The Duke My Father's Wrack': The Innocence of the Restoration *Tempest.*" *Shakespeare Survey* 43 (1991): 91–98.

Worsdale, James. *A Cure for a Scold: A Ballad Farce of Two Acts. Founded upon Shakespear's "Taming of a Shrew."* London, [1735].

Sticks and Rags, Bodies and Brocade: Essentializing Discourses and the Late Restoration Playhouse

Cynthia Lowenthal

*T*he late Restoration playhouse was filled with women—women playwrights, women performers, and women spectators. David Roberts disturbs many of the old assumptions about the nature of the late seventeenth-century audience when he constructs a full picture of the Restoration playhouse that was "rich indeed": in attendance could have been lady's companions and maidservants; female relatives of members of Parliament, professional men, and merchants; royal mistresses, duchesses, and the wives of the aristocracy; and a "conspicuous minority of women of all classes" who disguised themselves at the theater (94). The powerful influence of these female spectators, especially upper-class women, is discernible in constant references in epilogues and prologues to the "ladies" in the house. As Thomas D'Urfey's appeal in *Trick for Trick* (1678) attests, the "ladies" had become the arbiters of taste: "The poet now the ladies help does crave, / That with a smile or frown can damn or save" (cited in Roberts 34). The power attributed to these women is both royal and sexual, according to Roberts, because the lady, "regal in her [critical] detachment," is also "potentially alluring in her command of the favourable nod or glance" (34–35). More significantly, such appeals locate the "ladies" in a particularly theatrical position: in such moments, they themselves become the theatrical objects of view.

By the mid-1690s these same spectators would have had the opportunity to see the two most famous female performers on the late Restoration stage, Elizabeth Barry and Anne Bracegirdle, actresses who had become so famous—who were perceived to be so much a part of the repertoire and whose performances were so stylish and memorable—that a satire, *The Female Wits,* a 1697 rehearsal drama, targets the onstage behavior for which they were renowned. Parodied, for instance, were Barry's penchant for stamping her feet during ranting speeches and Bracegirdle's elegant manner of weeping onstage. The fact that such personal attacks were launched at these female performers is evidence of their "star" status, a phenomenon begun thirty years earlier from the moment actresses were first introduced to the English stage. We need only recall Pepys's enthusiastic responses to "my Lady Castlemaine" or the gossip surrounding Nell Gywn's liaison with the king to see just how quickly and powerfully the women players became objects of both specularization and speculation.[1]

Barry's and Bracegirdle's star status, however, generated for them both power and hazards. Because they participated in an event that displayed their bodies onstage, this visual availability, so essential to their representations of characters, translated into a communal, extratheatrical discourse filled with speculations about the offstage activities of their bodies. This essay examines these discourses first to determine the ways the bodies of the Restoration actresses were read—both as representations of ephemeral characters moving through an onstage space and as "known" objects moving through an offstage discourse. Second, it examines the ways such readings performed a larger and more powerful cultural function, one drawn from the subtle interdependence of class and gender definitions: by locating an essential female identity inextricably linked to the body, the discourse about the actresses served to reinforce aristocratic claims to an equally "essential" aristocratic identity, one that works to separate the "ladies" from their less aristocratic but equally spectacular counterparts.

Colley Cibber, writing in 1740, calls the public's interest in the lives of the players "natural": "A Man who has pass'd above Forty Years of his Life upon a Theatre, where he has never appear'd to be Himself, may have naturally excited the Curiosity of his Spectators to know what he really was, when in no body's Shape but his own." He concludes that the public has "a sort of Right to enquire into my Conduct" (3–4). Such an inquiry took shape, in the late seventeenth century, beyond the ephemeral form of communal gossip, in printed histories of the theater, verse satires, unauthorized biographies, and even Tom Brown's *Letters from the Dead*. Such information allowed an audience to believe that it had some special access, some "knowledge," about the performer that could indeed describe what an actor "really was." Yet even though Cibber attempts to create a difference between an authentic self and a role by pointing to the body as the source of the distinction, "when in no body's Shape but his own," his *Apology* goes on to present the discourse of a likable, charming—if often disingenuous—persona, a "Cibber" who is quick to cite his failures and successes in his public roles as theater manager and poet laureate.

For women working in the theater, both women players and playwrights, such access was almost solely constituted by knowledge about their private, sexual lives—knowledge that supposedly located and revealed an authentic self. Aphra Behn, whose specter hovered over all subsequent women writers, actively exploited this seventeenth-century inability to separate the professional woman from the prostitute. According to Catherine Gallagher, the culture heard very distinctly the "public" in *publication* and believed that a woman could not preserve a private body if she put her mind on public display: "The woman who shared the contents of her mind instead of reserving them for one man was literally, not metaphorically, trading in her *sexual* property. If she were married, she was selling what did not belong to her, because in *mind and body* she should have given herself to her husband" (27). Gallagher concludes that Behn intentionally sacrificed the ideal of the "totalized" woman in her aggressive assumption of identities dependent on multiple exchanges: in "literalizing and embracing the playwright-prostitute metaphor," Behn chose to "regenerate, possess, and sell a series of provisional, constructed identities" (28, 31).

As we might expect, a Restoration audience found it doubly easy to equate the actress with the prostitute: her job demanded that she present her body, feign desire, and display this divided female self; her profession required that she regenerate, possess, and sell a series of provisional selves. John Hill made that easy equation in 1750, when he wrote that an actress must guard against, even empty herself of, response to her own "trivial, domestick affairs." "The mistress and the actress," said Hill, "have only this in common, that it is the more easy to them to affect a passion, as they are less under the influence of its opposite one" (26). But it was not simply that an audience failed to distinguish between a woman's staging of her own reputed desire—as in prostitution—and a woman's participation in a theatrical event that itself stages a character's sexual desire. It is the very fact of female presence that evidenced pretense, generated tension, and confirmed the fear that a woman was capable of division or multiplicity. As Peter Stallybrass has noted, the relationship between "speaking" women—harlots, whores, and other public women—and their "silent" counterparts—chaste women, invisible within the domestic— began during the Renaissance: "The connection between speaking and wantonness was common to legal discourse and conduct books. . . . The signs of the 'harlot' are her linguistic 'fullness' and her frequenting of public space. . . . The [ideal wife], like Bakhtin's classical body, is rigidly 'finished': her signs are the enclosed body, the closed mouth, the locked house"

(126–27). Of course, Restoration actresses were, by definition and by necessity, such "speaking" women.

Yet similar claims for prostitution and implied division did not so readily attach themselves to male actors, as Katharine Eisaman Maus has elegantly pointed out (603). The public had not been particularly interested in the offstage lives of the earlier Renaissance actors such as Richard Burbage or William Kempe, nor was a Restoration audience particularly concerned with the offstage activities of the bodies of male actors. Edward Kynaston, for instance, could have aroused similar interest: famous for playing women's parts in the pre- and just post-Restoration theater, he is described by John Downes as being "a Compleat Female Stage Beauty, performing his Parts so well, especially *Arthiope* and *Aglaura,* being Parts greatly moving Compassion and Pity; that it has since been Disputable among the Judicious, whether any Woman that succeeded him so Sensibly touch'd the Audience as he" (19). Kynaston was often gathered up by ladies of quality after a performance, still in his female dress, to be paraded around Hyde Park, and there is evidence that he was himself "kept" by women in his offstage life (Cibber 72). Even Joe Haynes—who became notorious for once riding an ass onstage to speak an epilogue—was celebrated, not condemned, for his unsanctioned offstage behavior. Tobyas Thomas's *Life of the Late Famous Comedian Jo. Hayns* (1701) excuses Haynes's antics by apologizing for his irregularities this way: "His Frauds were rather to be call'd his Frolicks; Deception more then Deceipt. . . . his Designs and Strategems, aspiring more to an Aiery Feast, the pleasure of a Light Jest, than from any sordid hunger after an Avaritious Cheat" (Preface). Thomas describes Haynes's sexual escapades as giving him "a little too much of the Libertinism," even though the text contains a story—intended as comic, but horrifying to a modern audience—of Haynes's attempted rape of a young, mute serving girl. Charges were dropped after Haynes claimed to be secretary to the duke of Monmouth and when the young woman herself was physically unable to speak as his accuser (12–14).

Restoration actresses, however, were burdened with this additional definition established through a discourse concerning the private activities of their offstage bodies and their sexual, rather than theatrical or technical, "virtuosity." Thus the problem of female duplicity—always in danger of erupting in dominant male perceptions of women generally—was even more strongly reinforced when the "speaking" woman became "spoken of." Barry and Bracegirdle, who acted together in at least twenty new tragedies during the reign of William III, lived with such discursive definitions. Descriptions of Barry's rise to fame always cite her father's falling fortunes and her guidance, first, under Mrs. Davenant, who introduced her to the "company of the best sort," so that in time she was "soon

Mistress of that Behaviour which sets off the well-bred Gentlewoman"
(Betterton 13). Her second mentor, Lord Rochester, reportedly wagered
that he could make her the finest player on the stage. Through constant
rehearsal, especially of her voice (said to be flat and monotonous), he is
credited with helping her to achieve the Restoration definition of the best
actor: she could *become* the person she played (Betterton 14–16).

In well-known descriptions, Cibber praises Barry for being "gracefully majestick" and for creating "a Presence of elevated Dignity" in
characters of greatness (95), while Charles Gildon's *Life of Mr. Thomas
Betterton* recounts her onstage actions as "always just, and produc'd
naturally by the Sentiments": "She indeed always enters into her Part, and
is the Person she represents. Thus, I have heard her say, that she never
said, *Ah! poor* Castalio! in the *Orphan,* without weeping. And I have
frequently observ'd her change her Countenance several Times as the
Discourse of others on the Stage have affected her in the Part she acted"
(39–40). This becoming a self *to* the self creates a version of female unity
that might lessen the anxiety of a spectator who, perceiving the difference
between the actress and her character, is convinced of female duplicity.

Yet "becoming" the part also meant that an actress had to convince
her audience to forget, momentarily, the public discourse that subverted the
onstage sympathy. In Barry's case the obstacles to overcome were mighty,
for contemporary accounts of her offstage life were often harsh, abusive,
and even obscene. In *The Play-House, A Satyr* Robert Gould calls her a "Drab"
and "a Hackney Whore" and specifically equates her with a prostitute:

> So Insolent! there never was a Dowd
> So very basely born so very Proud:
> Yet Covetous; She'll Prostitute with any,
> Rather than wave the Getting of a Penny.
> [cited in Summers 311–12]

Tom Brown is equally specific: "Should you lie with her all Night, She
would not know you next Morning, unless you had another five Pound
at her service" (3:39). While Anthony Aston paints her as a "shining actress," with dark hair and light eyes, of a slightly plump "middle-size," he
describes her mouth as opening "most on the Right Side, which she strove
to draw t'other Way" (6–7). Curll's Betterton claimed that this irregularity
resulted in "[a] peculiar *Smile* . . . which made her look the most genteelly
malicious Person that can be imagined" (19). This same physical characteristic, however, was also used as a sign of her reputed sexual promis-
cuity, and it forms the basis of a contemporary attack on her personal
character: "With mouth and cunt, though both awry before, / Her cursed
affectation makes 'em more" (Wilson, *Court Satires* 78).

Such discourse concerning Barry's life accompanied her performances as much as Bracegirdle's reputed and much-discussed chastity did hers. The most tragic consequence of Bracegirdle's legendary purity resulted in the death of actor-playwright William Mountfort, who was killed while attempting to abort Captain Richard Hill's real-life abduction of Bracegirdle. Of her stage representations, Cibber claims that no other woman was "in such general Favour of her Spectators," because she was not "unguarded in her private Character," a discretion that made her "the Darling of the Theatre." He goes on to say that because she was "the Universal Passion, and under the highest Temptations," her resistance served "but to increase the number of her Admirers." It was, he adds candidly, a kind of fashion to lust after her (101).

Yet even these contemporary accounts also clearly focus on the activities of Anne Bracegirdle's body, constructing her sexual availability through her resistance. And they too go beyond merely reporting the "remarkable" absence of her sexual activity to inscribe meaning on her body itself, this time in signs of her virginal status, with an emphasis on sexual possibility. Cibber claims that, in her youth, she threw out "a Glow of Health and Chearfulness" (101), while Aston describes her beauty as a conventional kind of loveliness: she had dark brown hair and brows, "black sparkling Eyes," and fine, even white teeth. He goes on, however, to concentrate on the beauty of her involuntary physical responses, signs on her body that mark her sexually: she had "a fresh blushy Complexion" that, when she exerted herself, flushed her neck, face, and breast (Aston 9). Yet for all the celebration of her chastity, not even she escaped charges of sexual license. In Tom Brown's *Letters from the Dead* (1702) a fictionalized Mountfort intimates that he and Bracegirdle were lovers: complaining of a backache, he cries, "[P]ox on you . . . for a bantering Dog, how can a single Girdle do me good, when a Brace was my Destruction?" (cited in Holland 143).

Thus, when Peter Holland writes that in the Restoration theater "the actor precedes the role" (79), he points to a similarity shared by Restoration performers and modern celebrities whom Michael Quinn has described as possessing an overdetermined quality that keeps them "from disappearing entirely into the acting figure[s] or the drama" (155). They come equipped with such a powerful intertext—a conjunction of life and art, and a continuity of sequential roles—that it is difficult and perhaps even impossible "to sort out the personal from the referential" (Quinn 158). The Restoration actress, as such a celebrity, was always, at the same time, a body onstage (a visual phenomenon), the character she played (a representation in the minds of an audience), and an individual woman whose life in the "real world" came as part of the theatrical event (a verbal construct). But unlike the castrati, whose bodily difference was more than metaphorically inscribed and whose physical difference could be seen and heard, the ac-

S.Harding Delin.   *James Stow Sculp*

Engraving of Anne Bracegirdle, in Francis Godolphin Waldron, *The bio-graphical mirrour, comprising a series of ancient and modern English portrait of eminent and distinguished person, from original portrait and drawings* (London: Silvester and Edward Harding, 1795-1802), vol. 3, plate 4. By permission of the Special Collections Library, University of Michigan.

tresses were perceived through a different veil of "knowledge." Their bodies were "known" through an offstage discourse with a life of its own, a discourse often entirely unanchored, without a traceable source, and even an outright fabrication. It is the fact of its ubiquitousness that endowed it with the power of "truth" and with the status of a stable signifier. Thus, as Quinn has argued of all celebrities, the actress is both a sign object and a sign producer (157). Through the discourse, the Restoration audience essentialized the actress according to her sexual behavior as a means of coping with the apparent lack of female unity her role-playing displayed onstage.

When Quinn goes on to argue that the celebrity phenomenon appeals to a culture that "creates, maintains, and apparently requires celebrity actors to feed its desire for an aesthetics of familiarity, recognition, and fulfilment" (160), he sounds curiously like the *Players Tragedy,* an anonymous 1693 work that insists, "Reputation, as well as Person is exposed for the Pleasure, and Diversion of the Audience" (cited in Holland 143). Reputation, like familiarity, works to establish the "exposure" of the actress's "person" through an interest in her onstage beauty and her offstage body, both as sexual commodities in communal discourse and as sources of pleasure. Thus in the inevitable erotics of theater performance, visual spectacle read through an extratheatrical "knowledge" of female performance both confirms and disturbs notions of identity.

In its consistent essentializing, the discourse concerning the bodies of the actresses plays an important part in larger cultural and political attempts to locate the sources of identity: to determine where it resides, how to recognize it, and how to represent it. The "real-world" objects of multiple gazes were, of course, the aristocrats whose public performances displayed a power and an identity inextricably linked to a theatrical kind of presentation and spectacle.[2] Lawrence Stone, in *The Crisis of the Aristocracy,* cites conspicuous consumption as one aristocratic strategy used for securing an upper-class identity. Such display demanded the expensive maintenance of pomp and circumstance in royal service, the cost of attendance at Court in the hope of office, and the pleasures and vanities of London—and a "round of dissipation which in time inevitably undermined both the health and fortune." It also required an aristocrat "to keep open house to all comers, to dispense lavish charity, to keep hordes of domestic servants and retainers—to live, in short, as a great medieval prince." Such upper-class excess not only served a social function, "as a symbolic justification for the maintenance or acquisition of status," but also erected a strong barrier against "the lower orders," a means of keeping outsiders from encroaching on aristocratic privilege (184–87).

Yet as Christopher Hill has observed, the new roles available for aristocrats after 1660 were "precarious." Before 1640 the aristocracy had a discernible social significance, "if only as mediators working the court to procure monopolies for merchants" (328). After 1660, however, the restored aristocracy found itself playing a largely decorative role: "The aristocrats who regained their privileged position after 1660 had no significant role to play in the reconstructed social order. Flocking to the court, they ceased even to take their traditional part in local government; and at court their role was decorative rather than functional" (301). Even though courtiers like Rochester were free to indulge their passions, this only emphasized their social irrelevance, a situation that results in the condition of the "alienated aristocrat." Thus, Hill asserts, after the execution of Charles I, tragedy was replaced by heroic drama "in which kings concern themselves with imaginary points of honour in love and war because real political issues have become too hot to touch" (326).

Such observations are supported by Michael McKeon's arguments concerning the eighteenth-century aristocracy's "increasingly defensive awareness" that social hierarchy and exclusive class identity were "under assault." He concludes that this awareness resulted in an increasing "theatricalization" of social performance (151, 169). As an instance of a new philosophical ridicule of the aristocratic notion that honor is "biologically inherited," McKeon cites Daniel Defoe's attack on the supposedly essential identity of the aristocrat, " 'as if there were some differing Species in the very Fluid of Nature . . . or some *Animalculae* of a differing and more vigorous kind' " (154). The resulting attempts to naturalize aristocratic ideology take on not a biological but a theatrical component: status values commonly associated with aristocratic social relations—such as deference and paternalistic care—underwent an elaborate sort of "theatricalization," one that is "likely to occur whenever social convention is raised to the level of self-conscious practice" (McKeon 169).

Such theatricalization of aristocratic social performance and increasing self-awareness of aristocratic practice could be seen in large-scale public displays of shifting and multiple identities. Terry Castle's extraordinary documentation of the eighteenth-century masquerade provides ample evidence of a culture vacillating between pleasures and anxieties in the play of representations, the possibilities and the problems inherent in unitary notions of identity. At the masquerade, the cultural equivalent of the theatrical performance, "new bodies were superimposed over old; anarchic, theatrical selves displaced supposedly essential ones. . . . The pleasures of the masquerade attended on the experience of doubleness, the alienation of inner from outer, a fantasy of two bodies simultaneously and thrillingly present, self and other together, the two-in-one" (4–5).

The most powerful effects of such theatricalization depended on clothing to signal this doubleness, even this multiplicity. The question of fashion—as an external marker that could secure a particular identity—had important class implications in the late seventeenth century. Pierre Bourdieu makes explicit the power that such seemingly "insignificant" signs wield: "The social formation of the body (the details of dress, bearing, physical and verbal manner as the inscribed principles of the arbitrary content of the culture) is the more effective because it extorts the essential while seeming to demand the insignificant" (cited in Stallybrass 123). Castle goes further to comment on the "massive instability of sartorial signs" that accounts for the contempt for fashion in Western culture: "Clothing has always been a primary trope for the deceitfulness of the material world—a mutable, shimmering tissue that everywhere veils the truth from human eyes. Inherently superficial, feminine in its capacity to enthrall and mislead, it is a paradigmatic emblem of changeability" (56). She concludes that underlying the early eighteenth-century sumptuary laws and antimasquerade literature was the fear that when a commoner wore the clothes of a higher rank, even in jest, it incited in the wearer a desire to join that rank and receive its rewards: "Luxurious costume might invest the lower orders with delusions of grandeur. Worse, it could lead to the revolutionary notion that rank itself could be altered as easily as its outward signs" (92).

This anxiety about the performative quality of aristocratic status and its visibility in external signs is reflected in stories about Restoration actresses who had to be warned by theater managers not to wear their costumes outside the theater. J.H. Wilson reports that some of the clothing worn onstage came from "the castoff suits or dresses of ladies and gentlemen too proud to wear the same outfit more than once," and he calls the extratheatrical display of such costumes a "compensation" for the female players: "There was always the chance of slipping out after the play wearing one of the company's 'French gowns à-la-mode' or some other finery. The companies frowned on this practice, complaining that their clothes were 'Tarnished and Imperelled by frequent weareing them out of the Playhouse,' and fined the culprit a week's pay if they caught her in the act" (*King's Ladies* 38–40).[3] Managerial fiscal responsibility may be one practical reason for the injunction, but the prohibition also masks a deeper anxiety. Onstage, actresses, like aristocrats, were aware that they were always being watched; offstage, when both actresses and aristocrats paraded on public display the fashions that set them apart from "lower-order" spectators—clothing itself drawn from aristocratic models of ideal style—such fashion marked the wearers *outside* the theater with that particular status. Such an event comes disturbingly close to confirming the "revolutionary notion" Castle cites, "that rank itself could be altered as easily as its outward signs."

In fact, some actresses did indeed acquire more permanent "marks" of higher status outside the theater, as they moved from playhouse to townhouse, or even to country house, when they were courted or kept by the aristocrats for whom they played.[4] As Leslie Ferris acknowledges, "It was the expected custom for the men of the court to keep a pretty actress—just one of their many expenses in an age of public display" (70). Two of the most famous examples, of course, are Nell Gwyn and Moll Davis, who each became mistress to Charles II; Gwyn also gave birth to a son of the king, the first duke of St. Albans. Margaret Hughes was mistress of Prince Rupert, Anastasia Robinson was reported to have married Lord Peterborough, and Hester Davenport was tricked into a false marriage by the Earl of Oxford when he dressed one of his servants as a parson to "marry" them. Thus when Katharine Maus calls the actresses' upward mobility "unorthodox" (609), such a claim is true only if we think of class barriers as impermeable and of common women as barred not just from wealth but also from the cultural capital of the social graces, manners, fashions, and trappings inscribed in the aristocratic class. In tragedy especially, however, actresses took the parts of aristocratic and even royal characters. Like ladies of quality, they costumed themselves in finery and marked themselves as extraordinary in the same fashion as their more genteel counterparts. Onstage, and sometimes off, common women *enacted* the aristocratic imperatives supposedly denied them by their nonaristocratic status.

Yet when the same theatrical questions of role-playing, multiple identity, and performance are applied to aristocrats, they take on a very different resonance. The reasons are manifest in questions of class imperatives linked to notions of class essentialism. First, and most simply, people of rank did not join the theater. Cibber recounts the sad story of a young aristocratic woman who, as a result of being thrown out of her family after an "indiscretion," comes to the theater for a job; her relations prohibit her taking the stage by interfering behind the scenes. Cibber concludes that there was more dishonor to the family for her to be on stage as to sell "patches and pomatum in a Band-box" (46).

Second, and more powerfully, such dishonor can occur only when there is little acknowledged symbolic distance between a duke, for instance, and some separate, private self: he *was* his rank. And while some aristocratic behavior was indeed attacked—Steele (himself Sir Richard) despairs of the excessive affectation and violence inherent in the male upper-class codes—such writing rarely suggests that aristocratic men, in particular, were merely role-playing. The discourse of the era allowed them a simultaneity of identity: the Earl of Rochester, whose "real" name was John Wilmot, is essentially Rochester. On an even larger scale, the English had in previous years been engaged in their own turbulent political "dramas," to use Hobbes's theatrical metaphor: King Charles I had been beheaded, the rightful James II had been overthrown, and the foreign William III had been installed on the throne. Kingship was obviously subject to religious and political demands, and the old imperative—for an essential, traceable genetic royal line—had already given way to contemporary expediencies. Yet the notion that the "part" of the king had been played by a series of "substitutes" enters the discourse only as a means of confirming the status quo. The only "Pretenders" to the English throne were the family of James II, whose lineage should indeed have secured him the role but whose unpopular political and religious activities had caused his replacement by a more congenial Dutch understudy.

So when an aristocrat—or a monarch—lent his or her robes to an actor for a particular part (an event guaranteed to increase the box office), Restoration discourse did not publicly proclaim this as the division of aristocratic identity, the conclusion to which a modern audience immediately jumps. Nor did that discourse describe it as an undermining of aristocratic, or even royal, essentialism—an interpretation obviously available to the seventeenth century.[5] Instead it located the suspicion, the distrust, and the pleasures of divided identity in the playhouse, a difference that could be highlighted when the player wore the monarch's robes.

Thus the beautiful fashions, cultivated speech, and formalized gestures of the late seventeenth-century actors performed a double cultural function. Modeled on aristocratic notions of style and decorum, the actors' performance first offered a theatrical representation of "ideal" behavior and consequently helped to shape an audience's own self-definition.[6] Equally important, it reinforced the audience's belief that a *separable* self for the actor existed independent of the plot, a self available in and defined by an extratheatrical discourse. As we have seen, for women that separable self was described in the discourse as a sexually available body. So while the stylized performances of seventeenth-century actors cultivate and constitute the fiction, they also create a transparent structure through which an audience can replay the narratives of an offstage reality "masquerading" as a deeper "truth."

Only a naive reader of performance is tricked. Aston recounts the story of Betterton and a country gentleman's experience at a fair: The country gentleman thinks the puppets in the puppet show are real, and only after much convincing does he come to believe, as Betterton insists, that the players are "Only sticks and Rags." That night, after Betterton takes the gentleman to see his own production of *The Orphan,* when asked whether he liked the performance, the country fellow replies, "Why I don't knows, . . . it's well enough for *Sticks and Rags*" (Aston 5–6). The lesson is clear. A naive spectator first experiences an epistemological and ontological problem: failing to distinguish between the player and the part, entering wholly into the fiction of the spectacle, the spectator then encounters an aesthetic dilemma—how to distinguish a genuine performance from its poor imitation.

Readers of seventeenth-century culture, however, were put in an analogous but more precarious position: they had to enter wholly into the fiction of aristocratic spectacle; otherwise they might suspect that the bodies and brocade so visible in the upper ranks might be merely the sticks and rags of a cultural construct. Questions of identity were therefore displaced onto the safer territory of the playhouse, a space where differences were said to be leveled. As a watering hole for aristocratic men, who often sat on the stage and "contributed" to the dialogue, the playhouse was also a place where aristocratic women frequently attended performances dressed like the onstage princesses or masked in the same fashion as prostitutes. Pepys recounts a telling incident in this context, one concerning Frances Jennings, sister to the Duchess of Marlborough and resident in the house of the Duchess of York. When Jennings attended the theater "disguised" as an orange-wench, her impersonation was unmasked only by a too spectacular item of fashion: "What mad freaks the Maydes of Honour at Court have—that Mrs. Jennings, one of the Duchesses Maydes, the other day dressed herself like an orange-wench and went up and down and cried oranges—till falling down, or by such accident (though in the evening), her fine shoes were discerned and she put to a great deale of shame" (21 Feb. 1665). It is precisely this confusion of "women" that becomes the crucial issue: in the playhouse, ladies of quality could play down their rank, without the loss of their "essential" identity; yet when the status of the common woman player (and one powerful seventeenth-century meaning of the word *common* was "shared") rose onstage, even to the heights of majesty, it was an event the dominant class both demanded and feared and therefore one that the dominant ideology had to enact and resist.

And thus the contemporary accounts indicate that Mrs. Davenant did indeed train Elizabeth Barry to display "a Presence of elevated Dignity" and to be "gracefully majestick," training so effective that she was "soon Mistress of that Behaviour which sets off the well-bred Gentlewoman." Barry became a target of satiric abuse precisely because she cultivated a carriage so noble that her mean birth was in danger of being obscured.[7] The late seventeenth-century discourse about the actresses' sexual activities disguises this larger cultural anxiety—that the traditional "essential quality" of the aristocratic class might not be distinguishable from those persons who could so excellently and so convincingly mimic it—an anxiety worked through by essentializing the identity of the female players through the activities of their sexualized bodies as a means of confirming a class status quo.

Notes

1. Elin Diamond's insightful essay comments on the way Behn exploits and problematizes both the commodification of female players and the gendering of a set of spectatorial relations that reifies women by making them the objects of a new "spectator-fetishist's" gaze.
2. See Pye for a fascinating discussion of the ways that "sovereignty is an irreducibly theatrical phenomenon" (86) and the ways a monarch comes to possess an awesome and always visible presence.
3. Wilson cites an even more fascinating incident of the blurred lines between player and aristocrat in an anecdote concerning Kynaston's impersonation of Sir Charles Sedley: "When Edward Kynaston, who closely

resembled Sir Charles ('a handsome plump middle sized man') had the effrontery not only to get 'some laced clothes made exactly after a suit Sir Charles wore' but to appear so dressed on the stage, Sedley was annoyed and promptly hired 'two or three' bullies to chastise the player. The bravos accosted Kynaston in St James's Park, 'pretending to take him for Sir Charles,' picked a quarrel with him, and beat him so savagely that he was forced to take to his bed." Sir Charles, however, refused to sympathize with Kynaston, claiming that his own reputation had suffered more than "Kynaston's bones" (*King's Ladies* 29).

4. Straub argues that an actress's marrying respectably was the exception rather than the rule (155). Yet it is the public perception—the persistence of a discourse connecting actresses with aristocrats—that forms the focus of my concern.

5. Dr. Doran writes of one such incident involving Barry and the wife of James II: "Mary of Modena testified her admiration by bestowing on the mimic queen the wedding-dress Mary herself had worn when she was united to James II, and the queen of the hour represented the Elizabeth, with which enthusiastic crowds became so much more familiar than they were with the Elizabeth of history" (53).

6. Erika Fischer-Lichte writes that "the particular mode of [the actor's presentation of the body] onstage may contribute to this ongoing process by representing and propagating new models of self-presence and self-presentation for audience imitation" (23). Her essay provides a detailed discussion of the relationship between stage representations and larger cultural self-definitions.

7. A later eighteenth-century incident, concerning Anne Oldfield, is equally telling in this regard: "Notwithstanding these [her sexual liaisons with Maynwaring and Churchill] were publicly known, [Oldfield] was invited to the houses of women in fashion, as much distinguished for unblemished character as elevated rank" (Davies 2:434).

Works Cited

Aston, Anthony. *A Brief Supplement to Colley Cibber, Esq.; His Lives of the Late Famous Actors and Actresses.* N.p., n.d.

Betterton, Thomas. *The History of the English Stage, from the Restauration to the Present Time.* London: Printed for E. Curll, 1741.

Brown, Thomas. *Works.* 3 vols. London, 1715.

Castle, Terry. *Masquerade and Civilization: The Carnivalesque in Eighteenth-Century English Culture and Fiction.* Stanford, Calif.: Stanford UP, 1986.

Cibber, Colley. *An Apology for the Life of Mr. Colley Cibber, Comedian, and the Late Patentee of the Theatre-Royal.* London, 1740.

Davies, Thomas. *Dramatic Miscellanies.* 3 vols. London, 1784.

Diamond, Elin. "*Gestus* and Signature in Aphra Behn's *The Rover.*" *ELH* 56 (Fall 1989): 519–41.

Doran, Dr. *Their Majesties' Servants; or, Annals of the English Stage.* London: Allen and Co., 1864.

Downes, John. *Roscius Anglicanus; or, An Historical Review of the Stage*. London, 1708.

Ferris, Leslie. *Acting Women: Images of Women in Theatre*. New York: New York UP, 1989.

Fischer-Lichte, Erika. "Theatre and the Civilizing Process: An Approach to the History of Acting." *Interpreting the Theatrical Past: Essays in the Historiography of Performance*. Ed. Thomas Postlewait and Bruce A. McConachie. Iowa City: U of Iowa P, 1989. 19–36.

Gallagher, Catherine. "Who Was That Masked Woman?: The Prostitute and the Playwright in the Comedies of Aphra Behn." *Women's Studies* 15 (1988): 23–42.

Gildon, Charles. *The Life of Mr. Thomas Betterton*. London, 1710.

Hill, Christopher. *The Collected Essays of Christopher Hill: Writing and the Revolution in Seventeenth-Century England*. Amherst: U of Massachusetts P, 1985.

Hill, John. *The Actor: A Treatise on the Art of Playing*. London, 1750.

Holland, Peter. *The Ornament of Action: Text and Performance in Restoration Comedy*. Cambridge: Cambridge UP, 1979.

Maus, Katharine Eisaman. " 'Playhouse Flesh and Blood': Sexual Ideology and the Restoration Actress." *ELH* 46 (Winter 1979): 595–617.

McKeon, Michael. *The Origins of the English Novel: 1600–1740*. Baltimore: Johns Hopkins UP, 1987.

Pepys, Samuel. *The Diary of Samuel Pepys*. Vol. 4. 1665. Ed. Robert Latham and William Matthews. Berkeley: U of California P, 1972.

Pye, Christopher. "The Sovereign, the Theater, and the Kingdome of Darknesse: Hobbes and the Spectacle of Power." *Representations* 8 (Fall 1984): 85–106.

Quinn, Michael L. "Celebrity and the Semiotics of Acting." *New Theatre Quarterly* 6.22 (May 1990): 154–61.

Roberts, David. *The Ladies: Female Patronage of Restoration Drama, 1660–1700*. Oxford: Clarendon, 1989.

Stallybrass, Peter. "Patriarchal Territories: The Body Enclosed." *Rewriting the Renaissance: The Discourses of Sexual Difference in Early Modern Europe*. Ed. Margaret W. Ferguson, Maureen Quilligan, and Nancy J. Vickers. Chicago: U of Chicago P, 1986. 123–42.

Stone, Lawrence. *The Crisis of the Aristocracy: 1558–1641*. Oxford: Clarendon, 1965.

Straub, Kristina. *Sexual Suspects: Eighteenth-Century Players and Sexual Ideology*. Princeton, N.J.: Princeton UP, 1992.

Summers, Montague. *The Restoration Theatre*. London: Kegan Paul, 1934.

Thomas, Tobyas. *The Life of the Late Famous Comedian Jo. Hayns, Containing His Comical Exploits and Adventures, Both at Home and Abroad*. London, 1701.

Wilson, J.H. *All the King's Ladies*. Chicago: U of Chicago P, 1958.

———, ed. *Court Satires of the Restoration*. Columbus: Ohio State UP, 1976.

Contributors

Dagny Boebel teaches at Manchester College. She is the author of articles and papers on seventeenth-century writers, including Shakespeare, Milton, Bathsua Makin, and Giambattista Basile. She has also published essays on twentieth-century women poets, such as H.D. and Anne Sexton.

J. Douglas Canfield, Regents' Professor at the University of Arizona, is the author of *Nicholas Rowe and Christian Tragedy* (1977) and *Word as Bond in English Literature from the Middle Ages to the Restoration* (1989). With J. Paul Hunter, he coedited *Rhetorics of Order / Ordering Rhetorics in English Neoclassical Literature* (1989), and with Deborah C. Payne, *Cultural Readings of Restoration and Eighteenth-Century English Theater* (1995). His ideological analysis of Restoration comedy, *Tricksters and Estates*, is forthcoming from the University Press of Kentucky.

Robert A. Erickson, professor of English at the University of California, Santa Barbara, is the author of *Mother Midnight: Birth, Sex, and Fate in Eighteenth-Century Fiction* (1986) and is coeditor of John Arbuthnot's *The History of John Bull* (1976). He has also published articles on Cervantes, Behn, Congreve, Defoe, Richardson, Sterne, Scriblerian satire, and the British midwife books. His most recent book, *The Language of the Heart 1600-1750*, is forthcoming from the University of Pennsylvania Press.

James E. Evans, professor of English at the University of North Carolina at Greensboro, is the author of *Comedy: An Annotated Bibliography of Theory and Criticism* (1987). He has also published articles on eighteenth-century fiction in such journals as *Philological Quarterly, South Atlantic Quarterly,* and *Comparative Literature Studies.*

Pat Gill, assistant professor of English at Western Michigan University, is the author of *Interpreting Ladies: Women, Wit, and Morality in the Restoration Comedy of Manners* (1994) and of articles on Congreve, Haywood, and the origins of eighteenth-century bourgeois identity. She has presented numerous papers on revisionist readings of Restoration drama, Lacanian theory and feminism and film theory.

Cynthia Lowenthal, associate professor of English at Tulane University, is the author of *Lady Mary Wortley Montagu and the Eighteenth-Century Familiar Letter* (1994). She has also published on Manley's *Royal Mistress.* Her book in progress, *Performing Identities,* concentrates on late seventeenth-century and early eighteenth-century theater to determine the ways in which discourses and representations are interdependent in early modern British attempts to define categories of gender and national character.

Jean I. Marsden, associate professor of English at the University of Connecticut, is the author of several articles on Restoration and eighteenth-century drama and of a book examining adaptations of Shakespeare, *The Re-imagined Text* (1995). She is the editor of *The Appropriation of Shakespeare: Post-Renaissance Reconstruction of the Works and the Myth* (1991). Her performance history of Shakespeare's *Cymbeline* is forthcoming in the Plays in Performance series of Cambridge University Press. She is currently working on a study of women and the eighteenth-century stage.

Rebecca Merrens, assistant professor of Literature, Communications, and Culture at the Georgia Institute of Technology and former independent graduate fellow at Pembroke College, Cambridge University, is the author of papers and articles on intersections between gender, literature, and science in the Renaissance and Restoration.

Jacqueline Pearson, lecturer in English Literature at the University of Manchester, England, is the author of *John Webster's Tragicomic Endings* (1980) and *The Prostituted Muse: Images of Women and Women Dramatists, 1642-1737* (1988). She has also written a number of articles on science fiction, on Shakespeare and other Renaissance dramatists, and on seventeenth-century women writers, including Margaret Cavendish, Aphra Behn, and Aemilia Lanier. She is at present working on a literary history of women's reading in the seventeenth and eighteenth centuries.

Katherine M. Quinsey, associate professor of English at the University of Windsor, Ontario, has published several articles on Pope and on Dryden, as well as articles on seventeenth-century poet-translator Sir Edward Sherburne, on Canadian poet Margaret Avison, and biblical tradition in English literature. Her work in progress is *Tempting Grace: The Religious Imagination of Alexander Pope,* a historical-bibliographic-textual study of Pope's religious thought and language.

Laura J. Rosenthal is associate professor of English at Florida State University. Her book, *Playwrights and Plagiarists in Early Modern England: Gender, Authorship, Literary Property*, is forthcoming from Cornell University Press.

Peggy Thompson, associate professor of English at Agnes Scott College, has published articles on Wycherley, Southerne, Behn, and on the relationship between comedy and Christianity. She is currently working on a study of eighteenth-century theater and religion.

Index